LIVING SPIRITUAL PRAXIS

Living Spiritual Praxis

*Foundations for
Spiritual Formation
Program Development*

ERIC J. KYLE

☙PICKWICK *Publications* · Eugene, Oregon

LIVING SPIRITUAL PRAXIS
Foundations for Spiritual Formation Program Development

Copyright © 2013 Eric J. Kyle. All rights reserved. Except for brief quotations in critical publications or reviews, no part of this book may be reproduced in any manner without prior written permission from the publisher. Write: Permissions, Wipf and Stock Publishers, 199 W. 8th Ave., Suite 3, Eugene, OR 97401.

Pickwick Publications
An Imprint of Wipf and Stock Publishers
199 W. 8th Ave., Suite 3
Eugene, OR 97401

www.wipfandstock.com

ISBN 13: 978-1-62564-035-2

Cataloguing-in-Publication data:

Kyle, Eric J.

    Living spiritual praxis : foundations for spiritual formation program development / Eric J. Kyle.

    xii + 312 pp. ; 23 cm. Includes bibliographical references and index.

    ISBN 13: 978-1-62564-035-2

    1. Spiritual formation. 2. Pastoral care. 3. Theology, Practical. I. Title.

BV4501.3 K95 2013

Manufactured in the U.S.A.

To Ursula, Richard, & Sean

Contents

List of Illustrations   ix
Acknowledgments   xi

Introduction: The Need for Spiritual Formation Methodologies   1

Part One: Theoretical Foundations

1. Discerning Discernment: Detailing the Dynamics of a Spiritual Discipline   21

2. Embodying Praxis: Cycles toward Transformation   55

Part Two: Methodological Movements

3. Going Deep: Exploration and Analysis Methodologies   77

4. Building a Home: Design and Implementation Methodologies   132

5. The Cycles of Ministry: Assessment and Modification Methodologies   180

6. From Mustard Seeds to Apple Trees: Pulling It All Together   210

Conclusion: Living Spiritual Praxis in Retrospect   235

Appendix A: Various Steps to Discernment   243
Appendix B: An Introduction to the Basics of Modeling   251
Appendix C: Tom's Original Program   278
Appendix D: Tom's Revised Program   288
Bibliography   295
Index   307

Illustrations

FIGURES

1. Fields of Human Formation   5
2. Three Levels of Formative Foci   8
3. Some Multiple Ways of Knowing   29
4. A Schematic of Discernment   52
5. The Four Components of Praxis   60
6. Three Elements of a Model to Consider When Synthesizing   93
7. The Six Steps of Exploration and Analysis   130
8. Relationship between Interventions, Our Community, and the Ideals   134
9. Five Core Categories of Approaches   144
10. The Five Steps of Design and Implementation   178
11. The Five Steps of Assessment and Modification   209
12. Our Three Methodologies and Their Cyclical Nature   237
13. A Proposed Feedback Framework   239
14. Four Components of Models   256
15. Three Parts of Model Construction   260
16. A Mapping of Some of Our Ways of Knowing   263
17. An Example of Complex Modeling Foundations   267

Illustrations

TABLES

1. Steps to Action Research   63
2. Steps to Practical Theology   65
3. A Model Mapping of Groome's Biblical Ways of Knowing   118
4. Francis' Model Mapping   122
5. Min's Five Core Model Brainstorming Results   158
6. Min's Core Approaches Brainstorming   161
7. Compiled Goals and Approaches for an Introductory TSF Class   164
8. Min's Course Goals and Their Supporting Interventions   166
9. Min's Guideline Reflections   171
10. Tom's Brainstormed Interventions   219

Acknowledgments

I WOULD LIKE TO acknowledge all those individuals who have helped to shape both the content and character of this project. Specifically, I would like to thank Philip Clayton, Andy Dreitcer, and Frank Rogers Jr. for their continued willingness and ability to answer my unending questions, read my flowery ramblings, and ultimately help me to refine and clarify all that has emerged throughout this journey. Without their mentoring, critical insights, and attentiveness to the movements of vitality in my heart and in this work, these writings might never have come to fruition.

I would also like to thank my family, especially my wife, Teddi, and my children, Katie and Alex, for their love, support, and patience with my absent-mindedness and absorptions while pondering and painstakingly engaging with this material. Teddi's presence and compassionate willingness to listen to my, at times, endless murmurings have been and continue to be a stable pillar in my life and research. The playfulness and creativity that Alex and Katie fill our home with was an inspiration to many of the novel directions that my writing took.

Finally, I would like to thank God for and in whom this work finds its beginning and end. May this work become a humble part of all that our Creator and Sustainer is continually seeking to do in our lives and our world.

Introduction

The Need for Spiritual Formation Methodologies

Montague is the newly appointed pastor of a "dying" inner city church that has been a part of the local community for more than eighty years. Once having more than fifteen hundred people in the 1950s, regular church attendance now dwindles to less than fifteen dedicated members each week. Coupled with changing neighborhood demographics as well as racism and sexism that are present within the church, Montague wrestles with discerning what God's hopes and directions are for this small community. Should the church be closed or should he attempt a revitalization campaign? What does the future hold in store for them?

Francis is a senior minister in a local church and has been called upon by her friend Martha for help. Martha is nearing retirement and is looking forward to spending more time with her husband, Charles, of forty-three years around the house and on the kinds of sight-seeing vacations that they love to go on. However, with just two years left before they both exit the workforce, Martha's husband suffers a major heart attack in which his brain goes without oxygen for an unknown period of time. After being in a coma for more than a week, the result is that his behavior and personality were somewhat altered. He is no longer the active person that Martha once knew. Now, he is much more introverted, lethargic, and becomes frustrated and confused more easily. Traveling is therefore much more taxing and difficult for him and Martha struggles with how to talk

Living Spiritual Praxis

to him as he is often resistant and even combative at times when she tries. Mourning the loss of the intimate and open relationship they once had, Martha isn't sure what she can or should do in response to these changes. Turning to Francis, they both ask: What can Martha and Charlie do now? What kinds of support should they seek? How should their relationship be reconceived and addressed now?

Tom was born and raised in a metropolis located in the Bible belt of the United States. Having attended a Baptist summer camp, he accepted Jesus as his "Lord and Savior" according to this denomination's teachings. As Tom grew, he longed to deepen his relationship with Christ and he longed to help others to live lives of fuller joy, hope, service, and love. However, growing up in an agnostic and unchurched home, he received little support or guidance in how to do this. On into his adulthood, Tom struggled with the means and methods by which to help himself and others to come to live such a fuller and richer personal life in God. Now a seminary student, Tom wants to develop a contemplatively oriented spiritual formation program for his theologically diverse seminary context that will help students and laity to engage such diversity in personally transformative and enriching ways. But what does this mean more exactly? How can he pursue these ends? What practices and activities should his program consist of?

These three stories illustrate the kinds of struggles that those in spiritual formation ministry have to face on a regular basis. Primarily working with individuals, relationships, and whole communities, such ministers seek to discern what it is that God has been doing and where it is that the Spirit might be leading them. These are struggles with a world that is less than ideal, struggles with discerning what to do in difficult situations, and struggles with knowing what it is that God is inviting us toward. As spiritual formators, it is struggles such as these that we—like Montague, Francis, and Tom—need help and guidance with.

Looking to some of the literature, there are numerous resources that are available on the work of spiritual formation. There are texts that address what spiritual formation means when working with individuals.[1] There are books that offer insights into helping relationships from a spiritual perspective.[2] And there are resources geared toward helping whole

---

1. Hull, *Complete Book of Discipleship*; McCallum and Lowery, *Organic Disciplemaking*; O'Connell, *Making Disciples*.

2. Barrick, *Sacred Psychology of Love*.

communities as a spiritually forming endeavor.³ Resources such as these can provide us with some of the necessary insights into the nature and practice of spiritual formation at these three levels: individuals, relationships, and communities.

However, most of these resources do not lead the reader through a specific process of developing spiritual formation programs or sets of interventions from conception, through discerning which approaches to use, and finally to assessment and evaluation. For instance, what kinds of activities and supports, such as counseling, might Francis suggest that Martha seek to engage her husband with? How will she know if they are really working or not? And how can she continually improve upon them as time goes on? While some resources do exist in other fields to help their practitioners to address questions such as these, as are found in education and organizational development,⁴ no resources appear to exist for the field of spiritual formation.

This book therefore seeks to address this need. Those wrestling with spiritual formation questions can benefit from resources that will help them to better understand the nature and dynamics of a situation, discern specific formative interventions, and to continually assess and modify these understandings and approaches. Can Montague benefit from a set of processes that will help him to discern where it is that the Spirit is seeking to lead his community? Are there steps that Francis can follow as she seeks to help Martha work with the new relationship that she and her husband now have? Are there really methods that Tom can use to help him to develop his contemplative program? It is the assertion of this book that yes, such foundations do exist, and yes, situations such as these might benefit from their usage. However, in order to see how this can be, we must first consider the nature and location of the work of theistic spiritual formation as it is conceived of herein.

THE LOCATION, FOCI, AND NATURE OF CHRISTIAN THEISTIC SPIRITUAL FORMATION

The work of formation, as we shall presently see, can be conceived of quite broadly. However, this book comes from a much narrower branch of this larger field. It is in this section that we will therefore briefly survey the

---

3. Ackerman, *Listening to God*.

4. Beitler, *Strategic Organizational Change*; Diamond, *Designing and Assessing Courses and Curricula*.

fields of formation and locate this work within it. We will also see the three levels of formative foci that most spiritual formators find themselves working with and for whom this book is intended. Then, in order to help us to see that such program development methodologies are needed, we will briefly review the nature of Western Christian theistic spiritual formation as it is found in some of the literature. This section will therefore become the basis for the road that we will be journeying on throughout the remainder of this book.

Location: Soundings from the Fields of Formation

It has been asserted that all of creation is in a state of continual process.[5] It is one that is in constant flux and transformation. From the continual changes in our bodies and brains to the constant alterations that societies go through, much of our world is in constant transition.[6] These changes influence our lives and impact our world.

In the midst of them, there are many fields and disciplines that seek to intentionally engage these constant transitions. There are those who would dive headlong into the work of seeking to give a more intentional and desired shape to the directions that such continual processes yield. From farmers who cultivate the land to politicians who seek communal coherence, such work may be referred to as "formation." These are vocations that have an intentional direction in mind as they work to be a part of the continual changes of our world. They are professions that use specific approaches, mechanisms, and practices to influence these changes. In short, formation fields are those that strive to bring some kind of specific form to the parts of creation that they primarily work with.

As it relates to humans, formation fields are numerous and diverse. Doctors and personal trainers work with the physiology of the human body for health and vitality. Teachers strive to nurture the minds, hearts, and relationships of their students. Community organizers seek the good of the neighborhoods they are working with. Each of these professions is an example of the kinds of formative work that is being done with humanity all around our globe.

For the purposes of this book, I categorize such human formation work into two broad areas: secular science-based, and religious and

---

5. Cobb and Griffin, *Process Theology*, 7.

6. For examples of brain and societal changes, see such texts as: Bear et al., *Neuroscience*, ch. 23; Sztompka, *Sociology of Social Change*.

theological. Figure 1 below shows these categorizations and some of the subcategories for each. While there are exceptions to these subcategories, for there are such things as self-proclaimed "Christian atheists" and counselors who work from a religious/theological framework,[7] the goal here is to highlight some of the broad differences in worldviews that are generally found in our Western culture today.

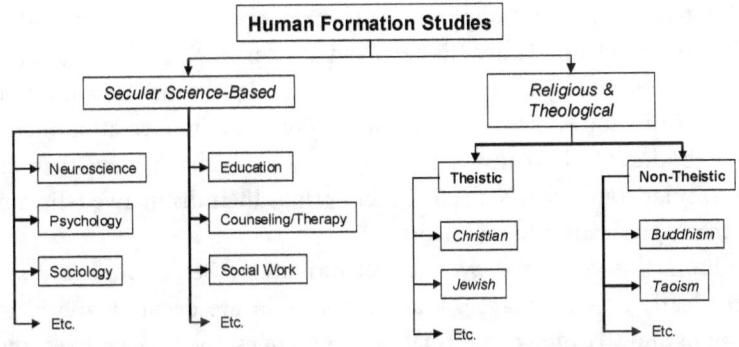

Figure 1. Fields of Human Formation

We can see that secular science-based fields are those relying on more contemporary scientific research methods and worldviews. Examples of these include texts that seek to understand the nature of human transformation from genetic,[8] neuroscientific,[9] psychological,[10] and sociological perspectives.[11] Such examples are also those whose primary foci and approaches are discipline specific such as are found in education,[12] counseling,[13] and community building.[14] These fields of human formation, as they are categorized here, are those that do not engage in their formative work from any sort of distinctive religious or theological worldview.[15]

---

7. For examples of each, see: Altizer, *New Gospel of Christian Atheism*; Barrick, *Sacred Psychology of Love*.
8. Dawkins, *Selfish Gene*; Wilson, *On Human Nature*.
9. Daugherty, *Power Within*; Siegel, *Mindsight*.
10. Kegan, *Evolving Self*; Mischel et al., *Introduction to Personality*.
11. Sztompka, *Sociology of Social Change*.
12. Mezirow, *Learning as Transformation*.
13. Kornfeld, *Cultivating Wholeness*; Mahoney, *Human Change Processes*.
14. Kretzmann and McKnight, *Building Communities from the Inside Out*.
15. There are, as mentioned above, individuals and communities who do engage in these areas from a religious and theological worldview. However, these fields are

Rather, they study and engage in formative endeavors from a more purely secular-scientific framework.

Alternatively, there are many formators and communities who do operate from a different set of paradigms and assumptions. In their non-theistic forms, of which some sects of Buddhism, Pantheism, and Taoism are found,[16] these approaches to human formation work do not assert or assume the presence or workings of any sort of transcendent Deity or God. Alternatively, theistic approaches to formation—such as are found in some circles of Christianity (Eastern and Western), Native/Shamanistic, Judaism, Hinduism, and Islam—do hold a central place for Deity as a core of their formation efforts.[17] Each of these approaches to formation therefore embodies an alternative set of worldviews and assumptions than do their secular counterparts. Each of them brings their distinctive religious and theological lenses to their work.

From this very brief overview of formation, we can therefore see more clearly how Montague, Francis, and Tom are deeply involved in questions and struggles of a formative nature. In essence, they are seeking to give some intentional form to the individuals, relationships, and communities that they are involved in. Not only are they well aware of their situations as they currently are, but they also have yearnings for how they would like to see things progress.

This particular book, as we shall see next, is primarily located in the theistic subcategory of the religious and theological fields. More specifically, it is primarily a Western Christian one. However, we will also be drawing extensively from and seeking a synthesis with some secular-science resources as we journey throughout.

Knowing one's location, and the sets of lenses that one brings to their formative craft, is important. Not only does it shape the kinds of work that we do, but also how we go about engaging with it. The contexts that we come from and the influences that have given form to our own lives will impact the directions that we will seek to give to the individuals, relationships, and communities to which we are called to formatively work with.

---

more commonly engaged from a Western secular-scientific perspective, as journals and introductory textbooks in each of these areas testify to.

16. For examples of such formation texts, see: Levine, *Pantheism*; Nhat Hanh, *Calming the Fearful Mind*; Reid, *Complete Guide to Chi-Gung*.

17. For formation examples from each of these traditions, see such texts as: Azeemi, *Muraqaba*; McCallum and Lowery, *Organic Disciplemaking*; Morinis, *Everyday Holiness*; Prabhupada, *Dharma*; Olomo, *Core of Fire*; Stevens and Stevens, *Secrets of Shamanism*; Ware, *Orthodox Way*.

The Need for Spiritual Formation Methodologies

Knowing the landscape of these fields of human formation and where our own vocation is located within it is therefore beneficial to our work.

Three Levels of Formative Foci

In the book edited by Jack Seymour, *Mapping Christian Education*, "spiritual growth" is primarily understood as the "personal dimension of learning" while the work of religious education is asserted to focus more broadly to include relationships, whole communities, and the wider world.[18] It is common today, as a review of the literature shows, to think of spiritual formation as primarily being oriented toward the level of the individual as we saw it being done in Tom's case.

However, such person-centered views are not the only way to think about our work. If we were, for instance, to more simply understand the term "spiritual formation" to be the work of being "formed in the Spirit," as we shall elaborate on more below, then our vocation should be focused wherever we perceive the Spirit to be at work. Following Seymour, and the contributors to his book, we can find God's work to be occurring not just at the level of the individual, but also at the levels of close relationships as it is in Martha and Charles's situation, in larger communities such as Montague's, and even in the wider environments and cultures of which we are a part. If this is so, then spiritual formation should be seen as more intentionally happening at these other levels—beyond the individual—as well.

As this book is written for those working primarily in congregational and nonprofit organizations, there are three primary levels toward which our formative efforts can be focused. These three levels can be thought of as ever widening circles of community and relationship: with ourselves, with one another, and with larger communities of which we are a part. Figure 2 below shows the three levels that this book will primarily focus on.

---

18. Seymour, "Approaches to Christian Education," 20–21.

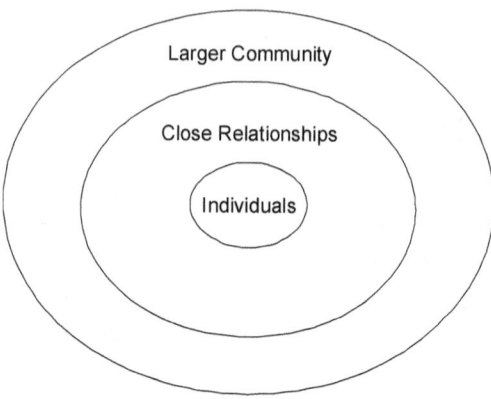

Figure 2. Three Levels of Formative Foci

The first level is the one already mentioned, and that is the level of the individual. At this level, as Seymour and his colleagues have noted, our focus is on individual persons and their growing life in the Spirit. It involves intentionality with both inner and outer aspects of each person's life for the purposes of helping them to grow spiritually as Tom will be seeking to do through his contemplative program. It is a focus that is primarily concerned with each person's private and public lives, helping them find and grow in their relationship with the God who is within all.

The second one is the level of close relationships and small groups. At this level, our spiritual formation efforts are focused more intentionally on the personal relationships that people, like Martha and Charlie, have with one another. It is oriented toward nurturing relationships that are loving, just, giving, and healthy (i.e., relationships that are more reflective and manifesting of the Spirit). Such close relationships include the intimate ones we have with significant others, the mentoring partnerships that we choose, the small groups we are a part of, and our families. At this level, our formative focus is therefore on nurturing the life of God within and among these close relationships.

The third level that we can intentionally focus on in our local contexts, is the level of the wider community. For spiritual formators and pastors working in a church, such as Montague, this would mean focusing on the congregation as a whole. For leaders at a retreat center, this would be the large groups that come for a visit. For those working in nonprofits and engaging in community building and organizing efforts, this would be the organizations or neighborhoods they are working with. At this

The Need for Spiritual Formation Methodologies

level, similar to the close relationship level, the focus lies in forming whole communities of justice, peace, harmony, order, et cetera, for their political, social, and economic dimensions. Here, the formator's eyes are oriented not so much on the individuals, relationships, and groups that make up the community, but rather more toward the overall dynamics of the larger community as a unified whole. This third level therefore focuses on the wider communities that we are in leadership with.

Of course, there are also even wider circles of influences that we can and should seek to address. We should seek to impact our cities, governments, and larger cultures. We need to actively pursue the health and vitality of our planet and its complex ecosystems. However, as spiritual formators working primarily in parishes and nonprofits (for whom this book is intended), many of us will formatively influence these wider circles mostly from our own local ministerial contexts. If we were a politician, however, then these wider circles could and should become the focus of our spiritually forming endeavors. It is, however, these three levels—individuals, close relationships, and larger communities—that most spiritual formators will find themselves focused on.

On the Nature of Christian Theistic Spiritual Formation

While these reflections might be helpful, knowing the overall location and foci of our work is not enough. We must also understand the more specific nature of theistic spiritual formation and the ends toward which it strives. As we look into some of the Christian spiritual formation literature, some intentionality is given to describing the nature of spiritual formation and discipleship. "Discipleship" is described as being "an intensely creative process," one that is not merely "a program or an event" but rather an entire "way of life."[19] It is described as a process of one being in a mentored relationship with a teacher.[20] It is a committed relationship that is intended to help the individual or community toward a greater life in God.[21]

Similarly, "spiritual formation" from a Western Christian perspective is understood as being an "ongoing journey of imagining, gaining insights,

---

19. Hull, *Complete Book of Discipleship*, 24; McCallum and Lowery, *Organic Disciplemaking*, 37.

20. Hull, *Complete Book of Discipleship*, 24; O'Connell, *Making Disciples*, 142.

21. Hull, *Complete Book of Discipleship*, 26–27; Law, "Serious Call to a Devout and Holy Life," 208, 241–47.

and deciding how to live as faithful and responsible Christians."[22] While there are many ways of approaching such formation, it is described as one that involves the entire community of which one is a part for the purpose of shaping and nurturing the whole of one's life.[23] Both of these concepts, then, depict something of the nature of theistic spiritual formation as being the intentional shaping and forming of one's life in God.

But toward what ends? In the literature, there are a number of ideals that are set forth for Christian spiritual formators working with individuals to strive for. As Christians, "attaining to the whole measure of the fullness of Christ" is set as a central goal.[24] Such an ideal generally means one of two things. First, it is often understood that a Christian will strive to imitate and embody the life and teaching of Jesus, for he is our example of an ideal life.[25] In this vein, it means that we will work toward achieving a "likeness" to him; that we will take on his character.[26] Second, it can mean that we come to share more fully in the divine life. Such a sharing is described in terms of our abiding more fully in God and God coming to dwell more completely in us.[27] This mutuality of sharing is an ideal that is foundational to the growing Christian spiritual life.

The results of such imitation and abiding life are that the individual's whole personality and character is to be transformed.[28] Descriptions for what a transformed character looks like are quite broad and diverse.

22. Wimberly and Parker, "In Search of Wisdom," 12–13.

23. Bidwell and Marshall, "Formation," 3; Dettoni, "What Is Spiritual Formation?," 11; Van Kaam, *Fundamental Formation*, chs. 3 and 4.

24. Lawrenz, *Dynamics of Spiritual Formation*, 21, 119.

25. Erasmus, "Handbook of the Militant Christian," 73, 88; Felder, "Counsel from Wise Others," 94; Hull, *Complete Book of Discipleship*, 114, 135; Law, "Serious Call to a Devout and Holy Life," 47, 75, 83, 321, 350; Lawrenz, *Dynamics of Spiritual Formation*, 145–46; Meye, "Imitation of Christ," 199; O'Connell, *Making Disciples*, 15–16.

26. *John Cassian: The Conferences*, 24, 43, 44, 163; Dettoni, "What Is Spiritual Formation?," 16; Erasmus, "Handbook of the Militant Christian," 92; Hull, *Complete Book of Discipleship*, 19; Lawrenz, *Dynamics of Spiritual Formation*, 144; Lightner, "Salvation and Spiritual Formation," 39; Willard, "Spirit Is Willing," 225; Wimberly and Parker, "In Search of Wisdom," 15.

27. Clark, "Spiritual Formation in Children," 235; Deison, "Spiritual Formation through Small Groups," 271; Hull, *Complete Book of Discipleship*, 28, 47; Jackson, "Forming a Spirituality of Wisdom," 154; Lightner, "Salvation and Spiritual Formation," 44; Payne, "Personal Healing and Spiritual Formation," 213; Pazmino, "Nurturing the Spiritual Lives of Teachers," 148; Wimberly and Parker, "In Search of Wisdom," 13.

28. McCallum and Lowery, *Organic Disciplemaking*, 39; O'Connell, *Making Disciples*, 82, 151.

The Need for Spiritual Formation Methodologies

They include such idealized traits as: greater independence, stability, and obedience; an increase in joy, peace, love, and humility in one's life; a calling to service, higher ethical ideals, and right beliefs.[29] Such a character is asserted to also manifest greater self-knowledge and integration, thereby leading one to becoming ever more fully and authentically human for some authors.[30]

Some also discuss ideals related to spirituality itself, the church, and one's communal environment. An ideal spirituality, for instance, is described as being one that is fully incarnational, present with the concrete "here and now" of our lives, as well as one that is liberating and empowering.[31] The ideal church is depicted as one that manifests Christ's life as a community through service and affection, one that embodies gospel values, and one that is ever "young, vital, and powerful," similar to the church depicted in the book of Acts, chapters 2–4, in the Bible.[32] Finally, the ideal communal environment is one that needs, according to at least one author, trust, grace, humility, submission, affirmation.[33]

From these theoretical discussions, we therefore gain a much clearer understanding of the nature and goals of Western Christian theistic spiritual formation. As a field of formation, it is about intentionally working to give a specific shape and form to the individuals, relationships, and communities that we are called to work with. It is one that is intended to result in a transforming way of life and being, but toward specific horizons. As a theistic field, it is one that seeks to do this from a religious and theological

---

29. *John Cassian: The Conferences*, 51, 329, 376, 419, 572; Erasmus, "Handbook of the Militant Christian," 41, 49, 73; Graham and Whitehead, "Role of Pastoral Theology in Theological Education for the Formation of Pastoral Counselors," 23; Hull, *Complete Book of Discipleship*, 47, 130, 139, 145; 149–51; Law, "Serious Call to a Devout and Holy Life," 82, 91, 96, 129; McCallum and Lowery, *Organic Disciplemaking*, 217, 225, 251, 260; O'Connell, *Making Disciples*, 12–13, 25; Pazmino, "Nurturing the Spiritual Lives of Teachers," 149–51; Piper, "God Is Most Glorified in Us When We are Most Satisfied in Him," 74.

30. Erasmus, "Handbook of the Militant Christian," 42; Jackson, "Forming a Spirituality of Wisdom," 155; Lawrenz, *Dynamics of Spiritual Formation*, 34; Payne, "Personal Healing and Spiritual Formation," 213; Van Kaam, *Fundamental Formation*, 61–62.

31. Felder, "Counsel from Wise Others," 99; Pazmino, "Nurturing the Spiritual Lives of Teachers," 150; Smith, "Forming Wisdom through Cultural Rootedness," 40.

32. Hull, *Complete Book of Discipleship*, 165; O'Connell, *Making Disciples*, 85–86, 128, 168; Radillo, "Model of Formation in the Multi-Cultural Urban Context for the Pastoral Care Specialist," 169; Schreck, "Principles of Church Renewal," 154, 156.

33. Hull, *Complete Book of Discipleship*, ch. 5.

orientation. God is viewed as being the foundation of these formative endeavors. More specifically, as Christians, such theistic endeavors are understood in light of Christ. Jesus of Nazareth holds a central place in our formation systems. He embodies the ideals toward which we strive, the character we seek to become like as individuals and communities, and the greater divine life into which we are called to participate. However, as Christians, we also recognize the greater role and relationship of Christ to the Trinity. It is from this larger perspective that this book will operate, therefore using such terms as "Spirit," "Sacred," "God," and "the Divine" to refer to this Trinitarian life.

Stated very basically then, *Western Christian theistic spiritual formation may be understood as our intentional efforts to partner with God's formative life and leadings in our local contexts.* More simply referred to as "spiritual formation" throughout the remainder of these pages, it is a craft of our working to discern and partner with the life of the Spirit as God continually seeks to transform our world. It is therefore essentially one in which we, as spiritual formation practitioners, strive with individuals, relationships, and communities toward greater attunement with and in the formative life of the Divine in our midst.

If such an approach were to be adopted by Montague, Francis, and Tom, this would mean that they would each seek to discern what is it that God is doing in their local context. With Christ as a model, in addition to the Christian tradition, they would be seeking to better understand what is happening in their programs, relationships, and communities and where it is that the Spirit seems to be moving. Montague would seek to know how the Spirit is yearning to respond within and through his struggling community. Francis would work to find the genuine movements of divine life in Martha's relationship with her husband. And Tom would strive to discern God's desires for the participants of his program. From this Western Christian theistic perspective, then, each of them would intentionally work to perceive and move in harmony with God's life in their unique and formative situations.

The Road Ahead: Discernment, Praxis, and Methodologies

While these theoretical foundations may be helpful, we can still ask how are we to proceed along these lines? If it is true that there is a need for methodologies that might help to guide the formative work that practitioners

The Need for Spiritual Formation Methodologies

like Montague, Francis, and Tom face, what are they? How can we begin to conceive of a set of practical steps that spiritual formators can follow in their craft?

From our explorations above, we can see that spiritual formation has at least two primary elements to it: spiritual discernment and the intentional work of transformation. Both of these are essential to spiritual formation program development and we therefore need to address them with care and intentionality.

If our craft really is one of perceiving the life and movements of the Divine in our concrete local contexts, then we therefore need some way of identifying these movements of the Spirit. Montague, for instance, needs to know how he can reflect on the historical and contemporary dynamics of his congregation from such a theistic perspective. How can he really know where it is that God is inviting them to move toward? Engaging in these kinds of reflections is a practice that is known as "spiritual discernment" and we will be exploring this in detail in chapter 1. It is an art of coming to see the Spirit at work in our own lives and in the world around us. We will be walking with Montague in this chapter as he seeks to discern where it is that he comes to believe the Spirit is leading the congregation.

As we shall see in much greater detail in chapter 2, "praxis" is understood as standing at the intersection of theory, practice, and reflection for the purposes of transformation. It is one in which transforming action emerges from the mutual dance of each of these three contributions. As a "praxis-oriented" field, spiritual formation is situated within the interplay between theory and practice for the purposes of transformation via the theological and religious traditions that it draws from and the approaches it implements in its local contexts.[34] In other words, any set of program development methodologies that we engage in will necessarily draw from such external resources as sacred texts, the teachings of our traditions, and the insights of other practitioners. However, just as it does for Montague, Francis, and Tom, it will also utilize the insights and understandings that come from our own observations, actions, and reflections on our local contexts. As a result, and similar to other praxis-oriented fields, spiritual formation is therefore interested in how the discerningly reflective interplay between theory and practice formatively interacts with our local contexts.[35]

---

34. For understandings of TSF as a field that stands in dialogue with both theory and practice, see such texts as: Van Kaam, *Scientific Formation*.

35. For examples of research into similarly praxis-oriented fields, see: Gall et al.,

Living Spiritual Praxis

In chapter 2, we will therefore explore the nature of praxis as it relates to the field of spiritual formation. From these explorations we will then derive three sets of methodologies for engaging in spiritual formation program development. Part 2 of this book will then explore and detail each of these three methodologies from a spiritually discerning perspective. The methods found in chapters 3, 4, and 5 are intended to help practitioners—like Montague, Francis, and Tom—to walk, step by step, through the entire process of deciding upon, implementing, and assessing a program or set of interventions in her or his local context. For each of these chapters, we will be following formators—such as Francis and two others—as they engage in each of these methodologies. Finally, in chapter 6, we will return to Tom's case as we watch him apply all of these methodologies to the contemplative spiritual formation program that he developed for his participants.

You will also notice that each of the first six chapters is divided into two sections. The first section of each chapter explores the theoretical foundations of the theme being addressed. For instance, in the first chapter we will be exploring some of the core fundamentals of spiritual discernment. These foundations are intended to elaborate on the necessary concepts which will be needed for the second section of each chapter: methodological movements. In this second part, we will then turn our attention toward how to practically embody the topic. In the case of spiritual discernment, we will then see how to engage in discernment through five specific processes.

In essence, then, this book seeks to provide some of the essential theoretical and methodological foundations for spiritual formation program development. Striving to follow a praxis approach that is thoroughly rooted in spiritual discernment, we will be reflectively exploring both the theory and practice of this craft in an effort to develop and clarify some of its practical steps to designing, implementing, and assessing our formative endeavors. In the end, our hopes are to better enable us to partner ever more fully with the transforming life of the Spirit as we engage with the struggles of the individuals, relationships, and communities that we are called to work with. This book is therefore not one that is intended to present a set of "dead" steps to be mindlessly followed, but rather one that will hopefully empower us to journey with the living Spirit who is ever at

---

Educational Research; McLeod, *Doing Counselling Research*; Reamer, *Social Work Research and Evaluation Skills*.

work in our midst. In short, then, we are seeking the foundations of our spiritually forming craft that embodies a living spiritual praxis.

A Final Word: The "KISS" Principle

At this point, we are ready to begin. Not only do we know where we are headed, we also know some of the means by which we will get there. However, the journey we will be embarking on will at times be a complicated one. Before continuing, then, there is a core principle that will help us to stay the course when things appear to be getting too complicated. It is known as the "KISS" principle.

Mark, Engineering, and Green Jello: A Story

For more than forty years, Dr. Mark Johansson has worked and consulted for such organizations as NASA while teaching in an engineering department at Texas A&M University. Developing detailed dynamic simulations for some of the most complex physical systems, Dr. Johansson's career has been one pushing the edges of science and engineering. Yet, his philosophy of life and engineering design work is surprisingly simple.

When I first came to Texas A&M as an engineering student in the fall of 1991, I was fully prepared and completely scared of what I was about to face. Chemistry, physics, partial differential equations, and complex dynamic systems would often leave my head feeling like a bowl full of lifeless green jello by the end of a long day of classes and studying. And then I had a class with a man who could fill multiple chalk boards with all of this complex information and then effortlessly tie them together into a coherent engineering design. Dr. Johansson, for me, was the embodiment of what I thought an ideal engineer should be at that time in my life: smart, filled with volumes of encyclopedic knowledge that is ever at his fingertips, and smooth in operation.

As the semester wore on, however, I increasingly had difficulty keeping up with trying to embody this ideal as a young student. Apparently not alone, my peers in this class expressed their concern for also not being able to manage all of this complex information. Things seemed to be reaching a boiling point of stress and fear for all of us until Dr. Johansson finally shared with us a core insight that he has gleaned from his many years of being immersed in the highly sophisticated world of engineering. He called it the "KISS" principle, and it stands for "Keep It Simple, Student."

Living Spiritual Praxis

In problem after problem, Dr. Johansson demonstrated for us what this principle is all about. No matter how complicated an engineering design project seems to become, there is always a core focus that will lead you through it.

Take a commercial airplane like the 747, for instance. Think of all of the parts, different kinds of materials, electronics, safety devices, et cetera, that go into making such an enormous and almost majestic presence in the sky. Just thinking about the number of parts alone, of which there are asserted to be more than six million,[36] can be enough to turn a young engineer's head into a bowl of green jello. And yet, when we think about it in its more basic form, in simpler terms, we can realize that the core engineering design problem for this complicated beast of an airplane is quite simply to comfortably move a group of passengers safely from point A to point B via the medium of flight. All other design problems related to the 747, and all of its six million separate parts, revolve around this central and simple goal.

The Principle in Practice

This is an example of the KISS principle in practice. It is a matter of returning again and again to the more basic and simpler core of what we are trying to accomplish no matter how complicated something may seem to be. Not only can this principle apply to the complex reaches of engineering design problems, as it has in Dr. Johansson's distinguished career, but also to our own lives and our world more generally.

For instance, think about the sometimes overly long list that is our "to do's." Like God, our to-do lists often appear to be both infinite and eternal. Glancing at my own, I sometimes wonder whether there aren't enough hours in my lifetime, much less the coming day, to complete all that is on it. And yet I also find that if I prioritize them according to what "absolutely has to be done" today and leave the rest in the "hands of God," somehow life moves more smoothly. By focusing on what is most essential for this moment, we are able—often with much help and supporting guidance—to complete the tasks that are really most needed. This is the KISS principle at work in our lives. It is our focusing on the core of what is most important and allowing everything else to rearrange around it.

In this book, we will at times be traversing what can seem like complicated methodologies and theories. When this happens, I will attempt

36. WikiAnswers, "How Many Parts Are in a Boeing 747?"

to, as much as possible, apply the KISS principle and redirect our attention to the core of what it is we are trying to do with all of it. I will attempt to refocus us on what our primary goals and intentions are. However, as the reader, you are invited to do the same thing. And that is to again and again ask yourself, whenever things start to seem too complicated, what is the more genuine core of what we're trying to do here, and then let this central focus be your guide as you proceed. By doing so, it is hoped that our aims will be met, that our goals will be realized, and that in the end the horizons toward which we are journeying here and where we currently find ourselves will eventually come together and, dare I say it? KISS!

PART ONE

Theoretical Foundations

WE BEGIN OUR JOURNEY in this first part of the book by exploring some of the core theoretical foundations for our craft of living spiritual praxis. In the first chapter of this section, we will be exploring the nature and role of spiritual discernment for our vocation. Not only will we seek to better understand what discernment is and what it is founded upon, but we will also explore its practical steps and key components. In the end, the hopes are to provide a strong theoretical framework and methodological basis for engaging in discernment in relation to spiritual formation program development.

In the second chapter, we will then turn our attention to some of the basics of praxis and its relation to the field of spiritual formation. Here, our task will be to better understand what praxis is, where it comes from, and how it is engaged by other praxis-oriented fields. From these discussions, we will derive three methodologies that will become the foundations for our approaches program development. These three methodologies will then be taken up in part 2 of this book. Overall, then, the goal of this first part is to lay a strong theoretical foundation for the second part of this book where we will be exploring the three spiritual praxis methodologies.

1

Discerning Discernment
Detailing the Dynamics of a Spiritual Discipline

TYPE "DISCERNMENT" INTO A book search engine, such as Amazon or Barnes and Noble, and you will find a couple hundred resources pop up. Discernment and decision-making has become a hot topic in recent years as leaders have sought to improve the quality of actions in churches, businesses, and ethical situations. In spiritual formation, its importance is no less central. For instance, early Christians, such as the writers of the *Didache* and the desert monastic communities, are found to emphasize the role of discernment.[1] But what is it exactly? What are some of the foundational elements that we need to know about in order to engage in spiritual discernment? What are some of the basic steps that we can discerningly engage in? Drawing from a small sampling of mainline Protestant,[2] Evangelical-Charismatic,[3] and Roman Catholic[4] sources, which represent both academic and practitioner perspectives,[5] we will be exploring questions and topics such as these in an effort to better know what discernment is

---

1. *John Cassian: The Conferences*, 59–63, 87, 92; Milavec, *Didache*, 387.

2. Ackerman, *Listening to God*; Edwards, *Living in the Presence*; Wolpert, *Leading a Life with God*.

3. Isenhower and Todd, *Living into the Answers*; Parker, *Led by the Spirit*.

4. Au and Au, *Discerning Heart*; Dougherty, *Group Spiritual Direction*; Hauser, *Moving in the Spirit*.

5. Sources from the academy include: Au and Au, *Discerning Heart*; Hauser, *Moving in the Spirit*; Parker, *Led by the Spirit*. Sources written by practitioners include: Ackerman, *Listening to God*; Dougherty, *Group Spiritual Direction*; Edwards, *Living in the Presence*; Isenhower and Todd, *Living into the Answers*; Wolpert, *Leading a Life with God*.

and how we might engage program development in spiritually discerning ways. While these explorations are by no means a comprehensive survey of the vast literature that is out there on this topic, they will help us to gain a deeper understanding into some of the basic theoretical and methodological movements of these all important processes of spiritual discernment. For, as we heard in the previous chapter, there can be no living spiritual praxis without them.

FOUNDATIONS OF SPIRITUAL DISCERNMENT

Before we can engage in a specific set of processes for discernment, it will be helpful to explore some of the foundations of the nature of discernment. In this section, we will review a few key understandings of discernment, consider some of the necessary theological and epistemological bases for it, and gain insights into some its dynamics, pitfalls, and intended results. Overall, this section seeks to investigate these foundations.

Defining Discernment

While discernment does have a general meaning, it can be perceived differently depending on one's worldviews. In an effort to move toward a working definition of spiritual discernment for our purposes in this project, we explore some of the different ways that theistic authors view it. In the end, we will come to understand spiritual discernment as a purposeful way of perceiving God's presence and movements in our world.

Generally, Theistically

At its heart, discernment generally has to do with distinguishing between various parts or sources.[6] Literally, writes Shalem Institute for Spiritual Formation's Sister Rose Mary Dougherty, it means to "perceive clearly" or to "judge accurately."[7] It is essentially the process of being able to "distinguish between alternatives" and "discover answers to the questions that arise from issues in our lives."[8] In its most generalized form, then, discernment is associated with our efforts to choose rightly from among

6. Ackerman, *Listening to God*, 79.
7. Dougherty, *Group Spiritual Direction*, 24.
8. Isenhower and Todd, *Living into the Answers*, 10, 22.

alternatives, thereby being able to discriminate one path or choice from another.

For theists, "spiritual" discernment is described in more explicitly theological terms. Stated most directly by spiritual director and Presbyterian pastor John Ackerman, "The process of discernment is that of distinguishing the Holy Spirit from other spirits,"[9] and it is a view supported by some of our Catholic and charismatic authors as well.[10] Rather than merely attempting to distinguish between two choices in a general way, then, theists seek to do so from their distinctively theological perspective.

Spiritual discernment is therefore ultimately about perceiving the movements of the Spirit in our midst, that we might live more in tune with God.[11] It is about one's quest to know and live in accordance with God's will for our lives and our communities.[12] Generally and theistically conceived, then, spiritual discernment seeks to discriminate among the various influences of our lives hoping to perceive the movements of God with greater clarity. As a result, there are two primary places that an individual can and should look to when discerning: their outer and inner lives.[13]

Outer Mandates and Guidance

Looking externally, spiritual discernment is sometimes conceived of as a quest to know "God's universal will" for our lives.[14] Couched in this way, discernment may be approached as a process of looking to external sources of authority, such as sacred texts or one's religious tradition, for guidance and mandates regarding this universal will.[15] For others, the external aspects of discernment are a process of "recognizing the kingdom in our midst,"[16] helping us to "spot the presence of God in the concrete events and experiences of ordinary life."[17] While for others, it is a quest for "some

---

9. Ackerman, *Listening to God*, 79.

10. Au and Au, *Discerning Heart*, 38; Parker, *Led by the Spirit*, 34.

11. Au and Au, *Discerning Heart*, 22, 73; Isenhower and Todd, *Living into the Answers*, 17.

12. Edwards, *Living in the Presence*, 100; Hauser, *Moving in the Spirit*, 7, 63.

13. Au and Au, *Discerning Heart*, 5, 50, 122–24.

14. Hauser, *Moving in the Spirit*, 61.

15. Au and Au, *Discerning Heart*, 122–23.

16. Wolpert, *Leading a Life with God*, 67.

17. Au and Au, *Discerning Heart*, 19.

PART ONE: Theoretical Foundations

guiding wisdom" that will help us in our daily lives.[18] Regardless of the reasons, looking externally to one's outer life is considered to be a central part of spiritual discernment.

Inner Movements

However, many of our authors also highlight the need to consider the inner movements of one's life as well. Here, an emphasis is given to our inward listening for God's yearnings and invitations for our lives.[19] Going back to early Christian communities, listening inwardly "arose out of the desire to sort out the movements within us."[20] As Ackerman writes, "Discernment is inviting the mind of Christ to decide on a basis other than ego-centered choice."[21] The hopes for our internal arena are that God will ultimately become the one moving and guiding us in our hearts, minds, and bodies.[22] Inner discernment is therefore primarily one of our learning "to recognize when the Spirit is and is not present and then to follow only those experiences that are from the Spirit."[23] Inner spiritual discernment is therefore viewed as a central component as well.

A Working Definition

Given this very brief exploration, we are now in a position to offer a working definition that will become the basis for not only the rest of this chapter, but also for how we will discerningly engage in our praxis methodologies in the next part of this book. As it relates to this project, *theistic spiritual discernment is defined as the intentional processes of perceiving the movements of the Spirit in specific areas of one's inner and/or outer life for the purposes of empowering a more spiritually attuned life.* It is one that discriminates these divine leadings from others that either do not seem to manifest God at all or do so to a much lesser extent.[24] As we continue with

---

18. Ibid., 28.
19. Isenhower and Todd, *Living into the Answers*, 15.
20. Edwards, *Living in the Presence*, 99.
21. Ackerman, *Listening to God*, 79.
22. Au and Au, *Discerning Heart*, 5; Hauser, *Moving in the Spirit*, 4, 23; Parker, *Led by the Spirit*, 14, 180.
23. Hauser, *Moving in the Spirit*, 29.
24. Parker, *Led by the Spirit*, 34.

these foundational explorations of spiritual discernment, the nuances and details of this definition should become clearer.

Theologies and Epistemologies

Having a working definition and basic understanding of the nature of spiritual discernment, our hopes are to now begin moving toward actually engaging discernment in our lives and our formative programs. In order to do this, however, there are two key areas that we must have a better understanding of because they are an integral part of theistic approaches to discernment. These two areas are theology and epistemology. Without understanding their roles, we may be entering into discernment more blindly than we should be.

The Centrality of Theology

"Consciously or not," write professors Wilkie and Noreen Cannon Au, "our God-images directly affect the way we think, feel, and act."[25] Shaped by many influences, such as early childhood experiences,[26] not only do our understandings about God influence how we will interact with God,[27] but they also determine the ways in which we will engage in discernment.[28] As we saw above, "spiritual" discernment (or, more accurately, "theistic spiritual" discernment) was distinguished from the more general understandings of discernment because it was defined in theological terms. We are not merely trying to discriminate one thing from another but, more specifically, we are attempting to distinguish those movements in our lives that are more "manifesting of God" than are others. In order to do this, as we shall currently see, the theologies that we assert about God's nature and God's relationship to creation (and human nature) hold a central place in our spiritual discernment.

---

25. Au and Au, *Discerning Heart*, 104, 113.
26. Parker, *Led by the Spirit*, 173.
27. Dougherty, *Group Spiritual Direction*, 26–27; Isenhower and Todd, *Living into the Answers*, 33, 38.
28. Isenhower and Todd, *Living into the Answers*, 27, 29.

PART ONE: Theoretical Foundations

God's Nature

If we believe in a God who judgmentally expects obedience and conformity under the threat of wrath, then how we go about engaging in discernment will probably be quite different than if we understand God to be a compassionate, cocreating God who longs to participate with us in the journeys of life.[29] For instance, Dougherty shares a personal testimony of how her own images of God distorted the ways she engaged in prayer and discernment. Basing her images on early experiences that she had with relatives, she remembers,

> My behavior toward God in prayer, even as an adult, was much like my behavior toward [my two cousins]. I was still sitting quietly on God's sofa in my scratchy crinoline, trying not to move. I was still being polite with God. I never asked for anything. I always said, "Whatever you would like, God, just tell me, just give me." I had learned from my cousins that if I wanted something God must not want it and what God wanted would be terrible.[30]

Her reflections are a testimony to the impact that our theologies of God's nature can have on our discernment processes. At this time in Dougherty's life, she still viewed God as being one who was not interested in her own passions and desires. For her, God was clearly conceived as having God's own will, completely independent of her own. The dominant image of God's nature here, then, is one of an external and dominating Presence in Dougherty's life.

As a result, her discernment was one of seeking to uncover the will of this demanding God. Clearly, her processes favored outer sources over inner ones for she assumed that God would most certainly not want what she wanted. We can therefore see how Dougherty's discernment was influenced by the theology she held at that time in her life regarding God's nature. We must therefore seek to be more explicit, as Dougherty was, about these views of the Divine in relation to our own lives and the communities we are working with for they can dramatically impact our discernment processes.

---

29. Au and Au, *Discerning Heart*, 121, 223.
30. Dougherty, *Group Spiritual Direction*, 26.

God's Relationship to Creation and Human Nature

Reflecting on the nature of God alone, however, is not enough. We may believe that God does care deeply about our wishes and desires but if we do not believe that God actually interacts with us and our world, then our discernment processes will reflect that. A cornerstone of spiritual discernment is therefore the assertion that God actually wants us to know God's desires and directions for our world and that God interacts with creation in ways that reveal these holy longings.[31] How we view God's relationship to creation and to ourselves therefore also has an influence on our processes of discernment. It influences the outer and inner sources that we turn to for our discernment.

For those that view God as seeking to impose a fixed and external will on creation, their processes—as did Dougherty's—may favor external sources.[32] We have already seen that such outer sources are important for discernment. However, they can only be so if we believe that God's life is present and active within and through them otherwise there is no need to turn to them.[33] For instance, if we did not believe that God's "Word" was somehow present in the sacred texts of our traditions, then we would not spend so much time and effort with them. Our theologies therefore need to have some understanding of the nature of God's relationship to creation.

For inner sources of individual discernment, we must also have some notion of how God relates to human nature. Most of our authors emphasized the active role of the Spirit in the lives of individual human beings. Depicted as friend, lover, omnipresent companion, guide, sanctifier, and core identity, each of them stressed the intimate relationship that God has with human nature.[34] While some considered human nature to be fundamentally good, and therefore a reliable basis for inner discernment work, others stressed the presence of dual influences of good and evil.[35]

---

31. Au and Au, *Discerning Heart*, 37, 121, 223; Hauser, *Moving in the Spirit*, 63; Isenhower and Todd, *Living into the Answers*, 39, 43; Wolpert, *Leading a Life with God*, 68.

32. Au and Au, *Discerning Heart*, 123.

33. Au and Au, *Discerning Heart*, 4–5, 79.

34. Ackerman, *Listening to God*, 9, 90; Au and Au, *Discerning Heart*, 50; Dougherty, *Group Spiritual Direction*, 30; Hauser, *Moving in the Spirit*, 24, 62; Isenhower and Todd, *Living into the Answers*, 39; Parker, *Led by the Spirit*, 33, 103.

35. Ackerman, *Listening to God*, 90; Hauser, *Moving in the Spirit*, 9, 10; Parker, *Led by the Spirit*, 180.

PART ONE: Theoretical Foundations

Nevertheless, the immanence of God's active life in humanity is therefore considered to be a central pillar for each of their discernment processes. We can therefore see how our theologies of God's nature and relationship to creation are central factors in spiritual discernment.

Spiritual Epistemologies: Holistic Ways of Knowing God

Our working definition essentially has two aspects to it. The first is the activity of the Spirit in our lives and our world. For this, as we just saw, the theologies we hold are central. The second, however, is our ability to "perceive" this Spirit's work. For this, we must now turn to what is known as "epistemology," which is our understanding of where knowledge comes from.[36] We may have certain beliefs about God's nature and how God interacts with creation and our lives, but if we also believe that we are not able to perceive these movements, then our discernment will have no grounds to stand upon. In other words, if we are completely blind to God's movements in our midst then there would be no basis for discernment.

From our authors, we find that different communities emphasize different ways of knowing in relation to their discernment. In a research study that professor of counseling and human services Stephen Parker conducted on Pentecostal approaches to discernment, he found that "Pentecostal discernment and decision making emphasizes, encourages, and legitimates an openness to affective, intuitive, and semi-conscious dimensions of knowing."[37] Rather than being a more purely rational-based form of knowing, Pentecostal discernment places a much greater weight on these "transrational psychic processes" and "heart-felt experience[s]."[38] In a similar vein, Ignatian approaches to spiritual discernment emphasize the role of affective "consolations" and "desolations."[39] Both of these communities assert that God's life and movements can be more clearly perceived by these affective ways of knowing and experiencing.

However, given that most of our authors also supported a theology of God's immanence throughout all of creation, we also find many of them to support the need for holistic approaches to discernment. These approaches stress the role of multiple ways of knowing in their processes;

36. Moser et al., *Theory of Knowledge*, 24.
37. Parker, *Led by the Spirit*, 111.
38. Ibid., 21, 108.
39. Ackerman, *Listening to God*, 87; Au and Au, *Discerning Heart*, 53; Hauser, *Moving in the Spirit*, 4, 23, 74.

those that engage our whole beings and lives.[40] Such holistic ways might include using reason, bodily sensations, external observations, affective movements, situational circumstances, et cetera, in ones discernment. The goal here is to draw from each of these and other epistemological sources for the purposes of integrating the insights about God's movements from each of them.[41] As shown below in figure 3, I have developed a template that depicts some of these multiple ways of knowing that we might draw from in our own discernment processes.[42]

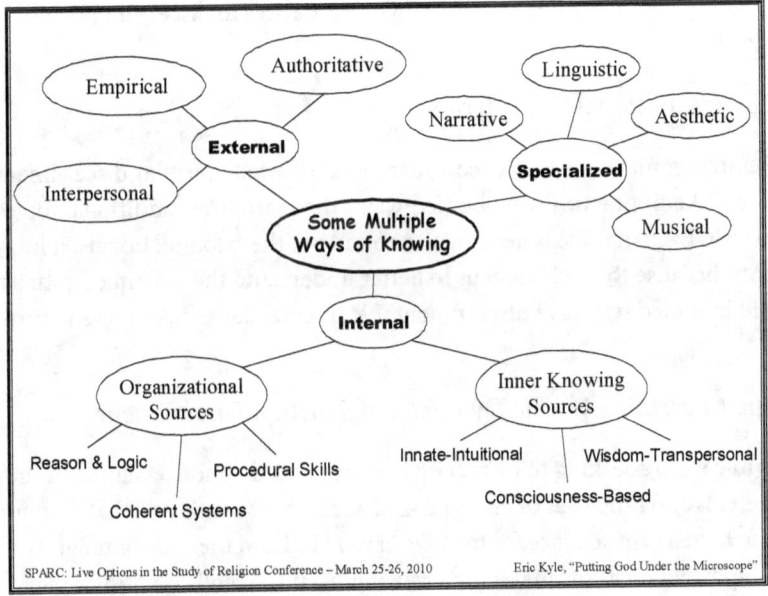

Figure 3. Some Multiple Ways of Knowing

Different communities, as we have already heard, will emphasize some of these ways of knowing more than others. Pentecostals and Ignatians, for example, tend to favor the "inner knowing sources," while those whose theology is more akin to Dougherty's above will favor "external"

40. Ackerman, *Listening to God*, 81; Au and Au, *Discerning Heart*, 9, 46; Isenhower and Todd, *Living into the Answers*, 86; Parker, *Led by the Spirit*, 176.

41. Au and Au, *Discerning Heart*, 47.

42. Kyle, "Putting God under the Microscope." To read a more detailed description of each of these ways of knowing in this paper, see the various papers posted at *Homebrewed Christianity*, online: http://homebrewedchristianity.com/2010/03/22/live-options-in-the-study-of-religion/.

sources more. The more explicit we are about which epistemological sources we and our communities favor, the better we will be able to engage in our discernment processes because we will know which sources we should spend more of our time with.

However, we must also, depending on our theologies, heed the admonitions of our authors and look to other and more holistic sources as well. Regardless of which ones we draw from, the epistemologies we have influence how we engage in spiritual discernment. We must therefore identify our own favored ways of perceiving God in the processes of developing and reflecting upon our own approaches to discernment.

Three Additional Considerations

Before we move on to our considerations of what spiritual discernment looks like in practically embodied ways, there are three additional topics to visit. Each of these is necessary to round out these foundational explorations because they will help us to better understand the dynamics, pitfalls, and intended results of discernment. Let us consider each of these in turn.

The Uncertain, Artistic Dynamics of Spiritual Discernment

While we are seeking to be precise in relation to the more essential fundamentals and processes of discernment, our authors remind us that we must also hold a central place for the mystery of God and therefore ambiguity in all spiritual decision-making.[43] Drawing from the biblical notion of Spirit being like the wind, blowing where it wills, our discernment must be open to novelty and will therefore be unpredictable to some extent.[44] No single external source or "guru" can ever tell us precisely what it is that God is doing in our lives or what it is we should do exactly in any given situation.[45] We must therefore allow for some lack of certainty in our discernment, never being 100 percent sure of the decisions that we make.[46] As a result, we should also expect a trial-and-error approach as we make mistakes as a result of this ambiguity and because of the distortions that are asserted

---

43. Au and Au, *Discerning Heart*, 37; Edwards, *Living in the Presence*, 101.
44. Au and Au, *Discerning Heart*, 14; Parker, *Led by the Spirit*, 202.
45. Au and Au, *Discerning Heart*, 100.
46. Edwards, *Living in the Presence*, 99; Isenhower and Todd, *Living into the Answers*, 25–26.

to be an inherent part of the human condition.[47] Spiritual discernment is therefore generally one of an uncertain and cyclical process.[48] Ultimately, it is therefore "both an art and a gift;" one in which Creator and creature dance toward the discerned horizons of the future.[49]

Potential Pitfalls When Discerning

In this dance, we must also be aware of some of the potential obstacles that can hinder our discernment. While they are numerous, our authors seem to focus on three. In essence, each of these potential pitfalls has the effect of either narrowing or distorting our abilities to perceive God's life in our own.

The first are the pre-expectations that we and/or the traditions of which we are a part hold in relation to the situations we are discerning over.[50] An example of this would be a centralized hierarchy of a denomination or religious tradition which asserts that it knows what is best for the whole of the denomination without considering local circumstances.[51] Such domineering influences may have the effect of turning our attention away from what God is doing in our local contexts toward what the hierarchy is demanding of us. We must therefore be aware of such pre-expectations and dominating influences, seeking to balance their expectations with all that we and our communities perceive God to be doing locally.

A second potential pitfall is the idea that we can always choose to not pursue the invitations and leadings of the Divine once they have been discerned.[52] We can choose to not follow after the Spirit or even to engage in any kind of explicit discernment at all. Such decisions may stem from fears that we have or our own narrower desires to move in a certain direction regardless of any considerations for others, the situation itself, and/or God in the midst of it all. An example of this would be a child who refuses to go to bed because he or she wants to stay up and play. Ignoring the weariness of her or his own body and the schedule set by the parents,

---

47. Au and Au, *Discerning Heart*, 97; Dougherty, *Group Spiritual Direction*, 30.

48. Isenhower and Todd, *Living into the Answers*, 9; Parker, *Led by the Spirit*, 110.

49. Ackerman, *Listening to God*, 81; Au and Au, *Discerning Heart*, 15; Isenhower and Todd, *Living into the Answers*, 23.

50. Wolpert, *Leading a Life with God*, 73.

51. Au and Au, *Discerning Heart*, 7.

52. Hauser, *Moving in the Spirit*, 29.

such a child focuses only on her or his individual wants to the exclusion of other considerations. In other words, we can choose to more narrowly focus our decisions on the choices that serve our own narrower wants and perceived needs to the exclusion of larger considerations.

A final obstacle that was noted in the literature is the presence of dominating affective influences that can distort our discernment. An example of this would be bad moods or emotional crises wherein we make our decisions under a cloud of negativity and darkness.[53] Such inner and overwhelming influences can obscure the way we see our lives and therefore distort our discernment. Part of our discernment processes should therefore be aware of these and many other potential pitfalls that more narrowly skew our decisions away from the genuine movements of the Sacred in our midst.

Intended Results: A Transforming Way of Life

A final consideration that it is important for us to address is the more primary intended results of all of these discerning practices. We have just heard that we should expect our approaches to be cyclical in nature. As we engage in spiritual discernment again and again, God not only guides us through the valleys and hills of life but also transforms us and parts of our world in the process as well. As retreat leaders Valerie Isenhower and Judith Todd write, "Our relationships with God and with other people will never be the same after we begin to live a life of discernment."[54]

Not only does it transform us into our more authentic identity and truer self in God, but we can also expect it to bring greater reconciliation, healing, and new ways of living to the communities that we are called to work with.[55] Living in spiritually discerning ways should foster greater love and service in the midst of a hurting world where these manifestations are needed.[56] In the unending end, spiritual discernment is intended to become not just one of many prayer practices that we engage in, but rather a fuller way of life that we lead. It is one in which we come to ever more

---

53. Hauser, *Moving in the Spirit*, 42; Isenhower and Todd, *Living into the Answers*, 19.

54. Isenhower and Todd, *Living into the Answers*, 16.

55. Dougherty, *Group Spiritual Direction*, 30; Isenhower and Todd, *Living into the Answers*, 22; Parker, *Led by the Spirit*, 180, 200.

56. Hauser, *Moving in the Spirit*, 8, 16.

fully and constantly find the Sacred in every part of our own.[57] Returning to our working definition, then, we can now see more clearly why it reads, "for the purposes of empowering a more spiritually-attuned life." Spiritual discernment is not merely a means to an ends, it is to also become a never-ending way of life in itself.

Core Components to Discernment Processes

With these foundational explorations in place, we can now begin to look toward concrete discernment processes that we might use for program development in our local ministerial contexts. However, because of the diversity of how various communities around the world engage in discernment, largely due to variations in the theological and epistemological considerations discussed above, it can be difficult to know what our own discernment processes should be. Nevertheless, there are factors that our authors assert that should be common to any such approaches. Even if you and the communities you are working with already have set discernment processes, I encourage you to read this section with your own practices in mind. If you are still searching for a set of steps to follow, the following components should aid you in your search.

Accounts for Diversity

In our discussions of theologies and epistemologies, we saw how variations in these can lead to different ways of both viewing and approaching discernment. Our processes must therefore account for diversity as God is asserted to lead different people and communities in different ways.[58] Such diversity may result from different significant religious experiences that people have had or from the different stages of spiritual development that people are in.[59] It might also stem from the different kinds of situations that we find ourselves facing. For instance, some issues, such as job changes, may require longer periods of time and more in-depth discernment than others, such as in deciding what to eat for dinner tonight.

---

57. Au and Au, *Discerning Heart*, 13; Dougherty, *Group Spiritual Direction*, 33; Isenhower and Todd, *Living into the Answers*, 11.

58. Au and Au, *Discerning Heart*, 5, 75.

59. Au and Au, *Discerning Heart*, 52; Dougherty, *Group Spiritual Direction*, 15.

PART ONE: Theoretical Foundations

The most commonly cited reason for accounting for diversity, however, is that different types of people and communities emphasize different styles of discernment.[60] The claim here is that different personality types have different strengths and weaknesses and therefore need to approach discernment from different angles.[61] For instance, Au and Au turn to Harvard Professor Howard Gardner's theory of multiple intelligences to show how different styles of learning (or "multiple intelligences") require different ways of engaging in decision-making.[62] Someone who is gifted in spatial intelligence will tend to favor visual sources while kinesthetic learners will discern more with their bodies. It is also asserted that whole communities, such as Pentecostals with their emphasis on "heart-felt experience," may favor certain approaches to discernment than do others.[63] Each individual and community must therefore come to discern, via trial and error, their own unique approach to discernment.[64] In essence, what we are attempting to discern here are the unique ways that God is seeking to lead and guide us and the communities we are called to formatively work with. As a result, any set of spiritual decision-making practices that are asserted must allow room for these kinds of diversity.

Articulates Needed Supports and Dispositions

It should already be clear by now that discernment is not a spiritual practice to be taken lightly. It is one that must be engaged with much care and intentionality. As a result, any set of processes should emphasize the supports that are needed to engage in discernment as well as the prerequisites that an individual or community should have as they enter them.

Necessary Supports

There are two primary supports that our authors highlight as being essential for engaging in the art of discernment. The first is the role and centrality of community. As Isenhower and Todd write, "Isolation is actually

---

60. Ackerman, *Listening to God*, 82.
61. Isenhower and Todd, *Living into the Answers*, 16, 27.
62. Au and Au, *Discerning Heart*, 78–94.
63. Parker, *Led by the Spirit*, 21.
64. Au and Au, *Discerning Heart*, 94.

not the best environment for personal discernment."[65] Whenever we are seeking to perceive God's movements in some part of our life, having a companion such as a spiritual director can be very beneficial.[66] We might also consider finding a small group that can help us to avoid self-deception and listen more attentively to the divine leadings.[67] Our traditions are yet another source of guidance that we can turn to for stability and insights.[68] Overall, then, community is viewed as an essential support for spiritual discernment.

A second set of supports that are noted are the spiritual disciplines that we have. Given the theistic orientation of these processes, prayer is highlighted as one such central and necessary practice.[69] Prayerful rest is another central practice as it fosters greater openness, listening, and receptivity to the divine leadings.[70] Given the ambiguity and unpredictableness of discernment, adopting such a receptive and "go with the flow" mentality can also be very beneficial, if not necessary.[71] Not only are these disciplines meant to empower our decision-making, but they should also transform our lives thereby helping us to further move toward the intended results of discernment discussed above, which is for us to continuously live spiritually discerning lives.[72] Overall, then, these and other supports are intended to help empower and guide our spiritual approaches to making decisions.

Desired Dispositions

In addition to these supports, any discernment process should address the dispositions that are needed in order to engage in its steps. As with the supports, there were two such prerequisites that were found among our writers. The first is that one must have the desire to follow God. If God is actively attempting to lead us, then we must have the intention to perceive these leadings and to follow them rather than to "simply have our own

---

65. Isenhower and Todd, *Living into the Answers*, 10.

66. Au and Au, *Discerning Heart*, 60–64.

67. Ackerman, *Listening to God*, 87; Dougherty, *Group Spiritual Direction*, 24; Edwards, *Living in the Presence*, 101.

68. Parker, *Led by the Spirit*, 36, 105.

69. Dougherty, *Group Spiritual Direction*, 25; Wolpert, *Leading a Life with God*, 70.

70. Isenhower and Todd, *Living into the Answers*, 24.

71. Au and Au, *Discerning Heart*, 32.

72. Isenhower and Todd, *Living into the Answers*, 43.

inclinations confirmed."[73] "Spiritual leadership from the perspective of the life of prayer," writes spiritual director Daniel Wolpert, "is about only one person: God."[74] This means that we must actively work to make God the true center of our lives.[75] While such a disposition may not come for some time until after an "awakening" or religious conversion happens, it nevertheless must become the cornerstone of how we engage in discernment if we are to have the kind of openness and dedication that discernment requires.[76]

The second prerequisite follows directly from the first and is known as "indifference" in Ignatian spirituality circles.[77] If we truly desire to follow God, the argument goes, and if God's will is ultimately a mystery that cannot be known with absolute clarity, then it follows that we must have some level of indifference toward the outcome of our decision-making from the start. Basically, it means that we should really be willing, from the beginning of our discernment, to follow the Spirit's blowing lead no matter where it might take us.[78] This means that we should be free from "inordinate attachments" and pre-expectations when entering into the process.[79] However, as we might expect our Pentecostals and Ignatians to quickly point out, that "indifference" does not mean that we do not feel anything, for the Divine may be found in our affective movements as well.[80] It just means that we are willing to go wherever it is our intentional and well-supported discernment may take us, enduring the ambiguity, darkness, and chaos that may sometimes arise with it.[81] These two sets of dispositions, the desire to follow God and an indifference toward wherever God may lead us, comprise necessary prerequisites that our authors highlight.

---

73. Au and Au, *Discerning Heart*, 2, 14, 55, 226; Hauser, *Moving in the Spirit*, 63; Isenhower and Todd, *Living into the Answers*, 51; Wolpert, *Leading a Life with God*, 67.

74. Wolpert, *Leading a Life with God*, 64–65.

75. Hauser, *Moving in the Spirit*, 36.

76. Au and Au, *Discerning Heart*, 55; Edwards, *Living in the Presence*, 100; Hauser, *Moving in the Spirit*, 5, 12; Isenhower and Todd, *Living into the Answers*, 43; Parker, *Led by the Spirit*, 104.

77. Isenhower and Todd, *Living into the Answers*, 63–64.

78. Wolpert, *Leading a Life with God*, 72.

79. Au and Au, *Discerning Heart*, 55; Edwards, *Living in the Presence*, 100; Hauser, *Moving in the Spirit*, 63; Isenhower and Todd, *Living into the Answers*, 63–64.

80. Ackerman, *Listening to God*, 88; Au and Au, *Discerning Heart*, 19; Isenhower and Todd, *Living into the Answers*, 64; Parker, *Led by the Spirit*, 21.

81. Hauser, *Moving in the Spirit*, 36; Isenhower and Todd, *Living into the Answers*, 22–23, 41.

Gathers from and Integrates Inner and Outer Sources

While there are communities and traditions that do stress one set of sources over another, our theologically diverse authors each emphasized the need for holistic approaches to discernment as we saw above. Based upon the epistemologies that we touched upon, every discernment process should be very explicit as to the sources it draws from and the ones that it emphasizes over and above the others.[82] The discernment process should also direct the practitioner in how to integrate all of this information thereby culminating in a decision that is asserted to be in harmony with the perceived "leadings of the Spirit."[83] Such an approach might mean looking for common themes, or might entail allowing the information to gel for a while until a dominant direction emerges.[84] Regardless of the details, the discernment approach that you choose should address these issues with some level of detail.

Sets Evaluative Criteria

While our epistemologies most directly influence the primary sources that we turn to in our discernment, it is our theologies that most directly determines how we will interpret this data.[85] Different views of God can lead to our viewing the movements within and around us in different ways as we have heard. For instance, in some traditions—such as Pentecostal ones—inner movements are seen as having their origins in one of three sources: "the Holy Spirit, oneself, or diabolical influence."[86] In order to know which of these sources may be acting, we must therefore have some criteria by which to evaluate them.[87] Every discernment process should therefore clearly define these criteria and identify the foundations upon which they are based. In effect, these evaluative criteria help us to know whether a particular movement is more or less "of God" and whether a specific decision we are considering is truly in tune with the Spirit.[88]

---

82. Edwards, *Living in the Presence*, 101.

83. Au and Au, *Discerning Heart*, 55, 125; Hauser, *Moving in the Spirit*, 5.

84. Isenhower and Todd, *Living into the Answers*, 102–3; Wolpert, *Leading a Life with God*, 74.

85. Hauser, *Moving in the Spirit*, 3; Parker, *Led by the Spirit*, 34.

86. Parker, *Led by the Spirit*, 34.

87. Edwards, *Living in the Presence*, 100; Parker, *Led by the Spirit*, 12.

88. Wolpert, *Leading a Life with God*, 68.

Examples of such criteria are numerous. They can take the form of listing what reliable and unreliable "signs of grace" are, or they can define what one's inner affective state of being should be like when acting in accordance with God's will—be it "consolating" or "desolating."[89] Some use Paul of Tarsus's "fruits of the Spirit" found in the New Testament, while others hold such ethical ideals as goodness, love, forgiveness, and service as guiding criteria.[90] Still others look to Jesus as a model of comparison, while authenticity is upheld as a pillar for some.[91] Regardless of the specific criteria we use, we should be explicit about them. Overall, these evaluative criteria essentially help us to better know where it is that we and our communities believe God is moving so that our discernment can proceed with greater clarity.

Emphasizes the Ongoing Nature of Discernment

A final key component that any discernment process should have is the emphasis on the ongoing nature of discernment. Essentially, the process should become not just a practice that we engage from time to time, but rather a way of life as was discussed above. Engaging in discernment in an ongoing fashion is important because of the "trial-and-error" nature of it. By looking back over certain periods of our life, we can sometimes see with greater insight how God was moving and working with us.[92] These insights are essential to the processes of discernment because they empower us to better know where and how God might be moving with us both now and in the future.[93]

Discernment is therefore one that improves as we continue to engage and reflect upon it.[94] It is therefore a practice that should become an ongoing and integral part of our daily lives thereby nurturing the transformation

---

89. Ackerman, *Listening to God*, 91–92; Edwards, *Living in the Presence*, 101.

90. Au and Au, *Discerning Heart*, 155; Edwards, *Living in the Presence*, 101; Hauser, *Moving in the Spirit*, 26, 30, 33; Parker, *Led by the Spirit*, 106; Wolpert, *Leading a Life with God*, 68.

91. Au and Au, *Discerning Heart*, 11, 155, 198; Edwards, *Living in the Presence*, 101; Parker, *Led by the Spirit*, 200.

92. Hauser, *Moving in the Spirit*, 34; Isenhower and Todd, *Living into the Answers*, 67–68; Wolpert, *Leading a Life with God*, 68.

93. Au and Au, *Discerning Heart*, 94; Parker, *Led by the Spirit*, 105; Wolpert, *Leading a Life with God*, 68.

94. Ackerman, *Listening to God*, 82; Au and Au, *Discerning Heart*, 16, 155.

Discerning Discernment

that discernment is intended to result in.⁹⁵ Each discernment process you consider should therefore emphasize this and be adaptable to your daily life habits of doing and being.

Suggested Discernment Processes

With these key components to discernment in place, we are now in a position to explore and develop a set of processes that we might adapt to our own lives and ministerial contexts for spiritual formation program development. If you already have a set practice, you might still be interested in reading through this section in an effort to further develop and deepen it. If you do not, the following is offered as a beginning in your own journey for discovering the unique ways that God works with and guides you and the community you are journeying with. At any rate, the following are the processes that will be used for engaging our spiritual praxis methodologies in the next part of this book.

Following in the Footsteps of Others

Appendix A shows the steps to discernment that seven of our authors recommend. In this section, we will briefly compare and contrast these various approaches to discernment with the intention of distilling some of their essential movements. These movements will then become the basis for the concrete processes that are presented below.

As we begin to look over these many different steps, we can see commonalities begin to emerge. Most of these include some intentionality in preparing for and exploring the issue to be discerned. Such preparations can include engaging in prayer and centering one's self for the discernment. Some of our authors also emphasize the need to walk through our discernment with a community or companion. We can therefore see how both of our supports are reflected in these steps.

We can also see that exploring the issue involves both inward and outward ways of knowing, looking to external sources such as "spiritual doctrines," as Ackerman asserts, as well as to the inner thoughts and feelings that we have in relation to the issue at hand. Some, such as Au and Au as well as Ishenhower and Todd, emphasize the need for uncovering the

---

95. Au and Au, *Discerning Heart*, 21; Isenhower and Todd, *Living into the Answers*, 15–16, 114; Wolpert, *Leading a Life with God*, 75.

underlying core values that we have. Others, such as Parker and Ackerman, encourage us to look to our traditions for additional insights and guidance. Regardless of the particular emphasis, however, each of our authors highlight such detailed inner and outer explorations.

From these reflections, these authors then encourage us to begin moving in the direction of making some definitive decision. While the specific paths that are recommended vary considerably, each of them does assert some form of theologically based evaluative criteria for moving in this direction. For Edwards, this entails prayerfully reflecting on the issue in the presence of God and noting any thoughts or feelings that arise. For Hauser, this partly means asking whether or not the potential decision brings greater glory to God or not. Some of our authors, such as Isenhower and Todd, recommend brainstorming as many different alternatives and possibilities as we can and then choosing from among them. It is then based on these criteria and processes that we can then ask the ultimate discernment question, to paraphrase Wolpert, "*Where is it that God seems to be inviting or drawing us toward?*"

There can be, however, one critique lodged against many of these suggested steps. While Isenhower and Todd do present their processes as "neither linear nor a checklist of items to be completed,"[96] most of our other authors do not appear to depict the ongoing nature of discernment as a transforming way of life in their steps. As we discussed above, this is something that is considered to be one of the primary goals of discernment. In our own processes presented below, then, we will be sure to address this deficiency in more explicit ways. Collectively, then, these seven authors provide us with the foundations for our own discernment approach.

Discerning Discernment: Our Synthesized Spiritual Processes

Based upon the work of these authors, and on the foundations which we laid in the previous sections, we are now in a place where we can suggest a set of concrete discernment processes. When beginning with any issue to discern, the following may be engaged in the order in which they are presented. However, acknowledging the ambiguity and non-linearity that has been asserted to be a part of the inherent nature of discernment, what is presented below needs to also be viewed more as interrelated processes and movements than distinctive and separate steps. While they do capture

---

96. Isenhower and Todd, *Living into the Answers*, 22.

Discerning Discernment

the general trend and direction of discernment, we must also remember that they happen simultaneously and cyclically in many cases.

For instance, I have presented "Coming to a Decision" as the fourth process because, under most circumstances, such a decision will only emerge after the three previous processes have been engaged to some extent. However, Ignatius of Loyola, Au and Au reminds us, acknowledged that there may be times when the Spirit "so moves and attracts the will that a devout soul without hesitation, or the possibility of hesitation, follows what has been manifested to it."[97] In other words, there are times when we make a decision to act in a particular situation because we just know that it is the right thing to do in that moment, with little processing coming before.

We must therefore remember that, when truly left open to God, these processes can intermingle in any number of different ways just as winds coming from different directions can mix together in unpredictable ways. We must therefore always leave a discerning and indifferent space for such novelty and ambiguity in our approaches. Nevertheless, I have chosen to present these processes in the following order because this resonates both with how our authors formulated their own steps and with how I have most commonly experienced spiritual discernment to unfold in my own life.

To help us to better understand each of these, we will also be walking with Montague as he reflects on the discernment processes he engaged in that led to the final decision that was made in relation to his congregation.[98] This United Methodist Church (UMC) was located in an urban setting and had been struggling with decreasing membership for at least the last twenty years as the demographics of the local neighborhood had significantly shifted. Montague had been appointed to this church with the expressed purposes of helping the local district and conference to discern which direction it should go in. Initially, Montague was told that there were three options that were being considered: (1) work with the current members to revitalize their church; (2) close the church as it was and attempt a new start-up congregation; or (3) close the church and sell the property. In what follows, Montague looks back and reflects on the decision that was finally made in relation to each of the processes pre-

97. Quoted in Au and Au, *Discerning Heart*, 52.

98. These reflections have been gathered from "Montague's" journal as well as from interviews conducted with him. As always, the names, some details, and locations have been changed to maintain confidentiality.

sented below. As the purpose of this case example is to illustrate these processes, this sketch will be brief, touching only on the relevant details of Montague's discernment. Montague's discernment also serves, as we shall see in chapter 3, as an example of the first step of program development: discerning and clarifying what the focus of one's formative efforts will be. It is therefore a valuable case study to explore.

Process One: Ensuring Foundations

One of the key components of discernment explored above were the supports and dispositions that we have in relation to our lives and the issue we wish to discern in particular. This first process therefore entails our working to ensure that these foundations are in place as we enter into discernment. This means finding communities and companions who will walk with us in supportive ways. It means discerning spiritual disciplines that can help to nurture and further deepen the dispositions that are needed for discernment, which are a holy longing for God's will and an Ignatian indifference toward the paths that God calls us toward.

As we look over the steps that our authors present in appendix A, we can see that this also means reflecting on the core values that shape and guide our lives. It means our working to cultivate a continual and fuller life with the Spirit throughout the whole of our own lives and communities: in the thought and feeling habits that we have, in the relationships that we keep, in the vocations that we choose to engage in, et cetera. Without the continual deepening and growth of these necessary foundations, we risk the narrowed distortions that can arise from the potential pitfalls of negative moods and pre-expectations that were discussed above. We must therefore intentionally and continually work to strengthen these foundations to help ensure sound discernment as well as a healthy spiritual life.

Montague's "Fear and Trembling"

Montague describes his own dispositions back then as one of "fear and trembling." Having just finished his seminary education, and this being his first appointment, Montague was very scared of what he was about to face as the new solo pastor of this struggling urban church. He did desire to know and do God's will for this congregation, but he was not sure what this might mean or where it might take him. Confessionally, Montague remembers that he did not have a genuine "holy indifference" to the outcomes of his discernment. Looking back now, he realizes that he had biased hopes of pastoring a congregation that was actively engaged in its local community. Though he did not realize it at the time, as we shall see below, he also had vocational hopes and expectations that were underlying how he both viewed and engaged in his discernment. Montague can now see how these pre-expectations skewed his views of the congregation and his discernment processes.

For supports, Montague feels that he was very well covered. He had a strong and daily life of prayer and discernment, and his immediate supervisor had assigned him a mentor that he would meet with on a monthly basis. The local UMC district also arranged for him to attend conferences that would help to provide him with the further education and resources he might need for this appointment. Overall, Montague recalls having a strong foundation to support him during these difficult discernment processes with this church.

Process Two: Exploration and Evaluation

With these foundations increasing, we can live our life in more discerning ways. A central part of this, of course, is that we seek to discern the life and leadings of the Spirit in specific areas of our own lives and communities. Clarification therefore involves our selecting a specific issue or situation to discern and exploring it in great detail. Looking to appendix A, we can see that such in-depth explorations involve the full range of inner and outer sources; they encompass truly holistic ways of knowing.

Inwardly, we at least need to attend to the thoughts, feelings, and bodily sensations that arise as we prayerfully sit with the issue being discerned. What arises within us as we consider it? How do we feel about it? What thoughts, dreams, and daydreams seem to emerge as we consider it? Do we feel any tensions and/or peace in parts of our bodies? How might we describe the situation or issue in our own words? Are there any insights or spontaneous promptings that have arisen? Each of these can provide us with a better understanding of the inner movements that are arising in relation to the situation under discernment.

Outwardly, we can also look to a number of sources for greater clarity. We can and should listen to the reflections and feedback of all those who are connected with the issue we are discerning. For instance, if we are trying to decide whether we should apply for a job in another city that would require a move, then we need to talk to those that we live with for they will be directly affected by our decision and therefore need to be a part of these discerning processes.[99] We should also discuss the matter with our spiritual community or companions that we are journeying with. Each of these individuals can be valued avenues through which God can further and more robustly lead us.

We can also look to additional sources, such as books, history, and factual data, to help us to further clarify the situation. If we were considering what kind of a bible study to lead our youth group through, for instance, we should consider at least a sampling of the youth bible studies that are available. We should also consider the Bible studies that have been offered in our community in the past: How were they engaged? What were the results of them? Sacred texts themselves are another valued external source of insight and wisdom for many issues. Finally, we can also describe the issue under discernment in more strictly factual ways—the who, what, where, when, why, and how of it. Turning to these can expand both the depth and breadth of our understandings thereby empowering us with greater clarity.

As we explore and clarify the issue, we will also want to begin applying our theologically based evaluative criteria. As we heard above, our views of God and God's relationship to creation and human nature are the basis for how we perceive God to be present within and to each part of our lives and communities. Since the ultimate concern in spiritual discernment, according to our working definition, is to "perceive the movements of the Spirit," we can begin reflecting on where and how we believe God is moving at this stage of the discernment. Which of these inner and outer movements seems to be more reflective of and in attunement with our Creator? Where does the Spirit seem to be more or less active and tangible? How does each one compare with the mandates and images of God presented by our traditions? These kinds of reflections can be engaged not only by us as individuals but also in conjunction with our supportive communities and companions. By engaging in them, we can clarify more fully where it is that the life of God is and/or needs to be according to these holistic ways of knowing and the evaluative criteria that we have come to choose.

Such explorations, as was mentioned above, should continue throughout the whole of our discerning journey. We can always know more about the situation than we currently do. We can always seek to perceive more clearly where it is that God is present or needs to be.

---

99. Au and Au, *Discerning Heart*, 63.

Exploration and evaluation are therefore an integral and ongoing part of discernment in general.

Montague's Immersion

When Montague arrived, he took the time to visit with each of the regularly attending members of the church in their homes. Through these discussions, he learned more about the church's history, the yearnings of the congregation, their frustrations and fears of the gradually declining membership and changing neighborhood demographics, and their unique personalities. From these conversations, he learned of the racist and sexist tendencies that some of his members had but also of some of the extraordinary lives that they had lived. With most of them now being retired, he also learned of their struggles with health issues, their difficulties in getting around, and he observed the fact that the majority of these Caucasian members did not live in the immediate and now largely Latina/o neighborhood of the church.

Montague also spent time in this neighborhood meeting local business owners, talking with his neighbors (his parsonage was only two blocks from the church), walking the streets and observing the kinds of people who lived there and how they seemed to spend their time, as well as reviewing recent demographic data about the community on the internet. From this, he noted the gang violence that gripped these streets as well as the racial tensions that existed between the now predominantly Latina/o residents and African and Asian Americans. Being a lower-income area, he also noted the beginnings of what is known as "gentrification," wherein young middle-class professionals were beginning to move into these kinds of communities to buy cheaper houses closer to the downtown area.

Next, in addition to meeting regularly with his mentor to discuss these matters, Montague also spent a considerable amount of time in personal reflection and prayer. Looking back now, he sees that there were actually two closely related internal issues that he was struggling with at the time. The first was the question of what God's will was for this small congregation and the neighborhood of which it was a part. The second one, which at the time was the more hidden yet more significant issue for him, was vocational discernment questions. Being right out of seminary, he was still not sure as to what his own vocational calling was. As a result, many of Montague's inner struggles were related not only to the future directions of this congregation, but also to his own life.

Internally, he therefore experienced much fear, uncertainty, and a lack of confidence in his abilities as a pastor. He struggled with whether he should be continuing the traditional ministries of the church as they had always been for now or whether he should attempt to go in new directions. Montague now believes that such doubts and questions about how to minister were related to his vocational struggles as much as they were to the discernment of this congregation's future.

Collectively, these were some of the outer and inner sources that he was immersed in as he continued through his discernment. At that time, Montague did not explicitly evaluate each and every one of these movements from a theological perspective. He did, however, believe as he experienced them that God wanted this congregation to be more involved with the local community in its struggles. He believed that the racism and sexism in the church was not reflective of God's will. And, finally, he did feel in his heart a growing compassion and empathy for his aging members as he came to know them more intimately, believing that God was seeking to care for them as well. This immersion and these reflections therefore formed some of the core foundations for Montague's ongoing discernment processes.

Process Three: Exploring Possible Paths

As we delve deeper into the issue, we will no doubt have ideas about how to act and respond. As these emerge, either spontaneously or with much intentional reflection, we are encouraged to keep track of them. Each of these essentially represents a possible path that God is inviting us to travel down. While part of us may desire to come to a decision as quickly as possible by simply choosing the first idea that arises and moving toward action, we are instead admonished to allow other possibilities into the conversation as well. Sometimes, like a river that is made up of the water from the many different creeks that feed it, the path we ultimately take is a conglomeration of the previous ones we have considered.

This process therefore entails our explicitly listing all of the possible actions that we might be able to take; all of the potential choices that are available to us. Again, these may come from a prayerful brainstorming session by one's self and/or with others. They can have their origins in the external resources we draw from such as our traditions. They might come as a bolt of inspiration in the middle of the night or while taking a shower. Or they may even be the result of much intentional reasoning and reflection. Whatever their source, however, we are invited to record and reflect on each of them.

Such reflections closely mirror some of the ones highlighted in the previous process. We can list the pros, cons, and possible consequences of each potential action. We should prayerfully sit with each one and note the thoughts, feelings, and sensations that arise for us. Again, our supportive communities and companions may be able to help us to further expand on each option and see it with greater clarity. Finally, we need to apply our evaluative criteria in an attempt to more clearly gauge the extent to which God seems to be present within and through to each one according to our theological and religious traditions. These processes are therefore one of considering the full range of possibilities that are available to us as we move toward transforming action.

Three Potential Paths

Montague knew, upon his appointment, that the local UMC district had three directions that they were considering for this congregation as discussed above. From his immersions in both the life of the church and in the local neighborhood, these were the three paths that he came to consider as well. Montague did, at various times, prayerfully consider each of these options.

The first option was to work with the current members to revitalize their church. After attending a couple of conferences and workshops on church revitalization in his first few weeks, Montague decided to attempt some of the vision casting techniques that he had learned. He put up banners that proclaimed the different foci of the church's mission, he preached on these topics, and he led a bible study that addressed these themes. While church members were open to and welcoming of these efforts, little else in the church seemed to change.

In reflecting on the viability of this option, Montague came to realize that these approaches to church revitalization require strong congregational leadership. He reflected on the ailing health of his members and the fact that many of these remaining members did not have a strong history of trying to reach out to the local community. He realized that much of their focus in the future would have to shift from being internal on the church itself toward evangelization and outreach to the neighborhood if the church was to revitalize. He noted that there did not seem to currently be the kinds of foundations to support this option. In talking with his members about some of this, they expressed hopes that the church wouldn't close but also that they were not the ones to embody these kinds of very active and outreaching kinds of ministries. As one member shared, being in their seventies and eighties they were "too old and tired" for these kinds of efforts. Believing that God seeks to care for these aging members, Montague affirmed these reflections.

The next path considered was to close the church and attempt a new start-up congregation. It is here, he now realizes, that Montague's own pre-expectations and vocational struggles most skewed his discernment. From the church start-up education that he had received through the local UMC conference, he had learned of the kinds of work that such start-ups require. They require spending most of one's time in the community, making friends, meeting connections, building alliances, et cetera. Such work is largely one of marketing, evangelization, and advertising.

While he affirms that such efforts are a movement of the Spirit, looking back Montague remembers the intense fears he experienced at the thought of doing this kind of ministry. Being much more introverted by nature, the images of being so active in the community and extroverted felt exhausting and draining to his energies. He now realizes that his tendencies then were to shy away from suggesting this option to his supervisor, for fears of becoming "chained down" to this kind of work. However, Montague did not fully admit that he had these fears at that time to himself, his mentor, or his supervisor. His vocational struggles therefore came to the forefront of these reflections thereby impacting his discernment, though he did not explicitly realize it at that time.

The final option that he considered with the local UMC district was to close the church and sell the property. In conversation with his supervisor, this was admittedly the least desirable one. Montague's immersion in the local neighborhood convinced him of the need for some kind of outreach and social-service ministries. This particular area had a large percentage of children and adolescents. However, there were very few resources available for them in a community that also had high rates of theft and violence. Inwardly, Montague felt that it was such a waste for the church's property, which remained empty for almost the entire week, to not be filled to capacity with after-school programs, social service supports, community-building meetings, fellowship opportunities, et cetera. For him, these were some of the visions that God had for this community. Historically, however, the church had also received very generous monetary offers from developers who wanted to tear the church down and build apartments in an already overcrowded neighborhood. Montague

Discerning Discernment

believed that if the UMC sold this valuable piece of land, they would probably never be able to recover it and few other properties in the area were available that could provide the kinds of ministries that this community needed.

These are therefore the three paths that Montague discerningly considered as his work with the congregation continued. We can already see at this point that one option seems to more viable than the other two. Without the current congregation having the necessary strong leadership and outreach foundations, as well as with the racism and sexism that some of the members expressed, the first option did not seem very likely. Similarly, the third option seemed to Montague like it would result in a loss that the local neighborhood could not afford; that there was still too much that a property such as this could offer. The option that therefore emerged was to close the church and attempt a restart; a choice that struck terror in Montague's heart.

Process Four: Coming to a Decision

In many discernment situations, but not always as we heard in the opening to this section, we can rely heavily on the previous processes for this one. If we do, we can now take a step back from all of the data and possibilities that we have explored, gathered, evaluated, and reflected upon until now and make a decision. Given all of this, there are at least two primary ways that we might come to a decision.

While these two ways are not necessarily distinct from one another, they do seem to represent two characteristically different ways that our authors have presented the decision-making process in their steps. As we move toward making our own decisions, we might find that different issues draw us to use one of these ways more than the other. As a result, we need to be aware of both of them, for in both cases the goal is the same: to act in accordance with the leadings of the Spirit in our local context.

INTEGRATING

The first is through a process of integration. Seen most clearly in the processes of Au and Au as well as Isenhower and Todd in appendix A, this approach involves stepping back and looking at the whole of all that has been gathered. In doing so, we seek to clarify any dominate themes and trends that seem to be emerging. We also seek to integrate the full range of

PART ONE: Theoretical Foundations

inner and outer sources that we have considered. Where does God seem to be moving most fully in all of this? How do my thoughts resonate with my feelings as well as with what my spiritual companions have said? The goal here is for us to seek a path that integrates the full range of all that we have considered to date. It is one that seeks to act in harmony with the life of the Spirit present in the whole of all that we have perceived.

Emerging

The second way to come to a decision is to actually do the opposite of the first. Rather than trying to engage all of the data from a more holistic and integrative perspective, we instead set it all aside and allow a single option to emerge and draw us toward it. Seen in the guidelines that authors such as Edwards and Hauser present, we "release the process to God" with the faith that the Spirit will draw us toward one direction more fully than any of the others. Emphasizing the role of affective movements in this process of decision-making, an emerging approach aims more for singularity of choice than for integration of the greater whole. Taken together with the other, it represents one of the two potential ways that we might be led to come to a decision.

The Church Closes

After five months of engaging in deliberate discernment, some in consultation with the congregation, some via trial and error with visioning processes, and some in dialogue with his mentors, Montague realized, with strong conviction, that the first option was not a viable choice for this current community. Without commitment and strong leadership, he felt that revitalizing a church that had been in longterm and sustained decline for more than twenty years was just not going to be possible. After discussing this matter with his supervisor, the decision was finally made by the local district to close down this United Methodist Church that had been in ministry for almost ninety years.

As we can see from the previous process, the journey that ultimately led to this decision was largely one of integration, though it culminated in an emerging conviction. By sitting with each one of the options, considering both inner and outer sources, Montague came to the realization that the church, as it currently was, could no longer embody the kinds of neighborhood ministries that he believed God was inviting them toward.

In other words, they could no longer fulfill the discerned mission of the church to this local community. All of this holistic and integrative work eventually led to the emergence of the strong conviction that Montague ultimately experienced and believed was a "Divinely given" affective confirmation of this decision.

As Montague looks back, he also learned more about his own discernment processes. In decision after decision, he sees more clearly that he generally engages in discernment as he did here. He needs to spend a significant amount of time immersed in the situation that he is discerning with. He needs to consider the in's and out's of each potential option. Finally, he needs to sit with the issue long enough for such a strong and confirming affective conviction to emerge. In short, reflecting on this final decision has helped him to better see some of the core ways that the Spirit works with him through these discernment processes.

Process Five: Discerning Action

Once a decision is made, we can then act on it. However, Hauser as well as Isenhower and Todd recommend our not doing so immediately if it is possible. Instead, they recommend what might be called a "holy pause." The purpose of such a pause is for us to live with the decision we have made for a period of time expecting God to further confirm the decision both interiorly and externally. Our thoughts, reasonings, feelings, conversations, resources, et cetera, should continue to deepen and reflect God's life within and through the particular choice if it truly is God's will. We should come to feel more at ease with the choice, it should make more sense to us and our communities, and the circumstances should come to support it more completely. If they do not, then we may need to reengage our decision-making processes. Again, the underlying theological assumption here is that if a choice is truly in accordance with God's leadings, then we will continue to be drawn ever more fully toward it.

Once a decision is confirmed, we can then act on it. However, this does not mean that we wildly run out and blindly enact our decision. Rather, as we recall that the intended result of all discernment approaches is to cultivate a transforming way of life, we need to act while continuing to engage each of the other processes discussed above. Figure 4 below shows a schematic of the overall flow of these processes as they have been presented herein and the continual feedback that happens as we discerningly walk with an issue.

PART ONE: Theoretical Foundations

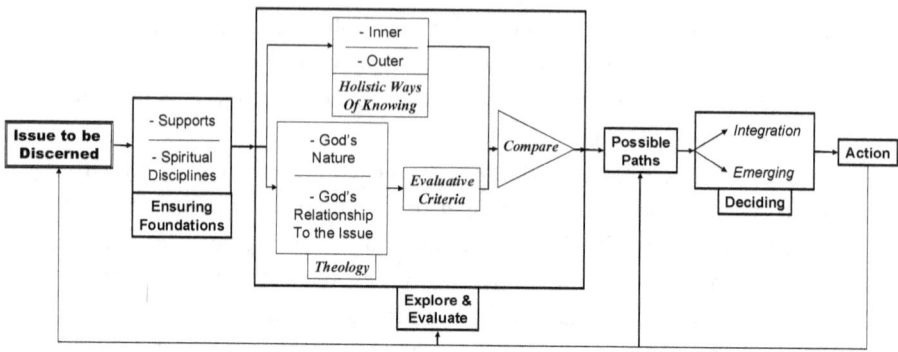

Figure 4. A Schematic of Discernment

As we can see, we need to continue to engage in the supports and maintain the holy dispositions. We need to continually gather and clarify inner and outer data in relation to the situation. We need to ever be open to, keeping track of, and reflecting on other possible paths. Finally, we can also regularly question whether or not the path we are journeying on, and even the issue we are discerning, is still the one that God seems to be inviting us down for these can change at any moment.

Spiritual discernment is therefore not a practice to be engaged in once and than left behind, but rather is it a way of life that is intended to transform the very nature of ourselves and our communities in an ongoing fashion. This final process is therefore intended to help us to enact our choices but in continually discerning ways. It is one that encourages us to persistently engage each of these processes as we carry out our decision. In short, it is one that should ultimately lead us to live a life of discerning spiritual action.

And Then... Montague?

While he did not wait for or even know about a "holy pause" before contacting his supervisor, Montague's discernment was confirmed by his supportive companions; both his mentor and his supervisor affirmed the choice. However, he still had to complete the difficult task of letting his member's know of this decision. Visiting each one in their homes just as he had greeted them when he first arrived, Montague told them the news. Driving to each of their houses, Montague feared their reactions and grief as some of them had been regularly attending this church for as long as eighty-five years. Surprisingly, however, there was a general sense of relief as he told each of them. Many of them said that they had been expecting this to happen for some time now. This feedback gave Montague further confirmation of the entire discernment process. He felt deeply in his heart now that they were acting in accordance with the leadings of God.

But now what? The decision is really only partly made because the decision still needs to be made as to whether the property should be sold or a new church created. Almost immediately after closing the church, Montague's supervisor asked him to write a proposal for a new church start at that location. In order for such an endeavor to be undertaken, it would need funding from the local conference to support it. Montague spent two months preparing this proposal, striving to put into words what a start-up campaign might look like in this neighborhood. As he worked on this proposal, he continued to deeply struggle with vocational questions and whether this was the kind of ministry he was called to. Fortunately, Montague began to share these struggles with his mentor and they began to talk together about what kinds of ministry he might see himself in. In effect, the discernment of the closing of the church led him more directly into the next major discernment process of his life: his vocation. That, however, would have to be another case example of these processes that will not be presented here.

In the end, Montague's proposal was denied and he was appointed to a large and vibrant church where he was able to engage in the kinds of educational ministries that he really felt called to. As for the members, Montague journeyed with each of them over the coming months to help them find and settle into new congregations in their area. The local conference had initially planned to use the property for a new church start-up, while renting out the facilities to another church in the meantime. More than five years later however, the property was still being rented out.

Closing Reflections

Spiritual discernment is the very core of the craft of theistic spiritual formation. If our goal truly is to partner with the Spirit's formative movements in the lives and communities of the people that we are called to work with, then we must have some way of perceiving that Spirit's life. As we have seen in this chapter, such perceptions are the goal and task of discernment. Not only does such spiritual decision-making depend upon the theologies that we hold about the nature of God and God's relationship

PART ONE: Theoretical Foundations

to creation, but it also stands firmly upon the epistemological sources that we rely upon to perceive the Spirit in our midst. Requiring an openness to ambiguity as well as needed supports and dispositions, spiritual discernment is ultimately intended to become a transforming way of life that we continually embody as we move from one decision to another.

As we look back over the five discernment processes, we can ask if whether or not these are sufficient for helping us to engage in spiritual formation program development. Might they be enough for formators such as Montague, Francis, and Tom to follow as they decide how to start a new congregation, transform the nature of a relationship, or design and implement a contemplative program? In a general way, "yes" these processes are sufficient, as we saw for Montague. Each formator can apply these processes to their specific situations in an effort to discern where it is that God seems to be leading them. However, these processes are also very general in nature; they are intended to be applied to a whole range of life situations.

One of the concerns that could therefore be raised is that there is still not enough detail and guidance in applying such processes to the work of spiritual formation program development. It is one thing for Montague to use them to decide where he believes God is leading his congregation in a general way, but quite another for him to know how to develop and implement a start-up congregation (if he were to stay and do this, that is). In order to address such specific concerns, we need to turn to other "praxis-oriented" fields. By doing so in the next chapter, in conjunction with the processes presented in this one, we will then be in a position to explore methodologies with enough detail to engage in program development in spiritually discerning ways.

2

Embodying Praxis
Cycles toward Transformation

WITH SPIRITUAL DISCERNMENT BEING the core of program development, we still need more concrete ways of engaging in it. To help us toward these ends, we look to a concept known as "praxis." In the introduction, spiritual formation was asserted as being a praxis-oriented field. But, what does this mean? How do we know that program development really is a work of praxis. It is therefore imperative that we expend some effort in exploring what this means more fully.

Our theoretical foundations therefore continue in this chapter with these explorations. Not only will we come to see what the nature of praxis entails, as the cyclical intersection of theory, action, and reflection for the purposes of transformation, but we will learn based upon this that spiritual formation program development is fundamentally a praxis endeavor. We will then explore what some of the fundamental movements of praxis are as it is embodied by two other praxis-oriented fields: action research and practical theology. By synthesizing these movements with those of our spiritual discernment processes, we will finally come to see what our detailed program development methodologies include for the craft of spiritual formation. These methodologies will then become the basis for the next part of this book where we explore each one in greater depth. In the end, we also shall come to see that the fundamental nature of our praxis-oriented program development is a cyclical one.

PART ONE: Theoretical Foundations

Essentials of Praxis

Before we can see that program development is a work of praxis, we must first have a fairly detailed understanding of what this concept means. In this section, we briefly explore some the essential characteristics that comprise the nature of praxis. After describing what a praxis way of being entails, and what its purpose is, we shall come to find that it basically has four essential components to it that are integral to our formative craft. It is based upon these four components that we will realize just how praxis-oriented spiritual formation program development is.

A Praxis Way of Knowing and Being

"Praxis" has been described to be more than mere intellectual or theoretical knowledge; rather, it is a lifestyle and way of knowing and being in the world. Dating back at least to Aristotle, praxis is understood to include the "sayings, doings and relatings" of people.[1] It is viewed as comprising the cultural traditions, habits, and activities of both individuals and communities.[2] For medieval Christian theologian Thomas Aquinas, it is "a knowing/believing that is embodied in a Christian lifestyle."[3]

As a result, praxis is considered to be a certain way through which we can know our world. Particularly, it is knowledge that is derived from our direct engagement with the concrete experiences of our local contexts.[4] By reflecting on these experiences, new insights about our world can emerge into our lives.[5] It is, in the words of Boston College Professor Thomas Groome, "a relational, reflective, and experiential way of knowing" that is intended to lead toward transformation in our world.[6]

Authors who explore the nature of praxis therefore distinguish praxis ways of knowing from other, and more theoretical, kinds of knowing. Noting the West's emphasis on rational, cognitive, distanced, and allegedly "pure" kinds of knowing, many of these authors criticize these types of truth claims.[7] The assertion is that rather than looking solely for abstract

1. Mattsson, "What's at Stake?," 5.
2. Ibid., 5–6.
3. Groome, *Christian Religious Education*, 160.
4. Hesslefors-Arktoft and Lindskog, "Connecting Theory and Practice?," 82.
5. Groome, *Christian Religious Education*, 153.
6. Ibid., 149, 156.
7. Graham, *Transforming Practice*, 88; Hesslefors-Arktoft and Lindskog, "Connecting Theory and Practice?" 78–79; Johansson and Sandberg, "What Knowledge

and more "universal" principles, there is also a need to consider the concrete and lived realities of one's local context, for knowledge about God and reality can and do come from these avenues as well.[8] Even more than this, some, such as practical theologian Elaine Graham, argue that an emphasis needs to be placed not just on intellectually grasping truth but actually living it out in our daily lives.[9]

A praxis way of being therefore does not decisively separate theory from practice. "Knowledge develops," one group of authors write, "through action and, as a result, theoretical knowledge grows from praxis and should be brought back to praxis."[10] Others, such as religious educator Daniel Schipani, assert that the clear demarcations that have been traditionally made between practice and theory have no scriptural grounds in the Christian tradition.[11] Theory and practice—knowing and doing—are therefore viewed as being mutually interdependent.[12]

Such a relationship therefore involves, so far, at least three elements: theory, practice, and reflection. Both secular and religious educators alike assert the need for students to blend "learning, teaching, and transformation."[13] Not only are students encouraged to engage already existing theoretical knowledge of their field, but to also reflectively engage with their actual communities in active ways.[14] Hence, not only is knowledge to be sought from theory, but also from the contextual experiences that one critically reflects upon.[15] The nature of praxis, as a way of being, therefore entails the theory, reflection, and actions or practices of us and our communities.

Develops from Participation in Practitioner-Oriented Research?," 157; Schipani, *Religious Education Encounters Liberation Theology*, 122–23.

8. Graham et al., *Theological Reflection*, 122–23.

9. Graham, *Transforming Practice*, 88.

10. Kemmis et al., "Reflections on 'Examining Praxis,'" 201.

11. Schipani, *Religious Education Encounters Liberation Theology*, 121.

12. Graham et al., *Theological Reflection*, 170; Groome, *Christian Religious Education*, 152.

13. Schipani, *Religious Education Encounters Liberation Theology*, 140.

14. Hesslefors-Arktoft and Lindskog, "Connecting Theory and Practice?" 81; Mattsson, "Degree Projects and Praxis Development," 70; Schipani, *Religious Education Encounters Liberation Theology*, 118.

15. Groome, *Christian Religious Education*, 149; Schipani, *Religious Education Encounters Liberation Theology*, 140.

PART ONE: Theoretical Foundations

The Purpose of Praxis

Given these three components thus far, we might additionally ask whether there is any specific purpose for praxis. Ultimately, a praxis way of being is to be oriented toward the transformation of our selves, our communities, and our world at large. In Christianity, such ends additionally take on a theistic tone as we seek to partner with the Spirit's life and work in our midst.

For all formators, specifically those in the educational fields, knowing how to engage with our constituents in efficient and effective ways holds a central place.[16] It is not enough to merely know about formation, we must actually be able to put our knowledge into action.[17] Being a central component, doing must be a core part of our praxis way of being.

However, it is not just action for the sake of doing something. Rather, it is for the primary purpose of further fostering liberation. Liberationist educator Paulo Freire, for instance, viewed education as a means by which "human beings actually make their own destiny" through social transformation.[18] Karl Marx's views of social progress, upon whom Freire based many of his assertions, comes via a praxis way of being as people critically and intentionally engage with their political and economic contexts.[19] More generally, educators are also encouraged "to challenge oppressive structures in real situations."[20]

Praxis is not to be a mode of living for educators and formators alone, however. The crux of world transformation at least partly lies in the hands of each human being.[21] As one author writes, ""Praxis" and "praxis development" should here be understood as a dialectical process in which humankind changes the world and the world changes humankind."[22] Each of us is therefore encouraged by the praxis perspective to tangibly engage

---

16. Hesslefors-Arktoft and Lindskog, "Connecting Theory and Practice?" 78–79; Mattsson, "Degree Projects and Praxis Development," 58.

17. Mattsson, "Degree Projects and Praxis Development," 58.

18. Groome, *Christian Religious Education*, 176; Schipani, *Religious Education Encounters Liberation Theology*, 118.

19. Groome, *Christian Religious Education*, 167; Schipani, *Religious Education Encounters Liberation Theology*, 118.

20. Kemmis et al., "Reflections on 'Examining Praxis,'" 193; Mattsson, "Degree Projects and Praxis Development," 69, 74.

21. Groome, *Christian Religious Education*, 170.

22. Mattsson, "Degree Projects and Praxis Development," 56.

Embodying Praxis

with the poor and oppressed in our world in order to bring about liberation and justice for everyone.[23]

In Christianity, such liberative ends can be fostered by the Christian story for the purposes of helping us to better partner with the Spirit's work in our midst.[24] For theologians such as Georg Wilhelm Friedrich Hegel, praxis is a way of coming to live more in alignment with "Geist"; with God's Spirit that is seeking to actualize Itself in human history.[25] For Christians, then, a praxis way of being is ultimately oriented toward a personal relationship with a God who seeks the liberation and emancipation of all of creation.[26]

The Four Components of Praxis

We can therefore see that the nature of praxis entails four essential components, as shown in figure 5 below: theory, practice, reflection, and transformation. We need to turn to the already existing models, theories, and knowledge that are available in order to help provide us with further insights into reality as it has been conceptualized by others. However, we also need to turn to the concrete experiences, actions, and practices that we and our communities have as well. With critical reflection and discernment as one of the means by which the dialectic relationship between theory and practice is fostered, our hopes are to work toward greater liberation and transformation in both our local contexts and our world in tangible and sustainable ways.

---

23. Graham, *Transforming Practice*, 113–14; Schipani, *Religious Education Encounters Liberation Theology*, 119.

24. Groome, *Christian Religious Education*, 149.

25. Ibid., 164.

26. Groome, *Christian Religious Education*, 145; Schipani, *Religious Education Encounters Liberation Theology*, 128, 133.

PART ONE: Theoretical Foundations

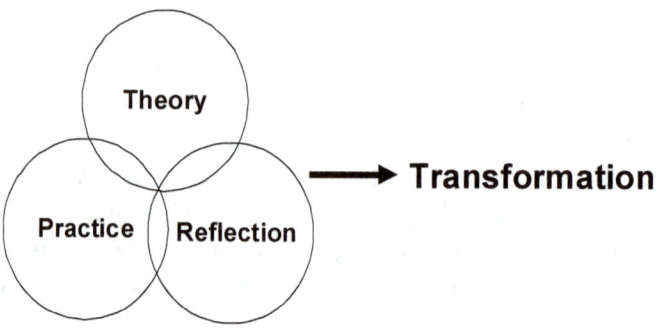

Figure 5. The Four Components of Praxis.

Spiritual Formation as Praxis

Of course, such is the core nature and purpose of theistic spiritual formation. A praxis way of being can therefore be a primary modus operandi that we follow whenever we ever seek to follow the formative leadings of the Spirit in our local contexts. We can see this praxis-oriented nature embodied in both the spiritual discernment processes that we explored in the last chapter as well as in the general nature and ideals of spiritual formation that we reviewed in the introduction.

It is at least partly because theistic formation fundamentally is rooted in spiritual discernment that it is a praxis-oriented endeavor. Looking to outer resources to inform and guide our discernment, as we just heard, spiritual formation embodies the praxis use of theories. But our spiritually discerning vocation looks to more than just these outer sources, for it also seeks to integrate the personal experiences and observations of ourselves and the communities that we are called to work with. Practice, in the experiential use of the word by our praxis authors, is therefore also an inherent part of spiritual formation program development.

Reflection is likewise central to our craft as we ever seek to discover the movements of God in our midst. As we saw, spiritual discernment considers both theory and practice, knowing and doing, to critically inform its evaluative and decision-making processes. Finally, the ultimate ends of all discernment are for the transformations that the Spirit is seeking to manifest through our decisions. We can therefore see, based upon spiritual discernment, that our vocation of spiritual formation is a praxis-oriented one.

However, we can also return to the nature and ideals of spiritual formation discussed in the introductory chapter where we find these four components to also be central. Clearly, the ultimate goal of spiritual formation, as with other praxis-oriented fields, is for the transformation of the people and communities we are called to work with. Given its theistic orientation, and therefore centrality of spiritual discernment as we have just heard, reflection is also a central part of this formative craft of ours. Theory and external resources are likewise crucial for spiritual formation program development as we need to look to our religious and theological traditions for guidance and insight into how the Spirit might be working in our midst. Finally, because we are primarily oriented toward walking with the life of God in our local context, we must consider the practices and actions that are found here as well.

We can therefore see that spiritual formation program development is an inherently a praxis-oriented vocation. This is important for our explorations here because it is now to two other praxis-based fields that we will turn to as we seek a set of more detailed methodologies to help guide the generation and embodiment of our spiritual formation programs and sets of interventions. While our spiritual discernment processes were too generalized, we will now see that when synthesized with the praxis methods described below we will find the additional direction we will need.

Methodological Movements: Embodying Spiritual Praxis

Given that program development is praxis-oriented, we can now ask, what does a praxis way of being really look like when it is embodied in practical ways? What are the major methodological movements that we can follow in order to bring theory, action, and reflection together with spiritually transformative results? To help us gain a better understanding of what praxis looks like in concrete ways, we turn to two other praxis-oriented fields: action research and practical theology. Both of these disciplines seek to embody praxis in their work and both will give us insights into how we might do so as well. As we shall presently see, however, we will need to synthesize the methods from both of these fields along with our spiritual discernment processes in order to develop our own praxis approach to theistic spiritual formation program development.

PART ONE: Theoretical Foundations

Exploring Two Praxis-Oriented Fields

Action researchers and practical theologians seek to transformatively engage with their communities by intentionally integrating theory, action, and reflection. By looking into the general movements that these two praxis-oriented fields engage in, we will gain a better understanding of some of the more detailed ways that we might begin to approach spiritual formation program development. We will therefore now consider the practical steps that each of these fields follow as they embody praxis.

Action Research

At its heart, action research is an endeavor that seeks to produce insights and understandings into a specific contextually located problem for the express purposes of enacting some sort of positive and progressive change.[27] In order to move toward such ends, action researchers engage both current research findings and models that are available as well as the contextual, or "ethnographic," observations and reflections that are made by both researchers and the communities they are working with.[28] Understood as a "researcher's long-term relationship with a problem," the process of action research is a spiraling one wherein there is an ongoing critically reflective movement from theory to practice and back to theory again for its intended transformative aims.[29]

An example of such approaches to research may be found in professional action researchers Jeffrey M. Duncan-Andrade's and Ernest Morrell's book, *The Art of Critical Pedagogy*, wherein they provide several examples of how these approaches are used to empower underprivileged youth.[30] These approaches are also being used in the fields of organizational development, social science, and education. Davydd Greenwood and Morten Levin, in their book *Introduction to Action Research*, provide de-

---

27. Cunningham, *Action Research and Organizational Development*, 67; Duncan-Andrade and Morrell, *Art of Critical Pedagogy*, 15, 126; Greenwood and Levin, *Introduction to Action Research*, 5.

28. Cunningham, *Action Research and Organizational Development*, 5; Greenwood and Levin, *Introduction to Action Research*, 3, 5, 107.

29. Cunningham, *Action Research and Organizational Development*, 4; Duncan-Andrade and Morrell, *Art of Critical Pedagogy*, 13; Greenwood and Levin, *Introduction to Action Research*, 102; Swinton and Mowat, *Practical Theology and Qualitative Research*, 255–56.

30. Duncan-Andrade and Morrell, *Art of Critical Pedagogy*.

tailed explanations and examples of how these methods are being used in social sciences.[31] Organizational development consultant Michael Beitler similarly outlines the applications of action research for use in corporate environments.[32]

In order to engage in such work, these action researchers generally outline a number of steps. Table 1 below shows the steps that are outlined by these authors and we can see some resonances and differences among them.

Table 1. Steps to Action Research

Greenwood and Levin, *Introduction to Action Research*, 142.	Beitler, *Strategic Organizational Change*, 24.	Duncan-Andrade and Morrell, *Art of Critical Pedagogy*, 12, fig. 1.1.
1) Creating a shared history and letting every participant understand how the world looks according to other groups of participants	1) Data Gathering—From Client Members	1) Identify a problem
2) Creating shared vision about what is a desirable future or solution to the focal problem of the group	2) Data Feedback—To Client Members	2) Research the problem
3) Creating a view of what would be the probable future if nothing were done; sometimes this perspective might be integrated into the work on desirable future	3) Diagnosis—With Client Members	3) Develop a collective plan of action to address the problem
4) Identifying action plans for addressing the focal problem	4) Action Planning—With Client Members	4) Implement the collective plan of action
5) Creating a collective prioritization process in which participants choose among alternative action plans	5) Action Taking/Interventions—With Client Members	5) Evaluate the action, assess its efficacy, and reexamine the state of the problem
6) Initiating concrete change activity and structuring a follow-up process aimed at sharing achievements and learning	6) Evaluating—With Client Members	

31. Greenwood and Levin, *Introduction to Action Research*.
32. Beitler, *Strategic Organizational Change*.

PART ONE: Theoretical Foundations

As we can see, these three models of how to engage in action research differ in some of the areas that they emphasize and focus on. For instance, Duncan-Andrade and Morrell have included, as a first step, identification of the problem to be focused on while the other two models do not. Also, we can see that Beitler's and Greenwood and Levin's models spend the first four to five steps, respectively, elaborating on the details of how to move from research to action planning whereas Duncan-Andrade and Morrell compile these into just two of their steps.

Despite these differences, however, there do seem to be movements that are common to each of them. Each of them does, though it is not captured in all of their models, assume that there is some problem that they will focus on. Each of them does address some sort of research and exploration of the problem. Finally, they all articulate the need for developing, carrying out, and then evaluating actions based upon these explorations. From this, we can therefore begin to see some of the necessary movements that will be needed for our own practical steps below.

Practical Theology

Turning now to the work of practical theology, we find some of the same methodological movements as in action research, but with additional steps that will be necessary for our theistic perspective. Similar to action research, practical theologians are primary interested in the reflective intersection of theory and practice for the purposes of transforming the local contexts they are working with.[33] However, practical theology differs from action research because of its distinctive theological location.[34] More specifically, practical theologians additionally turn to the theological and religious resources of their traditions in an effort to further understand and illuminate the transformative movements of God in the local contexts that they are working within.[35]

Examples of practical theologians who engage their work in these ways are Emmanuel Lartey, John Swinton, and Harriet Mowat. Lartey's steps to practical theology are outlined in Angie Pears book, *Doing*

---

33. Pears, *Doing Contextual Theology*, 33; Swinton and Mowat, *Practical Theology and Qualitative Research*, 255.

34. Swinton and Mowat, *Practical Theology and Qualitative Research*, 256.

35. Graham, *Transforming Practice*, 112, 134; Pears, *Doing Contextual Theology*, 37; Swinton and Mowat, *Practical Theology and Qualitative Research*, 6, 258.

Contextual Theology,[36] while Swinton and Mowat detail such methods in their own book, *Practical Theology and Qualitative Research*.[37] These methods provide us with insights into the nature of praxis, according to a practical theological perspective, and are shown below in table 2.

Table 2. Steps to Practical Theology

Lartey's Steps (see Pears, *Doing Contextual Theology*, 40).	Swinton and Mowat, *Practical Theology and Qualitative Research*, 94–97.
1) The pastoral cycle begins with an actual or 'concrete' situation	Stage 1: The Situation At this intuitive, pre-reflective phase we being to explore nature of the situation and work out what we think are the key issues. Here we note the situation as we see it in the present and articulate in some initial form what appears to be going on. We may want to explore the literature that surrounds this area, we may decide to do some provisional historical and cultural explorations. All of this will help us to gain an understanding of the situation at this initial level.
2) Here the situation encountered is analysed using different analytic tools and disciplines to try and discern the dynamics of the situation that demands some sort of response or in which an individual may find themselves	Stage 2: Cultural/Contextual Analysis Here we begin to deepen our initial reflections by entering into dialogue with other sources of knowledge which will help us develop a deeper understanding of the situation. At this stage we begin to engage in a disciplined investigation into the various dynamics (overt and covert) that underlie the forms of practice that are taking place within the situation. The intention here is to enhance and challenge our initial impressions and begin to develop a deep and rich understanding of the complex dynamics of the situation.

---

36. Pears, *Doing Contextual Theology*.
37. Swinton and Mowat, *Practical Theology and Qualitative Research*.

PART ONE: Theoretical Foundations

Lartey's Steps (see Pears, *Doing Contextual Theology*, 40).	Swinton and Mowat, *Practical Theology and Qualitative Research*, 94–97.
3) The situation is analysed from a committed or faith perspective	Stage 3: Theological Reflection At this stage we begin to reflect on what we have discovered from a theological perspective . . . Here we begin to focus more overtly on the theological significance of the data that we have been working with in stages 1 and 2, and how it can be used to develop our understanding of the situation we are exploring and the practices which emerge from the various practices we encounter. At this stage we begin to develop the conversation by drawing out the implicit and explicit theological dimensions of the situation, sifting through the data and exploring the ways in which they complement and challenge one another; searching for authentic revelation in a spirit of critical faithfulness and chastened optimism.
4) It is the faith perspective that is itself questioned by situational analysis	Stage 4: Formulating Revised Forms of Practice At stage 4 we return to the situation that we began with. Here we draw together the cultural/contextual analysis with the theological reflection and combine these two dimensions with our original reflections on the situation. In this way the conversation functions dialectically to produce new and challenging forms of practice that enable the initial situation to be transformed into ways which are authentic and faithful.
5) Exploration is then made of the options that are actually available to the individual who then, as a result acts accordingly	

We can see many similarities and differences between these two sets of approaches just as we did for our action researchers. The first three steps, as we can see, are essentially identical to one another, with both

Embodying Praxis

emphasizing the need to engage the local context with interdisciplinary analytical tools. However, while Swinton and Mowat have included the challenging of one's theological tradition as a part of stage 3, Lartey has chosen to separate this movement out into its own step. Both of these models end with the embodiment of transformed practice which will then later lead to a repeating of the entire praxis cycle of practical theology as one continues to work with their local contexts.[38]

Similarities, Differences, and Common Movements

Overall, we can see that these two sets of approaches to engaging in transformative ways of being have some methodological commonalities. Both action researchers and practical theologians emphasize the need for an in-depth exploration of ones concrete local context in relation to the issue that one is interested in changing. They both also emphasize the need for analyzing the dynamics one is noticing. Our practical theologians and action researchers also assert the need for developing and/or revising interventions in response to one's analysis. Finally, both fields highlight the need for carrying out these newly formulated actions.

In addition to these similarities, however, there are also several notable differences among these two fields. First, while Duncan-Arcade and Morrell did highlight this in their steps, our practical theologians seem to place a much greater emphasis on the need for turning to outside research and analytical tools to aid them in their critical reflections. Also, as was already noted above, practical theology stresses the centrality of one's theological and religious tradition in their analyses. Our action researchers, alternatively, distinguished action planning from implementation as separate and distinct steps whereas our practical theologians combined them as one movement. Finally, only the action researchers explicitly stressed the need for intentional evaluations to be conducted as the actions are being carried out. We can therefore see how these two fields help us to better understand some of the dominant movements of praxis, with its emphasis on theory, action, and reflection for the purposes of transformation.

Collectively, for our applications, we can assert at least three common movements to praxis based on these explorations. The first would be one of an in-depth exploration and analysis of the situation that we wanted to be a part of transforming. Such a movement would not only rely on our

---

38. See figure 4 in Swinton and Mowat, *Practical Theology and Qualitative Research*, 95.

in vivo observations and experiences but also on external sources such as research findings and our religious traditions. A second movement would be one wherein we then discern and develop a set of interventions in order to engage with our local contexts in transformative ways. Finally, we would then carry out these interventions, assessing their effectiveness and modifying our actions as things progressed.

These three movements therefore comprise the general ones that emerge from these two praxis-oriented fields. While some of our authors placed a greater emphasis on one of them more than the other two, and while some authors have chosen to divide them into separate steps, these general movements nonetheless capture the flow of praxis according to them. It is these three movements that will next become the basis for our program development methodologies.

Synthesizing Spiritual Praxis: Three Methodologies for Our Craft

However, we might still be wondering how such praxis might be embodied in our craft in spiritually discerning ways. How they might or might not fit with the spiritual discernment processes that were outlined in the previous chapter? Can we synthesize the common movements of these two praxis-oriented fields along with our discernment processes into a set of methodologies? I assert that we can and, after discussing such a synthesis, I will briefly describe the three methodologies that emerge from this synthesis. These methodologies will then become the basis for the next part of this book.

Spiritually Discerning Praxis

As we consider these three general movements of praxis along with the five processes of spiritual discernment from our last chapter, we can immediately see commonalities among them. Both of them have steps for exploring a situation or issue in detail based upon both external sources and local observations. Both of them also have some means for considering the possible paths and interventions that one might choose from. And, finally, both of them express the need for enacting the decisions that are made and assessing the outcomes of those actions. From these observations, it is clear that theistic discernment is a praxis-oriented spiritual discipline as we heard above.

Embodying Praxis

At this point, it should be obvious that the three common movements of praxis are sufficient enough to become the basis for our program development methodologies. They are not only asserted to foster transformation, but they are also very much in accordance with our discernment processes. Just as we can see that discernment is a form of praxis, we can also see that these three praxis movements are a form of discernment. In some sense, they are a simplified version of the five processes of spiritual discernment. Hence, we might be tempted to drop either these three movements or our discernment processes in favor of the other.

However, despite how closely aligned these two sets of approaches appear to be, I assert that in order to truly engage in spiritually discerning program development, we actually need to retain them both. To do this, our three praxis movements will become the three methodologies that we will explore in the next part of this book. In a sense, they will become the overarching guides for how we will develop our formative programs. As we shall see in the coming chapters, each of these three movements will have a set of specific steps that we can follow in order to help us embody them more fully. For instance, in the exploration and analysis methodologies we will learn of the steps that are needed in order to make the necessary contextual observations, select relevant external resources, and then synthesize both of these into a coherent description of our local context. These three praxis movements are therefore the overarching methodologies for exploring, implementing, and assessing a spiritual formation program.

But then where does that leave our spiritual discernment processes? In order to answer this question, we need to first revisit the definition of spiritual formation that was given in the introductory chapter. It is, we may recall, *our intentional efforts to partner with God's formative life and leadings in our local contexts*. This means that for each of these overarching praxis movements, and each of their detailed steps, our task is to intentionally seek to allow the Spirit to guide our use of them. In other words, we are called to engage in each of these meta-movements in spiritually discerning ways.

This is precisely where our discernment processes come into play. For each step of these three praxis movements, we are invited to embody them in prayerfully discerning ways, and the previous chapter can help us to do this. In effect, then, each step of our praxis methodologies becomes the focus of our discernment process. For each one, our task is to answer the ultimate discernment question, "What is God inviting us to do here, for this particular step?"

"Wow," you might now find yourself saying, because this seems like a lot. To engage in all five discernment processes for each of the steps for all three praxis movements (of which there are at least five steps for each movement) . . . That's a ton of steps (at least seventy-five to be precise)! Okay, so this is where the KISS principle comes in. So let's return to the core focus of both praxis and discernment. The purpose of these praxis movements is to help us to integrate theory, practice, and reflection for transformation in our local contexts. Whether or not we actually engage in each of their detailed steps or not, we can do this. And the primary goal of spiritual discernment is to allow the Spirit to lead us all along the way. Again, whether or not we actually engage in each of its five processes or not, we can seek to be ever open to God's leadings.

In other words, the many and detailed steps that are presented herein for both praxis and discernment are merely guidelines and aids to the spiritually forming work that we are already engaged in. As long as we keep these core foci in mind while journeying, we can trust that God will eventually take us to where we need to be with our communities. As long as we work to partner with the Spirit's transformative life in our midst, whether that involves each of these steps and processes or not, then we are headed in the right direction. With this said, we can now briefly describe the three methodologies that will become the basis of our explorations in the next part of this book.

Exploration and Analysis Methodologies

In this first methodological movement, we discern the specific issue or community that we will be engaging with in formative ways. For instance, we may discern the need to develop a marriage retreat for our parish couples, or for couples who are struggling such as Martha and Charles are. Our goal may be to provide them with a weekend away from their daily and weekly routines so that they may focus more fully on deepening their intimacy with one another. In this movement, then, we seek to clarify what our formative focus will be.

From here, as we can see from our action researchers and practical theologians, we then seek to explore our foci in much more detailed ways. To help us to do this, as we shall see more in chapter 3, we will turn not only to our own personal observations and reflections but also to those of the people we are working with to generate contextually rooted understandings. For the marriage retreat, we would therefore not only reflect on our own observations of the couples we anticipate attending, but we might also sit with them and help them to reflect on how their relationships are going and what they think they might need at this time in their journeys together.

We will also, as Lartey, Swinton, and Mowat encourage us to do, look to various external resources to help us to gain greater insights. Such sources may include secular scientific resources and/or they may include the reflections of fellow practitioners who have led similar marriage retreats themselves. As theistic spiritual formators, however, our religious traditions should also form a core part of these external aids. For our example, this might include turning to theological books on marriage counseling and development. Or it might mean looking for specific resources that discuss how to lead such a weekend retreat. We can also look to resources that explore intimate relationships from our own religious traditions.

Collectively, then, these local observations and external resources should give us greater insights into a number of areas. For instance, they should help us to better understand the local dynamics of the people and communities we are working with, which may be called "anthropologies." For our couples, this would be the current status of their relationships and how they are getting along together. These explorations can also help us to see the effects that one's larger environment has on the local context; which might be referred to as "cosmology." Marriages, for instance, are often influenced by the cultures in which they develop. As theists, our reflections can also give us greater theological insights into where and how the Spirit is working in our midst. Where, for example, do we see God at work in these specific marriages? It is models such as these that can help us to better understand how to foster transformation. As we shall see in chapter 3, looking into these and other areas can help us to develop a deep understanding of our local dynamics.

The primary aims of this movement are therefore twofold: (1) to gain more accurate insights into the dynamics of our local context and the issues we are seeking to specifically and formatively address; and (2) to better understand where and how the Spirit has been, is, and may be working therein. This exploration and analysis movement then becomes the foundation out of which the next one emerges as we seek to discern how to intervene in concrete and transformative ways.

PART ONE: Theoretical Foundations

Design and Implementation Methodologies

As we learn more about the community we are working with, and as we discern more clearly the divine movements in their midst, we can then begin to reflect on, plan, and implement tangible actions and interventions. For our marriage retreat, this would come as we make decisions relating to the retreat's content and format. Knowing what it is that we want our couples to experience while on retreat is central to our discernment of which kinds of activities we will have them engage in. While there may be a full range of possible approaches to choose from, this movement will seek to narrow our choices and focus in on which ones we will actually use. Once such decisions are made, we can then carry them out.

This movement therefore has two primary tasks, as we shall see more below in chapter 4: (1) deciding upon which specific interventions to use; and (2) moving toward implementing these interventions. For our marriage retreat, then, we would decide what the retreat's primary goals are, discern which activities we will engage before, during, and after the retreat, and then reflect on what will be needed to implement the entire plan. This movement is therefore one of moving from our more descriptive explorations and analyses toward more concrete transformative actions in our local context.

Assessment and Modification Methodologies

Our third and final movement is one that emerges as we actually implement our interventions. As we enact the marriage retreat, we can intentionally monitor and evaluate how it is unfolding. Are we achieving the ideals that we set out from the beginning? What is transpiring as we move through the activities that we had planned? Is it going as expected or are new and unexpected dynamics happening? Questions such as these can form the basis for how we track the progress of our programs.

This movement therefore has three primary elements to it, which will be discussed in much greater detail in chapter 5: (1) monitoring the dynamics that we are seeking to formatively engage with; (2) evaluating the progress of our communities; and (3) modifying both our understandings of the situation and the interventions we are using. It will be important to note that "progress" is always gauged in relation to the ideals that we had set out previously. The extent to which we are making such progress or not will then lead us back into the first movement of this cyclical praxis-based process wherein we continue to discern where and how the Spirit is ever leading us and our communities.

Closing Reflections

In this chapter, we have sought to gain some sense of what the nature and embodiment of spiritual formation program development is as a praxis-oriented vocation. Lying at the intersection of theory, action, and reflection for the purposes of transformation of one's local context, praxis is an integral part of our craft. In order to practically embody such praxis, we have conceived of three general movements that emerged from our explorations of the fields of action research and practical theology. Each of these movements is intended to help us to see more clearly what praxis might look like and mean for program development.

As we have journeyed throughout this chapter, we have also seen how closely related praxis is with the spiritual discernment. The processes of praxis and discernment are very reflective of one another. Both call for a deep dwelling and listening to a situation. Both strive for intentional action that results in the transformation of some part of our world. And both emphasize the need for evaluating our actions in an ongoing way.

For this book, however, we will be relating them to one another in a very particular way. The praxis methodologies that we will be exploring in the next part will comprise an overarching framework. For each of the three methodologies, we will be providing detailed steps that will better enable us to engage in our spiritually forming craft in praxis-oriented ways. The spiritual discernment processes will then provide us with the means to engage each of these steps that will be detailed in the coming chapters. In other words, for each step of our methodologies, we are encouraged to engage them in spiritually discerning ways. While this may seem complex, returning to our KISS principle, our ultimate goal is to allow the Spirit to lead us step by step through each of these praxis methodologies. Such is the fundamental nature of spiritual formation and it is one that is intended to become a *Living Spiritual Praxis* for our lives and our ministries.

PART TWO

Methodological Movements

IN THE FIRST PART of this book, we have been exploring the central role that discernment and praxis have in spiritual formation program development. From these explorations, three methodologies were derived that will be the focus of the next part of this book. For each of them, we will be seeking to understand not only their theoretical nature, but also the more fundamental and practical steps needed in applying them. The hope of this next part is therefore to develop a set of simple steps that we can concretely use in our local ministries to spiritually discern the programs that we develop.

In order to clarify what these discrete steps might look like, however, we must first understand some of the theoretical foundations that undergird each methodology. Each of the next three chapters therefore begins with these considerations. The overall goal for each chapter is to therefore provide us with enough theoretical and practical considerations to enable us to adapt these methodologies to our own unique local contexts.

This part of the book will then conclude with a chapter that pulls all three methodologies together by presenting a case example of how they might be embodied in a real-world situation. In this case, we will see how Tom used these methodologies for his contemplative spiritual formation program. Overall, then, we hope to provide the strong foundations that are needed for spiritual formation program development.

3

Going Deep
Exploration and Analysis Methodologies

HAVE YOU EVER STOOD on the shore of one of the mighty oceans of our world and wondered what it is really like out there, in the depths of that vast abyss? Or have you ever looked up at the extraordinary array of stars on a clear moonless night and thought about what it might be like to visit the outer reaches of our universe? While we can watch television programs that show us parts of these places, and such information is indeed insightful, until we have been there ourselves, we cannot more fully know what it is like. We stand on the beach or peer out from our back porch and wonder, but until we've taken the plunge or blasted off ourselves, our knowledge will be limited. In order to really know these far away places, we have to be immersed in them; we must go deep into them.

Our first set of program development methodologies are those related to exploring and analyzing the situation or issue that we are discerningly called to formatively interact with. In essence, they are our attempts to go deep into them, to understand them from both the information that we can collect about them as well as from our own abiding immersion in them with our local communities. Before we can begin the processes of designing and implementing specific interventions and programs, we first need to develop a deep and detailed understanding of the situation or issue. Each one of the praxis authors in the last chapter expended some time in exploring and analyzing their situations before acting. Developing such a deep understanding is therefore the overall aim of these first methodologies.

As we also heard in the last chapter, there are two primary goals that we are seeking to fulfill through these methodologies. First, we need to

PART TWO: Methodological Movements

have a detailed understanding of the situation, and its many interrelated dynamics, both historically and contemporarily. For instance, as heard in our chapter on spiritual discernment, before Montague could discern whether to close the church or attempt a revitalization campaign, it was very beneficial for him to spend some time exploring the church's history and how this community had come to the place where it currently was. It was helpful for him to expend some effort getting to know this group of dedicated members, who they are as individuals, what their relationship to the church had been, what their hopes are for the church, et cetera. It was also helpful for Montague to know more about the surrounding neighborhood and the many demographic, political, and economic changes that it had gone through over the life of the church as these had played a part to play in the church's history and progress as well. In other words, one of the primary goals of these exploration and analysis methodologies are to help us to gain a much deeper insight into the history, nature, and dynamics of the situation we are working with.

The second primary goal is for us to then discern where it is that we believe the Spirit has been active and manifesting throughout it all. Turning to our religious and theological traditions, as our practical theologians admonish us to do, we reflect on the histories and dynamics of the situation and ask, "Where has God been most present? Absent?" In Montague's case, for example, he found that the demographics of the surrounding neighborhood had radically changed from being primarily Caucasian to now being mainly Latina/o. And when this happened, the church, being predominantly Caucasian, made the intentional decision to close its doors and outreach programs to these new members of their neighborhood. If Montague came, as he did, from a theological tradition that values diversity and sees the Spirit as not only embracing but actually being the source of such diversity then he might be led to decide that such a closed-door policy was not a movement of God, which he did. This second main goal of these exploration and analysis methodologies is therefore for us to reflect on where it is that we believe the Spirit has been, to greater and lesser extents, active in the situation that we will be attempting to develop a program or set of interventions for.

In the coming pages, then, we will be exploring both the theoretical and methodological foundations that will better enable us to go deep by embodying this exploration and analysis movement of praxis. We will be learning of the kinds of information that we need to consider in our exploration. We will further investigate how to theologically reflect on our situations as we did in our spiritual discernment chapter. We will see how to synthesize external resources with our own contextual observations. And finally, we will come to see the concrete steps by which to embody all of this in our local communities. In the end, this chapter will provide us with the tools we need in order to go deeply enough into our situation in order to participate with God's formative life in our midst. It is then from these deep encounters that our program design and implementation can emerge in the next set of spiritual praxis methodologies.

Theoretical Foundations

In order to help us, like Montague, Francis, and Tom, to delve deeply enough into our local situations, we need to understand some of the basics of what exploration and analysis entails. First, we need to know the kinds of information that we can and should be exploring in relation to our local context. What do we need to know about it? What types of information should we be focusing on? Knowing this, we can then ask where we might turn to in order to gather these kinds of insights. What sources will be helpful for us in gaining a deeper understanding of our contexts? Which resources should inform such explorations? Next, we can ask how we might begin to theologically reflect on it? Upon what bases does our discernment of the Spirit's movements stand? Finally, how do we begin to synthesize and integrate all of this information and insight into a more coherent and unified picture? It is these questions that this section will be exploring as a necessary theoretical foundation for the practical steps that will be outlined below.

Where to Dive: The Kinds of Information to Explore

"Diving deeply" into a situation may be a helpful analogy for us, but it will also be useful to know the general kinds of information and insights to explore. This data should help us to better understand the situation from the inside out and the outside in. It should help us to understand both the internal dynamics of the issue we are formatively working with as well as the contextual influences that have and continue to contribute to the situation. It should also help us to be able to better perceive how God has been and continues to be active. Overall, this information should provide us with the deep and necessary foundations that the design and implementation of our program will need.

PART TWO: Methodological Movements

As we look into spiritual formation literature, we can find five kinds of information that we can gather to give us insight into the deeper nature and dynamics of our local context for the purposes of program development. To help us better understand the nature of each of these and their importance for our deep understanding, we turn to historical and contemporary writers in our field. Taken collectively, these five areas of consideration should develop a foundation that will become the basis for the interventions that we consider in the next program design and implementation phase. Let us, then, consider each of these five areas in turn.

Anthropologies: Schematics for Our Work

As you might imagine, it is important that we understand the inner dynamics of the situations we are formatively involved with. Just as we would want a vehicle repair manual to be both detailed and accurate before popping the hood of our car, we need to be more clear about what we are working with before we begin designing and implementing a spiritual formation program. Such is the nature of our "anthropologies." These are the theories and models that we have of the individuals, relationships, and communities that we are working with. They are intended to give us deeper insights into the workings and dynamics of our situation.

For instance, having a better understanding of individual human nature can be tremendously beneficial in our formative work.[1] We humans, one author asserts, are considered to be very complex indeed.[2] The anthropological models found in spiritual formation texts range in complexity from Erasmus's two part model of an inner and outer person to the "physical, intellectual, psychosocial, spiritual, social, and emotional" model that has been developed by others.[3] Some of these models stress the idea that humans are made in the image of God and that we have the capacity to

---

1. O'Connell, *Making Disciples*, 28.
2. Van Kaam, *Fundamental Formation*, 60.
3. Clark, "Spiritual Formation in Children," 237–39; Driskill, "Spirituality and the Formation of Pastoral Counselors," 80; Erasmus, "Handbook of the Militant Christian," 42–43, 47; Radillo, "Model of Formation in the Multi-Cultural Urban Context," 169; Van Kaam, *Fundamental Formation*, 58, 60.

personally experience our Creator.⁴ Others, however, stress that humanity is also in need of salvation and redemption.⁵

From all of these discussions, we can see more clearly how central to spiritual formation such anthropological models can be. As schematics, they not only give insights into the nature and workings of the individuals, relationships, or communities that we are working with, but they can also help us to know how to approach our interventions with them, as we shall see in the next chapter. Such anthropological schematics therefore comprise an important part of our gaining a deeper understanding of our situation for the purposes of program development.

Theories of Change: Are We There Yet?!

A second set of considerations is related to how change happens for our communities. These "theories of change" are important because the fundamental nature and purpose of all fields of formation, as we heard in the opening chapter, is one of transformation. It therefore behooves us to deeply explore how such changes transpire for the people and communities that we are working with. Such understandings will become a central part of how we choose which interventions to use in our design and implementation methodologies in the next chapter.

In the literature, spiritual growth changes for individuals are conceived of as being a time-laden occurrence (i.e., changes that happen only gradually over the course of many years).⁶ Such growth is conceived of as a "progressive patterning of a person's inner and outer life" that takes much time and effort.⁷ Just as human nature is complex and unique, so

---

4. *John Cassian: The Conferences*, 374; Driskill, "Spirituality and the Formation of Pastoral Counselors," 80; Law, "Serious Call to a Devout and Holy Life," 322; Lockerbie, "Living and Growing in the Christian Year," 130; Van Kaam, *Fundamental Formation*, 59, 63.

5. *John Cassian: The Conferences*, 100, 156, 254, 257–58; Erasmus, "Handbook of the Militant Christian," 55; Lightner, "Salvation and Spiritual Formation," 39–40; Payne, "Personal Healing and Spiritual Formation," 219; Willard, "Spirit Is Willing," 227.

6. Hull, *Complete Book of Discipleship*, 125; Law, "Serious Call to a Devout and Holy Life," 59; Lawrenz, *Dynamics of Spiritual Formation*, 17, 33, 137; McCallum and Lowery, *Organic Disciplemaking*, 269; O'Connell, *Making Disciples*, 39; Wimberly and Parker, "In Search of Wisdom," 17.

7. *John Cassian: The Conferences*, 43–44, 46, 253, 377, 379, 383, 475, 514, 520; Law, "Serious Call to a Devout and Holy Life," 148; Lawrenz, *Dynamics of Spiritual Formation*, 15.

PART TWO: Methodological Movements

too are the changes and growth patterns that accompany each individual's journey.[8] Some see this journey as a gradual awakening, while others view it more as a redemptive one.[9] Regardless of one's views of the nature of the formative changes, they are asserted to happen at least partially via crises and temptations.[10]

In addition to describing the nature of spiritual growth, some authors also spend time exploring the developmental stages by which our journeys unfold. These stages can depict one's dispositions as a disciple, or they can capture the moral, intellectual, or other stages by which one changes over the course of their lifetime.[11] Other models explore the steps that one moves through as they grow in their communal relationships, while still others outline the stages of discipleship training.[12] Each of these models essentially attempts to identify the core movements, or phases, by which an individual's, relationship, or community's journey progresses through in some fashion.

Finally, these views of the nature of change also often deeply explore some of the reasons for their being a lack of progress in an individual's life. They highlight the reality that "breakdowns" occur along the road to God.[13] They also note that such regressions can occur anywhere along the way, whether one is a novice newly starting out or a seasoned disciple.[14] They also address the reality that sometimes there are various kinds of blocks, potholes and barricades if you will, that need to be addressed before we can continue on our journeys with and into God.[15]

Overall, then, we can see that theories of change are central to our work. In order for us to discerningly know how to engage with the

8. Graham and Whitehead, "Role of Pastoral Theology," 10; McCallum and Lowery, *Organic Disciplemaking*, 56.

9. *John Cassian: The Conferences*, 250; Erasmus, "Handbook of the Militant Christian," 40; Jackson, "Forming a Spirituality of Wisdom," 157.

10. Erasmus, "Handbook of the Militant Christian," 49, 77; Graham and Whitehead, "Role of Pastoral Theology," 21; Law, "Serious Call to a Devout and Holy Life," 332; Lawrenz, *Dynamics of Spiritual Formation*, 43; Van Kaam, *Fundamental Formation*, 61.

11. Hull, *Complete Book of Discipleship*, 256–60; O'Connell, *Making Disciples*, ch. 4.

12. Hull, *Complete Book of Discipleship*, 166–67; McCallum and Lowery, *Organic Disciplemaking*, ch. 4.

13. McCallum and Lowery, *Organic Disciplemaking*, 169.

14. *John Cassian: The Conferences*, 167, 263, 411, 523; Erasmus, "Handbook of the Militant Christian," 38.

15. Law, "Serious Call to a Devout and Holy Life," 98, 104–5, 149; O'Connell, *Making Disciples*, 34.

Going Deep

individuals, groups, and communities that we are working with, we must have some notions of how progressive transformation transpires. While the literature reviewed herein has focused on such changes for individuals, there are similar sets of literature for relationships and communities. These theories of change are therefore another important area that we need to deeply explore and analyze.

Cosmologies: The Ponds in Which We Swim

Next, is our understanding of the contexts in which we find ourselves, and the people we are working with, in. These "cosmological" models also capture what we and our communities believe about the more fundamental nature of reality. They are important because they enable us to see more deeply how wider influences beyond our local contexts may be influencing them. If such influences really are significant, then any programmatic development needs to take them into consideration. There are, as was just mentioned, two sets of cosmologies that we can explore.

The first set has to do with the nature of life and reality that we and the people we are working with believe in. Such models may describe life as "sad and miserable, short and quick" or they might highlight the finiteness of it all.[16] Others might assert the inherent moral nature of creation or they could highlight the "invisible" and sacramental aspects of our world.[17]

Many spiritual formation systems also describe the nature of sin and evil. For instance, spiritual formator Mel Lawrenz asserts, "Sin is a law at work in the sense that it is universal, persistent, and chronic," and this is a viewed shared by others.[18] For some, such as the early desert monastics, sin is also at least partially the result of demons at work in the world.[19] Sin is also viewed as something that we need to do battle with in order to overcome it.[20] As we can see, these sorts of cosmological views therefore

---

16. Erasmus, "Handbook of the Militant Christian," 83; Law, "Serious Call to a Devout and Holy Life," 72, 270; O'Connell, *Making Disciples*, 21, 23.

17. Erasmus, "Handbook of the Militant Christian," 61, 64, 76; O'Connell, *Making Disciples*, 25; Ryken, "Puritan Model of Spiritual Formation," 50–51.

18. Erasmus, "Handbook of the Militant Christian," 41; Law, "Serious Call to a Devout and Holy Life," 336; Lawrenz, *Dynamics of Spiritual Formation*, 49.

19. *John Cassian: The Conferences*, 164, 254, 264, 269. See also Law, "Serious Call to a Devout and Holy Life," 236.

20. *John Cassian: The Conferences*, 100, 156, 161–62, 254, 257–58, 334; Erasmus, "Handbook of the Militant Christian," 28, 31; Hull, *Complete Book of Discipleship*, 292–93; Law, "Serious Call to a Devout and Holy Life," 51, 196, 243; McCallum and

seek to describe what we believe is the more fundamental nature of life and reality. These are important for our thick descriptions and deep understandings because such views influence how we think and act.

The second set of cosmologies that we must consider is related to our concrete settings. Contextually speaking, the people we are working with are situated within larger social, political, and economic contexts. Our spiritually forming endeavors can therefore not neglect these wider sets of influences.[21] Our communities can be places where transformation becomes reality, where we are enculturated into new and better ways of being, and where we can receive the support and guidance we need to grow.[22] These wider influences can also be places of destruction and demise as well. The communities of which we are a part therefore play a powerful role in the formation of individuals, relationships, and congregations. We therefore need to have some understanding of what these wider cosmological beliefs and influences are in relation to the spiritual formation programs that we are seeking to develop.

Theologies: "And God Said..."

We have already seen the centrality that theology has to spiritual discernment. In the literature, we also find the importance of being explicit with our theologies in relation to spiritual formation.[23] If we truly are seeking to better understand where it is that the Spirit has been and is active in our local situations, then our theologies must have a central role in such reflections.

In spiritual formation literature, we find the same two sets of theological models that were central to spiritual discernment: God's nature and God's relationship to our specific situation. Erasmus of Rotterdam, for instance, puts forth a model that asserts, "God is mind, the most pure and

---

Lowery, *Organic Disciplemaking*, 136; Piper, "God Is Most Glorified in Us," 78.

21. Bidwell and Marshall, "Formation: Content, Context, Models and Practices," 4; Jackson, "Forming a Spirituality of Wisdom," 162; Lawrenz, *Dynamics of Spiritual Formation*, 19; Van Kaam, *Fundamental Formation*, 57; Wimberly and Parker, "In Search of Wisdom," 13.

22. *John Cassian: The Conferences*, 263; Hull, *Complete Book of Discipleship*, 188–89; Lawrenz, *Dynamics of Spiritual Formation*, 96; O'Connell, *Making Disciples*, 85–86.

23. Felder, "Counsel from Wise Others," 105; Lawrenz, *Dynamics of Spiritual Formation*, 109; Townsend, "Theological Reflection and the Formation of Pastoral Counselors."

most simple mind of all."[24] Others, such as the Puritans, describe the omnipresence of God in relation to all of creation.[25] Some authors explore the forcefulness and non-forcefulness of God's dealing with creation,[26] while still others see interpersonal relationships as one of the means through which God transforms lives.[27] Also, given the centrality of Christ, some writers discuss the nature and role of his life and death in relation to the redemption of creation.[28]

Overall, these theological models seek to establish the more general nature of God and God's relationship to our specific situation. These views will become the basis for how we reflect theologically on our models, as we shall see below. In short, these theological explorations should help us to think about on where and how God is more or less active in our concrete local contexts. They therefore comprise yet another important area that we need to deeply explore in preparation for program development design and implementation.

Formative Ideals: The Horizons toward Which We Journey

Finally, any program development journey typically begins with some initial set of ideals or aims that we will be striving toward. Before we can begin with developing a program, it usually helps to have some idea of what the program will be about and what our initial hopes for the program might be. Where do we currently believe that God might be wanting to take this individual, small group, or community toward via our formative work? Where is it that we feel called to go as a community? In Martha's case, her present "ideal," or hope, is to recapture something of the relationship that she and her husband once had. For Tom, his hopes are to introduce and transform his participants through contemplative practices and reflections on their lives.

---

24. Erasmus, "Handbook of the Militant Christian," 69. For similar views, see *John Cassian: The Conferences*, 257.

25. *John Cassian: The Conferences*, 55; Law, "Serious Call to a Devout and Holy Life," 76, 317, 350; Ryken, "Puritan Model," 52.

26. *John Cassian: The Conferences*, 157; Law, "Serious Call to a Devout and Holy Life," 129, 319; Lightner, "Salvation and Spiritual Formation," 39.

27. McCallum and Lowery, *Organic Disciplemaking*, 13–14.

28. *John Cassian: The Conferences*, 472, 474; Erasmus, "Handbook of the Militant Christian," 30; Law, "Serious Call to a Devout and Holy Life," 336; Lawrenz, *Dynamics of Spiritual Formation*, 141; Lightner, "Salvation and Spiritual Formation," 45.

PART TWO: Methodological Movements

As we may recall from our introductory chapter, spiritual formation literature asserts a number of ideals that are set forth for individuals. Imitating Christ and attuning to his divine essence were mentioned. Ideals may also be set for relationships, groups, and whole communities as we also heard. Another area to explore, then, are the ideals that we initially set in front of us and work to strive for through the programs we are going to develop. They essentially constitute the general horizons toward which we initially believe we may be journeying.[29]

However, we also need to expect these horizons to change as we proceed through each of these praxis methodologies as new insights and information emerges for us. Not only will our clarity about them expand, but we may come to discern a different direction altogether. Hence, while they therefore provide us with initial ideas of where to focus our attention, we need to be open to their changing in radical ways as our exploration and analysis, and the coming methodologies, unfold.

An Overview and Order to Engaging These

The five areas, these five core models, therefore capture some of the essential kinds of information that we need in order to deeply explore and analyze our contexts. The anthropologies provide us with the necessary insights that we need to better understand the inner dynamics of the individuals, relationships, and communities that we are working with. The cosmologies help us to better understand the role that wider influences have on our constituents. The ideals are the horizons that we anticipate heading toward together. The theories of change are essentially our maps for how we believe our journey toward these horizons will progress. And our theologies help us to see where and how God is a part of it all. Collectively, then, these five core models cover many of the necessary bases that our design and implementation methodologies will need in order to discern which interventions are likely to be most transformative.

Also, with spiritual discernment being the core of our craft, we should be open to exploring and analyzing these five areas in any number of different ways. However, my experiences have generally led me to engaging these in a certain order, which you may find helpful. Typically, I have found it most helpful to begin with the anthropologies, cosmologies, and theories of change—in that order. Essentially, these reflections

---

29. Hull, *Complete Book of Discipleship*, 30; McCallum and Lowery, *Organic Disciplemaking*, 57–58, 269.

help me to gain a solid grounding in the dynamics of my local context. I then use these foundations to help guide my theological explorations. Specifically, as we shall see why in greater detail below, I seek to discern theological models that can provide me with insights into where and how the Spirit may be active in these more foundational dynamics.

Finally, I turn my attention to the ideals that my program or set of interventions has. By looking back over the anthropologies, theories of change, cosmologies, and theologies, I am usually then in a better position to explore the horizons toward which I discern God inviting us toward. This, however, is merely one suggestion for the order in which to engage in these reflections. You should, as always, discerningly seek to find the order that works for you both generally as well as for each specific application.

Resourcing: Where to Turn to for These Deep Insights

These five areas of exploration therefore comprise the bulk of the in-depth understandings of our local situations that we are seeking to formatively interact with. However, we can now ask how to actually go about gathering this information. It is one thing to know what we need, but it is quite another to know where to go to find it. For our program development purposes, there are two primary sources that we can turn to for deeper insights into each of the five areas above; sources that we have repeatedly heard about in the two previous chapters.

External Resources

The first obvious place that we can look to for insights is external resources. In fact, we have just done this. By considering what various authors writing about spiritual formation had to say for each of these five different areas, we were turning to outside resources. Similarly, anytime we turn to the sacred texts or to the hierarchies of our religious traditions for guidance in what to do or how to be, we are turning to models and theories that come from sources other than within our local context. Such resources can come in the form of books, movies, other communities, spiritual mentors who are not a part of our community, et cetera. Any resource that can help us to more deeply understand any of these five areas is a potential candidate.

These external resources can inform and guide how we view and approach spiritual formation in extensive ways. For example, authors, such as psychiatrist and spiritual formation consultant Gerald May, turn to contemporary psychological understandings of human nature to inform their formative endeavors. May differentiates between mind and consciousness, attention and awareness, and discusses three different personality styles in accordance with his psychiatry background.[30] He also discusses some of the deep psychological longings and needs of humans such as the need for something deeper,[31] for acceptance,[32] love,[33] and to just be.[34] However, also drawing from contemplative traditions, May asserts that the ultimate human longing is to forget ourselves and to surrender to something greater.[35] Fulfilling these needs, May claims, is not easy because of the many and various repression mechanisms that contemporary psychology has reported to uncover, as well as our fears of self-sacrifice.[36] May asserts, however, that it is love that overcomes these fears and repression mechanisms as we work with our emotions through the various stages that he defines.[37] May's approaches to spiritual formation are therefore informed by these contemporary psychological resources and historical contemplative traditions. We can therefore see how such external resources can be a central part of our craft.

But how do we know where to look for such resources? How do we know which external resources will best help us to gain deeper insights into our local dynamics and all that God is working to do there? How can we choose resources that will truly deepen our understandings of each of the five areas above for our local context? In essence, they should help us to gain a better understanding of the actual dynamics of our situation.

For instance, dramatic differences in models of moral development came about because of the differences in the kinds of people that Harvard's ethical researchers Carol Gilligan and Lawrence Kohlberg were studying: Gilligan working primarily with women, and Kohlberg primarily with men.[38] For Kohlberg, the resulting emphasis was on an ethic of justice and rightness, while Gilligan found that the women she studied

---

30. May, *Will and Spirit*, 39, 46, 75.
31. Ibid., 70.
32. Ibid., 73, 83–85.
33. Ibid., 85.
34. Ibid., 87.
35. Ibid., 1, 89.
36. Ibid., 93, 103, 107, 112, 114, 164.
37. May, 130, 135, 179, 201, 225, 233.
38. Gilligan, "Different Voice in Moral Decisions," 175.

placed a greater emphasis on an ethic of care and relationships. If we were seeking to intentional work for the moral formation of a group of youth, for instance, we would therefore need to consider which of these moral emphases seems to have a greater importance for our adolescents. Do they seemed to be more concerned about being right, or are they more interested in maintaining relational harmony? Knowing this about them would help us to better determine which of these external resources—Gilligan's or Kohlberg's model of moral development—to turn to. Or, if we were intentionally seeking to foster both kinds of ethical development, then we could use both models. As we continue through these discussions, the selection of external resources will become clearer, and when we proceed to the actual steps of these methodologies we will spell it out with greater detail.

Overall, however, we can already see that the primary goals in our selection are for us to choose external resources that give us insights into: (1) the actual dynamics and influences of our local contexts; and (2) how the Spirit is active within and to them. These resources can be drawn from our own theological traditions, or they may be drawn from secular sources or other religious traditions. However, as we shall now see, it is the second primary source—our local context—that gives rise to and guides the selection and use of this first one.

Contextual Sources

While external resources can be very helpful, some would caution us against using such outside models without any consideration of our local contexts. There has been the tendency at times in the West for external models to be accepted as being "universally true."[39] The basic assertion in doing this is the belief that the dynamics the external resource proclaims to capture is valid everywhere regardless of the particularities of any local context or community.[40] For instance, Kohlberg's original model of moral development was considered by many to be universally true for all people—men and women—until Gilligan found otherwise through her research.[41] The act of divorcing a model from the contexts in which it was

---

39. Britt, *Conceptual Introduction to Modeling*, 76–77; Pears, *Doing Contextual Theology*, 8.

40. Britt, *Conceptual Introduction to Modeling*, 112.

41. Gilligan, "Different Voice," 175.

originally constructed and then using it in other contexts has therefore been challenged.[42]

In addition to using these external resources, therefore, we must also turn more directly to our local contexts in order to seek some of the necessary insights that our programs will need in order to be discerningly developed. In essence, we need to create models for each of the five areas discussed above based directly on our local experiences and contextual observations.

Modeling with the context in mind essentially means "creating more detailed, factually accurate descriptions of the dynamics of situations."[43] It entails a trust that our experiences and those of our communities can and should be a part of the grounding for the insights that we are developing.[44] Doing so will help us to guard against some of the abuses that have resulted from the use of "universally true" models, to avoid oversimplifications, and to gain a richer and much more detailed understanding of our local community.[45]

As we shall see in our practical steps below, there are two places we should turn to in developing such contextually immersed understandings: our own observations and reflections, and those of the people we are working with. So, for instance, in developing his contemplative spiritual formation program, Tom should not only draw from authors such as Gerald May. He also needs to spend some time observing and talking to the people with whom he will be journeying in his program. It will also be very helpful for him to write out his own reflections in relation to each of the five areas above. These local observations and experiences should be just as central to his deep exploration and analysis as are his considerations of external resources. In fact, as we just heard, it is these local insights that will help to guide his choices of which outside sources to turn to.

We should therefore not rely only on the models that others beyond our local contexts have generated, whether they are asserted to be "universal true" or not.[46] We must additionally turn to the ever unfolding and actual dynamics of our local ministerial contexts in developing the insights and theories that will inform our practice.[47] These two sets of sources—ex-

42. Pears, *Doing Contextual Theology*, 17, 21.

43. Britt, *Conceptual Introduction to Modeling*, 77.

44. Elaine Graham, *Transforming Practice*, 161; Pears, *Doing Contextual Theology*, 14.

45. Britt, *Conceptual Introduction to Modeling*, 114, 121–22.

46. Duncan-Andrade and Morrell, *Art of Critical Pedagogy*, 105.

47. Pears, *Doing Contextual Theology*, 44.

ternal resources and local observations and experiences—therefore comprise the primary sources that we can turn to help us to deeply explore the five central areas above that we will be using to inform and guide our program design and implementation in the next chapter.

Synthesizing These Sources

With these two sets of sources informing our explorations and analysis, we might have questions about how to integrate it all. If we have, for instance, our own personal reflections, the input of our communities, and three external resources on human nature for our program, what do we do with all of it? How can we bring it all together into a more coherent and unified anthropological model that we will then use for our design and implementation efforts? In order to answer questions such as these, we will need to explore some of the basics of what "synthesizing" is and how it can be accomplished. It is therefore in this section that we will be addressing these considerations.

Synthesizing Defined

When we talk about "synthesizing" in this book, we are primarily talking about a process of drawing together and integrating two or more models or sets of data. In their book, *Handbook for Synthesizing Qualitative Research*, healthcare researchers Margarete Sandelowski and Julie Barroso assert that such processes are "aimed at systematically reviewing and formally integrating the findings in reports of completed qualitative studies."[48] Synthesizing processes are depicted as being creative and interpretive as their final goals are not intended to create something that is merely "the sum of the parts" of the models and data being synthesized.[49] It is also therefore contrasted with what are called "metasummaries," wherein one merely seeks to summarize the themes of the models and theories that are being considered.[50] Instead, synthesis integratively strives to generate a new model that more accurately represents the area we are interested in

---

48. Sandelowski and Barroso, *Handbook for Synthesizing Qualitative Research*, 17.
49. Ibid., 18
50. Ibid., 151.

based upon the contributing external resources and contextual observations that we have made.[51]

For example, if we were trying to formulate a set of ideals for our community, our chosen synthesizing task might be to look to a range of relevant external resources and then bring them together with our contextual observations in a way that more accurately depicts the horizons toward which we believe God is inviting us. We might take the developmental trends that Kohlberg and Gilligan outline along with the contemplative ideals that May details, for instance. However, rather than merely choosing these three sets of ideals and then uncritically sticking them together in a piecemeal fashion, performing a synthesis would entail the process of more deeply sitting with and listening to each of these models and striving for a more integrated and coherently harmonized unity. Synthesis is therefore a necessary process that we need to engage in if we are to develop the kinds of deep explorations and analysis that are needed for spiritual formation program development.

Three Elements to Synthesize

Given that synthesis requires a detailed analysis of both the outside models we are drawing from and our local contexts, we can ask the question of what we should be considering for such processes. In appendix B, an introduction to the essentials of model construction is provided. This appendix outlines the basics elements of a model, how they are constructed, and what some of their inherent limitations are. When synthesizing, there are three basic elements of any model (shown below in figure 6) that need to be considered in order for synthesis to be carried out.

---

51. Ibid., 18, 199.

Going Deep

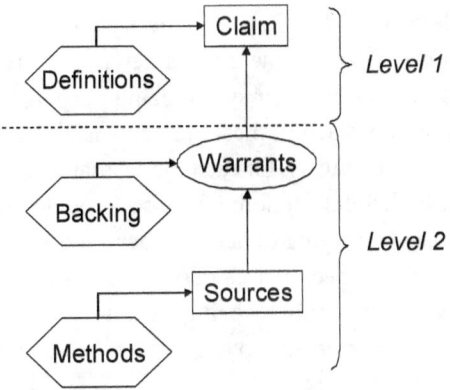

Figure 6. Three Elements of a Model to Consider When Synthesizing

Specifically, when synthesizing our chosen external resources along with our contextual observations, we need to be more intentionally cognizant of their claims and definitions, the sources and methods they are based upon, and the warrants and worldviews that inform them. By exploring each of these in turn, we will be in a better position to understand how a full synthesis can take place in the practical steps of the next section of this chapter.

CLAIMS AND DEFINITIONS

Let's say that we wanted to synthesize a view of spirituality. There are many different ways of defining and understanding that term. In order to synthesize some of these various views about the nature of what spirituality is, we would first need to track what each of these authors/communities mean by this term. In other words, we would need to be very clear in our understandings of how they each define "spirituality" and how they are using it because their definitions might be very different from those of others. Additionally, we also need to clarify what we and our local communities mean by this term, because it may differ significantly from the definitions provided by any of these authors.

A primary consideration when synthesizing, then, are the claims that are being made by a model—be it our own or another's—and the definitions that accompany those claims. These claims can be related to the specific elements of a model or their interrelationships. For instance, if

93

we were exploring various external models of human nature, we would need to be very clear as to what they mean by each term—such as "mind," "body," "spirit," et cetera—and how these different aspects of human nature are related to one another. For synthesizing purposes, then, we need to better understand how each of these elements is understood and what the nature of their relationships is for each model that we are considering.[52]

It would not be helpful for someone else to be describing an apple while we were focused on trying to better understand an orange. We may also come to find that someone else's descriptions and claims challenge our own, or vice versa. It is only by being clear as to what we are talking about that we will be in a position to begin the process of synthesizing in light of our local context.

Sources and Methods

We cannot be content with considering only the claims of a model that we are considering; be it a locally generated one or one from an external resource. We must also give some attention to the level 2 considerations shown in the figure above. These two sets of considerations—the sources/methods and warrants/worldviews—are often overlooked. Nevertheless, both of these are just as important, if not more important, for our synthesizing efforts.

The first of these are the sources upon which the models we are using are based upon and the methods that were used to access them.[53] For instance, as we heard, dramatic differences in claims about moral development came about because of the differences in sources that Gilligan and Kohlberg were working with: Gilligan with women and Kohlberg with men. Not only do we therefore need to track the definitions of the model's components, and their various relationships, but we also need to be cognizant of the data from which these claims are drawn.[54]

Why are such considerations important for our synthesizing purposes? Physicist-turned-theologian Ian Barbour notes, for example, the differences between religion and science in relation to the kinds of data that they access.[55] For some groups, such as scientific materialists, the primary source of data for their assertions comes from the observations of

---

52. Britt, *Conceptual Introduction to Modeling*, ch. 3.
53. Ibid., 29.
54. Ibid., 159.
55. Barbour, *Religion and Science*, 95.

physics and chemistry (i.e., material reality).[56] Biblical literalists, on the other hand, turn primarily to the Bible, which is taken to be inerrant.[57] If we look at their views of creation and evolution, we find two conflicting models of how creation came to be and how it continues to unfold.[58] Some scientific materialists assert that evolution, which has been happening for millions of years, has no purpose or direction to it, while some biblical literalists have claimed that the world was created only "within the last few thousand years" by God.[59] A foundational part of such conflicts are the differences not just in the claims that these two communities are making but also in the sources that they are turning to as the basis for these claims.

When synthesizing, then, some consideration must be given to the sources that are being drawn from, as well as to the methods that are used to access them.[60] We can and should note not only the sources and methods of the outside resources we are drawing from, but also the preferred ones of our local community. What kinds of sources might we turn to in order to give us a better understanding of what it is we are trying to create a model for? Do we favor more secular-science sources or biblically literal ones? What kinds of sources and methods does my local community turn to for insights most often? How do these compare with those of the external resources that I am using? Questions such as these can help us to shed light on some of the similarities and differences between the observations we make locally and the claims of the external models we are turning to for additional help. They can therefore help us in discerning which outside models to turn to as we shall see in the practical steps outlined below.

Warrants and Worldviews

Warrants, the stated reasons that link the sources to the claims,[61] are a final consideration for these synthesizing methodologies as are the worldviews that inform them. Such warrants can be inductive or deductive in formulation. We can either generalize from a smaller set of information (inductive

---

56. Ibid., 78; Barbour, *When Science Meets Religion*, 11.
57. Barbour, *Religion and Science*, 83; Barbour, *When Science Meets Religion*, 15.
58. Barbour, *Religion and Science*, 78–84; Barbour, *When Science Meets Religion*, 11–17.
59. Barbour, *Religion and Science*, 80, 83.
60. Britt, *Conceptual Introduction to Modeling*, 142.
61. Booth et al., *Craft of Research*, 114, 152; Murphy, *Reasoning and Rhetoric in Religion*, 14.

reasoning), or we can apply an already accepted broader generalization to a specific instance of it (the deductive movement).[62] For instance, we can assert the general deductive principle, "where there's smoke, there's fire,"[63] and then make the more specific claim that there must be a fire somewhere in our house because we see smoke coming from it. In this case, our claim is that our house is on fire, the source is the smoke that we see coming from it, and the warrant is the general deductive principle just mentioned. When considering multiple external models or observations of some part of reality side by side, then, we need to be cognizant of the particular kinds of warrants that are being utilized.

For example, in asserting his own views in relation to those of scientific materialists, Barbour challenges their inductively formulated claims. "In their metaphysics," he writes, "these authors have extended scientific concepts beyond their scientific use to support comprehensive materialistic philosophies."[64] His contention with such claims, we can see, are primarily with the warrants that these scientific materialists are using. These authors, he asserts, are inductively drawing upon scientific sources in order to formulate their theories about the more fundamental and metaphysical nature of reality, which is inherently beyond both the scope and study of physical science. Barbour challenges these linkages, and therefore their resulting claims, and goes on to articulate his own cosmological theory based upon the very same sources as these scientific materialists but using different kinds of warrants.

Finally, as this example begins to illustrate, we must also consider how the worldviews of those creating the models influences the theories that they construct. Barbour's exploration of the theories constructed by scientific materialists and biblical literalists is an example of this. Scientific materialists have one set of worldviews, biblical literalists have another, and the models that both communities have constructed are very different partly as a result of this.

Models are therefore, it is asserted, to be "paradigm-dependent."[65] This means that they are laden with the worldviews and assumptions that have been an inherent part of our thinking as we construct and formulate the models that we use.[66] Not only do such models therefore have the

---

62. Britt, *Conceptual Introduction to Modeling*, 38.
63. Ibid., 155.
64. Barbour, *Religion and Science*, 82.
65. Ibid., 125–29.
66. Ibid., 93–94; Britt, *Conceptual Introduction to Modeling*, 29, 158.

interpretations of those who originally constructed them, but they will also embody the worldviews and cultures of those who use and further synthesize them.[67] In our synthesizing approaches, then, we must therefore give ample consideration to the worldviews and underlying assumptions, as well as to the warrants, that have gone into the construction and modification of the models we are drawing from.

Three Synthesizing Possibilities

With these three elements of a model to consider, whether the models are externally and locally constructed, we are now in a position to see that there are essentially three possibilities for synthesizing a set of two or more models. Each of these essentially represents the kinds of influences that models can have on one another as we perform a synthesis. These three possibilities for synthesis will become the basis for one of our practical steps below. It therefore will be helpful to briefly explore each of them in turn.

Stepping back for a KISS moment, we must remember what the core focus of our efforts here are. Overall, we are striving in these exploration and analysis methodologies to generate enough of a deep understanding of our local contexts so that we can design and implement a formative program or set of interventions that partners with the Spirit's formative work in our midst. Our five core models, we have asserted, are intended to provide us with such deep insights. The primary purpose of these synthesizing efforts, with as complicated and detailed as they are, is to enable us to bring together all that we have gathered—contextually and externally—into a more unified picture of our community. These three possibilities are therefore intended to help us toward these KISS ends.

Linking Puzzle Pieces: Complimentarity

One possible way that two or more models/theories can be related to one another is complementarily. Such a relationship is one in which the models and data being considered do not overlap in any significant ways so that no synthesizing integration or modifications are necessary between them. The models are simply linked together like a jigsaw puzzle.

---

67. Pears, *Doing Contextual Theology*, 18; Sandelowski and Barroso, *Handbook for Synthesizing Qualitative Research*, xvi.

PART TWO: Methodological Movements

For example, dualistic views of the nature of the relationship between the body and the soul were present in early Christianity and were later more fully developed by philosophers such as Rene Descartes.[68] Similar dualistic views of the mind and the brain have also been contemporarily proposed.[69] At its heart, dualism holds that there is no overlap between these two different parts of reality. In this view, the body is considered to be completely separate from the soul, and the mind has no relation to the brain. Such worldviews therefore allow the models of these various parts to be held completely independent from one another. If we were to adopt such a perspective as our own, we could therefore take our models of the body and join them piecemeal wise to the models of mind that we wanted to use.

These two sets of models could, in other words, remain fully intact and be joined together like puzzle pieces with no modification to either of them. Their relationship is therefore described here as *complimentary*, meaning that these models compliment one another with no integrative changes being needed at all.[70] Such complimentarity might be asserted based upon the claims themselves or upon the sources that are being used.[71] In our synthesizing methods, then, we need to have some way of determining whether two or more models can simply be joined together as they currently are, with no changes being needed, or whether they need further modification.

Minor Modifications

In the event that the external models and contextual experiences we are drawing from are not completely independent from one another, and therefore complimentary, some integrative changes may need to be made to them. However, such changes may only be minor ones.[72] Bringing models together into a dialogical relationship with each other may result in one or both of the models being slightly expanded upon only in certain and limited areas. Rather than uprooting and structurally reshaping either

---

68. Barbour, *When Science Meets Religion*, 130–31.

69. Ibid., 131–32.

70. Barbour describes such relationships as Independent because the models are viewed as being independent of one another. See Barbour, *Religion and Science*, 84.

71. Barbour, *Religion and Science*, 85–86, 88.

72. Britt, *Conceptual Introduction to Modeling*, 78, 80.

Going Deep

of the models in significant ways, which will be discussed next, here the synthesizing changes are quite narrow.

An example of this may be found in the theology of Roman Catholic Karl Rahner.[73] Rahner, Barbour asserts, upholds the "classical doctrines of human nature and of Christology" but turns to the sciences and its evolutionary assertions only for greater elaboration.[74] For Rahner, science cannot provide the whole picture of reality because it is primarily oriented toward matter and not spirit. As a result, Rahner turns to "Scripture and tradition" as the primary sources for knowing about God,[75] while the sciences are viewed by him as merely expanding on these sources.

Such is an example of how one model, in this case Rahner's doctrinally based theology, is informed and modified by another, that of evolutionary theory, in only minor ways. These modifications are not major because Rahner asserts the Bible and the Christian tradition as being the more significant sources for his theological formulations. This is an example of how one set of models influences another, but in only minor ways.

Major Overhaul: Full Integration

Finally, the last kind of relationship that two or more models can have is when they fundamentally transform one another in major ways.[76] This kind of synthesis occurs when structural changes are made that significantly affect the models involved. Referred to by Barbour and by Sandelowski and Barroso as "integration," such changes are more considerable than complimentary or minor ones; they are more than a mere "sum of the parts" or only limited elaborations.[77]

An example of such a full integration may be found in chapter 2 of Bill Hull's book, *The Complete Book of Discipleship*. In this chapter, Hull reviews the origins of discipleship in the early Christian tradition beginning with Greco-Roman and Jewish views of discipleship. In a Greco-Roman context, being a disciple essentially meant being a follower and learner of a great master.[78] Similarly, for Jewish rabbinic traditions, a disciple

---

73. Barbour, *Religion and Science*, 92.
74. Ibid.
75. Ibid.
76. Britt, *Conceptual Introduction to Modeling*, 81, 85, 170, 181.
77. Barbour, *Religion and Science*, 98; Barbour, *When Science Meets Religion*, 27; Sandelowski and Barroso, *Handbook for Synthesizing Qualitative Research*, 18.
78. Hull, *Complete Book of Discipleship*, 54.

was one who learned from and sought to imitate their "teacher's life and character."[79] For Hull, these models become the basis for his understandings of the approaches to discipleship that Jesus took.

However, he also notes that the primary purpose of Christian discipleship is to become a follower of Jesus and not another human being.[80] These Greco-Roman, Jewish, and Christian models of discipleship are then synthesized by Hull when he goes on to assert that "a disciple is someone who submits to at least one other person in a healthy and appropriate way as a means of support and accountability to develop fully as a follower of Jesus."[81] Rather than the Christian disciple seeking to learn the teachings and ways of life of their mentoring teacher, they are instead to be learning about the teachings and ways of Jesus.[82] However, such disciples are not to "fly solo," but rather are they to be involved in mentoring relationships with communities who can help to disciple them along their path toward Jesus.[83]

This is an example of a fuller synthesis because Hull has taken the Greco-Roman and Jewish models of discipleship and changed them in significant ways by bringing them into dialogue with his own model of Christian discipleship. Being a Christian disciple means to follow the ways and teachings of Jesus, not another human. This model of Christian discipleship (i.e., being a follower of Jesus) was likewise significantly altered by considering the Greco-Roman and Jewish models, which placed a heavy emphasis on the role of a mentoring teacher. Hull's resulting model of Christian discipleship therefore emphasizes the need for mentors as well as for remaining focused on Jesus. We can therefore see how models, when brought into dialogue with one another, can significantly influence one another resulting in new and more fully integrated theories.

Theologically Reflecting on Our Context

Once we have synthesized a set of five core models (ideals, anthropologies, etc.), we are not quite finished with our deep explorations and analysis. As we repeatedly recall throughout this chapter, our two primary KISS goals are to: (1) better understand the dynamics of our local context, and (2)

79. Ibid., 62–64.
80. Ibid., 28, 67.
81. Ibid., 67.
82. Ibid., 68.
83. Ibid., 67.

discern where it is that God is, to more and lesser extents, a part of them. Three of our five areas that we will be synthesizing models for are directly intended to accomplish the first goal: anthropologies, cosmologies, and theories of change. Collectively, these are intended to give us greater insights into the inner dynamics, surrounding influences, and modes of transformation that are operative in our local context. We therefore need to theologically reflect on each of these, in order to accomplish the second goal.

It may also be that some of the external resources we are drawing from either embody theological perspectives that are not fully in accordance with our own or are from secular sources, such as Kohlberg's and Gilligan's models. As a result, our synthesis may yield anthropological, cosmological, and transformation models for which it might not be clear to us where and how God is embodied in them (or not) according to our own traditions. In other words, how might we know where and how God is moving in our situation based on these synthesized models? This is where the theological models that we have synthesized come into play.

In order to help us to understand how such theological reflection processes can occur, we might turn to resources that can help us to do this. Practical theologians Elaine Graham, Heather Walton, and Frances Ward and their book, *Theological Reflection*, is one example of such a resource. Here, they seek to explore and elaborate on a set of various methods for engaging in theological reflection based upon the Christian tradition. For them, "theological reflection is an activity that enables people of faith to give an account of the values and traditions that underpin their choices and convictions and deepens their understanding."[84] In essence, they are interested in uncovering some of the different ways that various communities have sought "to connect theological discourse about the nature of God to the exercise of faith" in their local contexts.[85] Their explorations are therefore relevant for our purposes because they are interested in some of the concrete methods by which we can construct and utilize the theologies that undergird our lives, communities, and practices in reflecting on the dynamics of our contexts.

As an example of how such reflections occur, in a chapter on conducting research with marginalized people, Swinton and Mowat deeply explore and analyze the lived experiences of persons with learning disabilities.[86]

---

84. Graham et al., *Theological Reflection*, 5–6.
85. Ibid.
86. Swinton and Mowat, *Practical Theology and Qualitative Research*, ch. 8.

Both the external resources they gathered and the interviews they have conducted with these persons revealed that they are often outcast and excluded from their local and larger communities.[87] Stepping back and theologically reflecting on these synthesized results, Swinton and Mowat turn to the resources of their Western Christian tradition. Looking to the Bible as well as to contemporary authors writing about hospitality, they not only conclude that such communal exclusions are not a movement of God but that hospitality and inclusion is actually a "biblical imperative."[88]

This is an example of the kinds of reflections that we can use our synthesized theological models for. As we explore and analyze our own theologies, we therefore need to seek those sources that can aid us in these kinds of reflections for our programs. As we shall see in the next chapter, such reflections will be an essential part of helping us to choose the interventions that we ultimately discern and implement.

However, as a side note, such theological reflections are not meant to only be a one way interaction. The outside and contextually constructed models we have might also challenge or question our own theological models and even those of our larger traditions. Practical theologians encourage these kinds of mutual and two-way interactions. Graham, Walton, and Ward, for instance, find such dialogues to be an intimate part of the history of Christian theological reflection. For instance, they note of third-century theologian, Origin, that he "was not afraid to break new ground, and to enlist Greek philosophy and metaphysics in the service of the further elucidation and development of Christian theology."[89] Nor was Thomas Aquinas afraid to draw upon Aristotelian philosophy to further inform and guide his systematic theology.[90] We also find religious educators, such as Thomas Groome, to encourage the mutual dialogue between the views and experiences of our local communities and the wider traditions of which they are a part.[91] Here, we see the intimacy of a dialectical dance unfold between the various models and sources that we are drawing from and our own religious traditions. Such theological reflections are, therefore, a two-way street with our local contexts having the potential to challenge and transform the theologies that we and our communities adhere to just as much as the latter can influence the former.

---

87. Ibid., 233, 245, 247.
88. Swinton and Mowat, *Practical Theology and Qualitative Research*, 246.
89. Graham et al., *Theological Reflection*, 206.
90. Ibid., 144–45.
91. Groome, *Christian Religious Education*, 122.

However, for our purposes here, we must remember the primary purpose for such all mutual dialogues and theological reflection efforts: they should help us to better understand how God is present within and to our local contexts so that we might partner ever more fully with the Spirit's formative life through our programs and interventions. We therefore need to look to the resources of our own traditions—in ways that authors such as Graham, Walton, and Ward have outlined—in order to better know how such reflections might proceed in concrete ways.

Methodological Movements

From these extensive theoretical foundations, we now have a better understanding of the five core models (ideals, anthropologies, theories of change, cosmologies, and theologies) that we are seeking to synthesize in order to more deeply explore and analyze our local situation. We also now know that we can turn to two primary sources for each of these: external resources and contextual observations/experiences. We have learned, in theory at least, how to synthesize the information from these two sources so that we have a more unified picture according to each of the five core areas. And we have again touched upon how theological reflection and translation can occur, just as we did in our chapter on spiritual discernment. Collectively, then, these provide the necessary foundations that we will need in order to engage in the program design and implementation methodologies of the next chapter.

However, it might still be unclear to us as to what the major movements are that we want to embody if we were to attempt such detailed explorations and analyses ourselves. What are the practical steps for fully embodying this first praxis-oriented set of methodologies? In this second section of the chapter, therefore, we will be doing just this. As we shall presently see, there are six major movements involved in drawing from and synthesizing our two primary sources for each of the five core areas. These six movements are intended to capture the most essential steps needed in exploring and analyzing our local context in preparation for the program design and implementation that will transpire in the next chapter.

It should be noted that these steps can be independently applied to all five core models that we are interested in. In fact, they are also general enough to engage in synthesizing any two or more sets of models that we might be considering. These six movements are being presented in this

PART TWO: Methodological Movements

general way because there may be additional kinds of information that you need to synthesize for your own program development, as it may differ from what is being presented in this book. These six steps should therefore be discerningly tailored to fit the specific needs of your own contexts.

Furthermore, not every program development endeavor will necessarily embody every step to the extent that it is described below. Due to time and resource limitations, we may not conduct them in precisely the same way for every program or set of interventions that we develop. Practitioners are instead encouraged to spiritually discern and modify these movements as they see fit to. These steps, then, are merely intended to draw out and give some kind of order to the major processes that are involved in the deep exploration and analysis of our local contexts.

In addition to outlining these steps, both in this and in the next two chapters, we will also be exploring a detailed case example in order to more concretely see how each of these steps may be embodied. Here, we will be following the efforts of Francis, the senior pastor to whom Martha turned for counsel in her situation. Having intimately known this couple for more than thirty years, Francis agreed to help Martha as much as she could.[92] What follows below are the exploration and analysis movements that Francis engaged in order to help her to more deeply understand the dynamics of Martha's situation with her husband, Charles, and to better counsel her in what might be done in response. For the purposes of brevity, only a portion of the actual exploration and analysis is presented.

Step One: Discern and Clarify Our Foci

Whenever beginning any exploration and analysis endeavor, we must first know what it is that we will be focusing on. There are two kinds of foci to consider here: the program we feel called to develop, and each of the five core areas to explore and analyze (ideal, anthropologies, etc.). This first step therefore entails our choosing and then clarifying each of these foci.

---

92. The reflections contained herein were gathered from the research notes and journal reflections that "Francis" made as she sought to journey with "Martha" and "Charles." Of course, the names and details of this case example have been changed in order to maintain confidentiality.

Discerning a Program to Develop

The first obvious step in working toward developing a program involves identifying the focus of formative endeavors. Are we trying to develop an action research-based youth program that raises the critical and social consciousness of youth as Duncan-Arcade and Morrell have, or are we seeking to better understand and intervene in the lives of those who struggle with depression as Swinton and Mowat did?[93] Are we being invited by the Spirit to develop a moral formation program for our youth group or revitalize a bible study for our seniors?

We saw Montague engage in our five discernment processes to help him to discern what his formative focus might have been. With the decision being ultimately made to close the church and attempt a restart, he essentially discovered what his next move was to be. At this point, Montague's development of this new congregation could have then followed the steps outlined in this book. However, his personal vocational discernment, in the end, led him down a different path. Nevertheless, Montague's case is an example of how the discernment processes can be applied to this step. It is this kind of discerning deliberation that each of the steps presented here and in the next two chapters may be approached with.

In addition, as we've seen, our programs can be oriented toward the levels of individuals, relationships, or communities. They can also focus on specific topics such as scriptural and doctrinal studies as they do in churches. This first part of this step therefore entails our identifying what the central focus of our formation interventions and programs will be. What is it, more precisely, that we are seeking to partner with God to spiritually form?

Identify a Specific Area to Explore and Analyze

Once we have discerned the kind of program to develop, we can then begin the process of more deeply exploring and analyzing each of the five core areas discussed above. Our focus therefore shifts to each one of them in turn. As far as which one(s) to choose, whether we take them one at a time or simultaneously, is open to discernment. For our purposes here, however, it will be assumed that we have chosen only one of these five

---

93. Duncan-Andrade and Morrell, *Art of Critical Pedagogy*, ch. 6; Swinton and Mowat, *Practical Theology and Qualitative Research*, ch. 4.

PART TWO: Methodological Movements

areas to explore and analyze in much greater detail.[94] Once we have chosen a specific area, we may then proceed to the next step.

Francis Clarifies the Issues

Francis's first step entailed sitting down with Martha to clarify what her hopes and dreams as well as her struggles with Charles were. Martha expressed her yearnings for a more talkative and engaging relationship. She talked about her fears that Charlie's status might in the future begin to deteriorate and Martha would be "chained down" in order to care for him. She shared her hopes that their retirement years would be full of vitality and activity through the many trips that she had been planning. Martha also cried over mourning the "loss" of her husband as he had been prior to his heart attack.

From these discussions, and as a result of engaging in her own spiritual discernment processes, Francis decided that she should be trying to discern a set of interventions that might help Martha and Charles to make the best of their relationship as it currently is. Rather than trying to recapture what once was, she felt it might be better for them to be present to what they have now and to proceed from their. Of course, Francis knew, facing the past and the feelings of mourning that Martha was experiencing were going to be a necessary part of these interventions. Nevertheless, Francis still initially felt that the best route was to do what she could to help them to make the best of what they currently have. Toward these ends, and for our purposes here, Francis decided to begin with researching and developing a synthesized anthropological model of Martha and Charles's relationship. It is these explorations and analyses that we will therefore be focusing on for the remainder of these steps.

Step Two: Construct a Contextual Model

Once we have discerned which area to focus on, we are now in a position to begin the process of gathering contextual data. As we look to both action research and practical research literature, there are two primary sets of sources that we should draw upon in building a "bottom-up" understanding of what we are interested in. The first are from our own personal observations and reflections, while the second are based upon the

---

94. Sandelowski and Barroso, *Handbook for Synthesizing Qualitative Research*, 23.

experiences and observations of the communities that we are working with. It is based upon this contextual data that we can then construct our own contextual models for use in the synthesizing processes described below.

What Do We Think We Know and See?

A first approach to gathering data is by our taking the time to clarify, as succinctly as possible, what our own views of the area currently are. As Sandelowski and Barroso write, "you cannot proceed with your search without having a working definition of your topic."[95] If we were seeking to explore and analyze human nature as it relates to our program, for instance, we might begin by sitting down and writing out what we currently think all of the different anthropological parts and relationships are. In the case of a developing a bible study for a group of second generation Asian American youth, for instance, this would mean that we first describe all that we personally know about the lived experiences and inner dynamics of these youth. These initial reflections will not only help us to clarify our own position, but they will also become a part of the contextual template from which to search for and choose the external resources that we will be drawing from.

Such personal reflections, however, are not the only way to gather such data. We can also engage in more formal observations and intentional experiences that give us further insights into what we are seeking a deeper understanding of. There are numerous texts on qualitative and quantitative research methods already available that explore many of these approaches in much greater detail, so I will not seek to repeat them here.[96] However, all of this research, action researcher J. Barton Cunningham writes, "encourages the researcher to experience the problem as it evolves."[97] The more connected and immersed that we are in our local contexts, the more fruitful and helpful will this personal data be for our exploration and analysis efforts.

---

95. Sandelowski and Barroso, *Handbook for Synthesizing Qualitative Research*, 36.

96. See such texts as: Braud and Anderson, *Transpersonal Research Methods for the Social Sciences*; Cohen et al., *Research Methods in Education*; Cunningham, *Action Research and Organizational Development*; Greenwood and Levin, *Introduction to Action Research*; McLeod, *Doing Counseling Research*; Schmuck, *Practical Action Research for Change*; Swinton and Mowat, *Practical Theology and Qualitative Research*; Williams et al., *Research in Social Work*; Yin, *Case Study Research*.

97. Cunningham, *Action Research and Organizational Development*, 5.

PART TWO: Methodological Movements

What Does Our Community Perceive?

As we know, we are not the only ones that have insights into the dynamics of our local contexts. Everyone who is immediately connected to the spiritually formative work of which we are a part can also be a source of contextual insight and understanding. Practical theologians and action researchers, as we heard above, emphasize these potential resources as an intimate and necessary part of their transformative work.[98]

For instance, liberation theologians, such as Gustavo Gutierrez, look to the lived experiences of oppressed people and communities to shape and mold their claims.[99] While Gutierrez also drew heavily on the external resources, such as Marxism and Vatican II,[100] he also held the lived experiences of oppressed persons as a key partner in this dialogue. "Theological reflection," Angie Pears observes of Gutierrez, "relies not only on tradition and revelation but also on experience, on the experiences of people today and in history."[101] In our own attempts to construct the contextual models that will be a part of these methodologies, we too need to give a central place to lived experiences and insights of our local communities.

Such considerations are essential in order to work more productively with our communities. For instance, we might be seeking to construct a cosmological framework within which to work in our ministries. Their input is essential, in this example, because if we are going to base our formative interventions on such worldviews, they will need to agree with such a scheme. For example, let's say that our cosmology includes a place and role for angels and demons, as many Christian worldviews have.[102] If we plan on explicitly engaging with these extra-material beings, then the people we are working with will at least have to believe in them as well before they will allow us to proceed with such interventions—such as prayer and laying on hands.

It therefore behooves us to look to the insights and observations of our communities for at least two reasons. The first is so that our understanding of what we are seeking to explore and analyze is broadened and deepened. And the second is so that the core models that we finally settle

98. Duncan-Andrade and Morrell, *Art of Critical Pedagogy*.

99. Pears, *Doing Contextual Theology*, 64.

100. Ibid., 66–67.

101. Ibid.

102. *John Cassian: The Conferences*, 164, 254, 264, 269, 351; Erasmus, "Handbook of the Militant Christian," 29, 35; Law, "Serious Call to a Devout and Holy Life," 91, 100, 236; McCallum and Lowery, *Organic Disciplemaking*, 136.

upon help us to facilitate our formative interventions in more harmonious ways. In order for our interventions to be more effective, it helps if the people we are working with consent to them. As we found throughout the theoretical foundations section above, such contextual data is one of the two central pillars that undergirds these exploration and analysis methodologies. We must therefore be very intentional in gathering this data. Overall, our spiritual discernment question is: "What is it that God needs us to know about our context in order to proceed with our design and implementation?"

Constructing a Contextual Model

In appendix B, as we've heard, we can learn some of the fundamental basics of what models are and how they are constructed. It is here in this step that we can now put all of this theoretical understanding into concrete practice. The qualitative and quantitative resources that were noted above are good resources to help guide this kind of constructive work. In addition, there are also other resources, such as Britt's *Conceptual Introduction to Modeling* and Jaccard and Jacoby's *Theory Construction and Model-Building Skills*, which can help to further guide these efforts as well.

While we will not be exploring these resources in detail, there are two important points to review from them and the extensive discussions found in appendix B. The first is that our claims should be clearly backed by the sources/methods and warrants/worldviews that undergird them. If we are making the claim that demons and angels play an active part in our world, as an example, upon what are we and our communities basing such claims? Or if we believe that our second-generation Asian American youth group is struggling with the tensions between the current US culture and the culture that their parents are from, how do we know this to be the case? We must therefore have some foundations and some reasons for making the contextual claims that we are.

The second, which is related to the first and draws upon scientific methodology, is that we can also look for patterns in the data that we have collected to support our claims. For instance, are there consistencies between the ideals that we personally think our local community should be striving for and what others in this community think? Do our Asian American youth agree that they are wrestling with bicultural tensions? Such affirmations, known as triangulation in scientific research, can help

PART TWO: Methodological Movements

to further confirm the claims that we are making.[103] Once we have the backings and confirmations of our models, then we are ready to begin looking for external resources.

Francis Develops a Deeper Understanding of the Relationship

True to the movements of this step, Francis spent some time in both reflection on Martha and Charles's relationship as well as in conversation with Martha. Having known this couple for so many years, Francis was able to reflect on the personalities and the dynamics of their relationship. She noted that both Martha and Charlie had very strong tendencies toward independence and individualism. For Martha, Francis also observed how rationalistic she was in her thinking both as a scientific researcher but also in her daily activities. She also noted the perfectionist tendencies that Martha expressed toward herself and others.

For Charles, before his heart attack, Francis reflected on his introverted and more solitary nature. He was not a person who talked very much in conversation with others. However, he used to open up to and share with Martha on a regular basis. Charles could also have an explosive temper at times, though he was not physically violent. After his heart attack and the brain injuries that it may have permanently caused, however, Francis observed that Charlie's tendencies toward quietness became much more pronounced not only toward other people but now also toward Martha. Charles also used to creatively express himself through photography and had his own hobbies, but now he was mostly contented with watching television in the evenings. Overall, Charles appeared to Francis to be much more passive and "simple."

Francis also spent much time talking with Martha as well as with Charles, though to a much lesser extent as he seemed to her to be less willing to discuss such matters. From these conversations, she learned that the doctors were unclear as to the areas of the brain that had been affected by the temporary loss of oxygen or to what extent they might have been impacted. In addition to the information she obtained previously, Martha also talked about their relationship dynamics. Charlie, she related, seemed to not have any strong desires to do anything now on the weekends. Overall, Charles seemed to Martha to be less energetic, opinionated, and

---

103. Cohen et al., *Research Methods in Education in Education*, 37; Neuendorf, *Content Analysis Guidebook*, 15; Swinton and Mowat, *Practical Theology and Qualitative Research*, 50; Yin, *Case Study Research*, 97–99.

proactive. Charles also has a tendency to become more easily frustrated with Martha when things were not going the way he had expected them to. He seems to also become confused more often and more easily, especially when traveling to new places.

From all of these observations, discussions, and reflections, Francis began to formulate her own ideas about the dynamics of their relationship. In other words, for our purposes here, she contextually constructed an anthropological model of their relationship. Francis sees clearly that the heart attack has significantly affected Charles's brain functioning enough to alter his personality, though not in major ways. She wonders, because of their more individualistic and independent personalities, whether Charles and Francis struggle with self-differentiation and emotional development issues; something that she believes is important for couples to have based on her own experiences in marriage as well as with other couples. It is clear, however, that their communication dynamics are not what they once used to be, and Martha is now struggling to adapt to these changes. While not comprehensive, such reflections do enable Francis to begin to gain deeper insights into some of the salient dynamics of their relationship. These beginning insights then further help her to search for and select the external resources that will provide her with even greater insights.

Step Three: Search, Select, and Detail External Resources

Once we have moved to a place where we have a contextually constructed model for the core area that we are focusing on (theories of change, theologies, etc.), we can then proceed to the process of seeking outside models that help us to gain further understanding. Now, at this point, we might be tempted to simply jump onto the internet and start searching for such resources. For instance, if we were interested in developing a group discernment process for our local church's administrative bodies, we might begin looking for resources that talk about group discernment. However, there are actually two sets of considerations to make before beginning: search parameters and evaluative criteria. Only then can we begin to gather and detail the kinds of external resources that will be most helpful.

PART TWO: Methodological Movements

Establishing Search Parameters

The first is for us to establish some set of parameters by which to conduct our search.[104] For instance, how many models do we hope to find and work with? With one source being the obvious minimum, following the general research guideline known as triangulation, discussed above, using three models is also a good starting place because it can allow us to see more commonalities and differences between these resources while also not becoming too overwhelming for us to handle in the midst of our busy ministries.

We can also determine the amount of time that we want to spend looking for models and where we will focus our search.[105] In the context of an active ministry, this is an essential element to consider and it may be helpful to carve out some intentional blocks of time to spend in searching for external resources. We also need to think about where we will conduct our searches. In addition to the numerous resources and search engines on the internet and at one's local library, we can also look to the bibliographies of promising resources we have already come across,[106] or we can begin to ask others for which ones to consider. The goal here is to strike a balance between considering enough resources so that we have a general sense of what is available to us while not allowing the search to become overwhelming.[107]

Set Evaluative Criteria and Conduct the Search

A second helpful consideration is for us to establish a set of criteria for how we will select which external resources to explore in more detail from among the many more that we might come across in our extensive searches.[108] In effect, we are trying to decide which of these resources to keep and which to pass up.[109] Such criteria can address such factors as the definitions that the resources are using in relation to our own contextual

---

104. Sandelowski and Barroso, *Handbook for Synthesizing Qualitative Research*, 23, 35.
105. Ibid., 17.
106. Ibid., 41–42.
107. Ibid., 35.
108. Ibid., xv, 82.
109. Ibid., 50.

models, the sources they draw from, the worldviews and kinds of warrants they use to justify their claims, et cetera.[110]

For instance, a biblical literalist will probably not be as drawn to the models about evolution that have been formulated by scientific materialists. As we heard above from Barbour, the sources and worldviews that these two communities draw from are very different. However, if one had the stated purpose of attempting to synthesize both of these seemingly divergent sets of theories, as Barbour attempts to, they might then intentionally search for both of these kinds of external resources.[111]

It is here that the clarification processes of the first two steps become helpful to our knowing what kinds of resources to draw from. However, we must also remember that our evaluative criteria are not set in stone. In other words, we can and should modify them as we move through our search thereby seeking to further clarify what it is we are looking for and why.[112] Ultimately, we are seeking to spiritually discern those external resources that will most help us to further clarify what we and our communities think we are seeing and experiencing in our local context.

For instance, does the external resource seem to further validate or challenge the contextual models that we have already constructed? If it validates them, then it might be a good candidate to consider. If it challenges it, however, it might still be a good one to use because such challenges can help us to see dynamics that we had not considered before. For example, if the youth minister of the Asian American youth group was Caucasian, she or he might not have originally been aware of the bicultural struggles of the group's members. Finding an external resource that teaches her or him about these dynamics might therefore initially be challenging, but ultimately helpful for program development. It is therefore with much care and spiritual discernment that we must engage this valuable step.

Detail the External Models

Once we have chosen our external resources, we can then engage them. Doing this entails noting the three elements of a model that we can: claims/definitions, sources/methods, warrants/worldviews. Basically, we are now interested in what it is that these resources have to say about each of the five core areas (anthropologies, theologies, etc.) that we are interested in. It

110. Ibid., 202.
111. Barbour, *Religion and Science*, 105.
112. Ibid., 75, 77–79.

is here that the parameters we set above, particularly in terms of time limits, becomes important. Our research here needs to be thorough enough to gather the insights and information that will be helpful for our program development, but not so much so that it becomes too burdensome on us. Again, spiritual discernment is an essential part of this and each of these steps.

Returning again to the primary KISS goals of these exploration and analysis methodologies, these external models should help us to: (1) gain a much more detailed and accurate understanding of the actual dynamics of our local communities in relation to the program we will be developing, and (2) develop a clearer vision of how the Spirit is at work within and to them. This third step therefore has to do with our efforts to more systematically and discerningly conduct our search for relevant external resources and engage them in illuminating ways.

Francis's Brain and Relationship Resources

Being in full-time ministry with all of its busy administrative, counseling, and pastoral duties, Francis realized that she did not have very much time to spend on researching outside resources that could help her to gain insights into Martha and Charles's situation. Having a doctorate of ministry (DMin) degree in religious education, however, she was already familiar with many resources that might be relevant. Given her background and her time constraints, Francis made the decision to begin her search with these sources. She realized, in doing this however, that she might be missing some additional and valuable insights that other sources might offer her. Nevertheless, she began her search here allowing herself no more than a few hours to look through them.

As evaluative criteria, Francis knew that she was primarily interested in at least two kinds of resources: those that might give her a further understanding of the general workings of the brain and therefore Charles's condition, and those that would help her to better understand the nature and dynamics of relationships. Since Charles did not have a stroke that affected a specific area of his brain, Francis could not turn to research or literature on stroke therapy. As a result, she decided that a general resource on brain physiology and its relationship to behavior and personality might be sufficient.

Also, Martha and Charles's relationship did not seem to have any unusual characteristics, other than Charles's heart attack, so she decided to look to a general text on relationship health and development. Being in ministry, Francis also hoped to find books that addressed these issues from a theistic perspective. With these criteria in mind, she began to look through the resources that she was already familiar with.

For the neuroscience resource, Francis was unable to find a text that addressed general brain-behavior dynamics from a theistic perspective. There were, however, numerous resources available that did so from a secular-scientific worldview. From the resources that she was familiar with, she chose a book entitled, *Evolve Your Brain*, written by chiropractor and neuroscience researcher Joe Dispenza.[113] From this text, Francis learned of the three basic parts of the brain—the cerebellum and brainstem, the midbrain, and the neocortex—and their basic functions.[114] From these, she particularly learned of the frontal lobe and its relationship to willful, purposeful action and planning as well as its relationship to personality and identity.[115] Reading this, Francis began to wonder whether Charles had experienced a decrease in functioning for some of these frontal parts of his brain. Finally, she learned that with sustained effort through different approaches, particularly in relation to the frontal lobe, we have the ability to develop the various parts of our brain. Francis also noted that Dispenza, appearing to operate from a secular-scientific worldview, turned again and again to neuroscience research, as well as to his personal and work experiences, in order to support the claims that he was making.

Turning next to relationship resources, Francis was able to find a source that discussed relationship dynamics from a theological perspective: *Sacred Psychology of Love* by longtime relationship therapist and former professor of psychology Marilyn Barrick.[116] From Barrick, she learned that working with relationships involves working with the "three parties to a marriage: husband, wife, and the marriage relationship itself."[117] Each person must therefore work for their own self-realization and differentiation from the other as well as for the good of the relationship as a whole in order for it to thrive.[118] She read that men and women often approach relationships in different ways.[119] For both, however, relational develop-

---

113. Dispenza, *Evolve Your Brain*.
114. Ibid., ch. 4.
115. Ibid., 139–41, ch. 10.
116. Barrick, *Sacred Psychology of Love*.
117. Ibid., 204.
118. Ibid., 26, 35, 188, 196, 206–7.
119. Ibid., ch. 14.

PART TWO: Methodological Movements

ment is asserted to be a process of "integrating one's other half," one's feminine or masculine sides.[120] Francis considered Barrick's claims that it is through relationships that couples seek to fulfill their yearnings for union with the Divine.[121] And she pondered Barrick's claims that we must pray to be more open to God's selfless love to be in us as we work on our intimacy with one another.[122] God is not only the source of such relational love, according to Barrick, but also of the journey of individuation that each partner is on themselves.[123] Finally, Francis noted Barrick's reliance on her extensive personal work with couples, psychodynamic literature and sources, and mix of Christian and New Age worldviews. Taken with Dispenza's text above, these two external resources provided Francis with additional insights that not only confirmed some of the contextual data she had gathered, but also further enlightened them.

Step Four: Perform a Detailed Analysis and Synthesis

Once we have settled on a smaller set of external resources to explore in more detail, we are now in a position to engage in the fourth step of our exploration and analysis efforts. This step first entails conducting a detailed analysis of each of these external models in relation to our own contextually constructed one, specifically noting the similarities and differences among them,[124] and then performing a synthesis. Our goal here is to draw together all of the insights and information that we have so far and begin the processes of synthesizing them into a more integrated and unified picture of our local community. As Sandelowski and Barroso write, "Once findings have been grouped, you will then be able to determine whether they confirm, extend, refute, or complement each other."[125]

To do so, following in accordance with the KISS principle, we must remember that the primary purpose for all of these sometimes intensive methodologies: to synthesize a set of core models that better enables us to partner with God's spiritually formative movements in our local context. This entails more accurately representing the dynamics of our local

120. Ibid., 117, 123–25.
121. Ibid., xvii.
122. Ibid., 8, 68.
123. Ibid., 10, 56.
124. Britt, *Conceptual Introduction to Modeling*, 22, 25; Sandelowski and Barroso, *Handbook for Synthesizing Qualitative Research*, 201.
125. Sandelowski and Barroso, *Handbook for Synthesizing Qualitative Research*, 82.

context, and God's relationship to them, so that we might better understand and work with it all. This step therefore has the intention of drawing on the work of each of the previous steps in order to provide us with the kinds of insights that can further empower and guide our craft. In order to help us to do this, we can note that there are three distinct movements to this step.

Model Mappings

The first is for us to create a mapping for each of our models.[126] We have already seen an example of a similar kind of mapping above in the previous chapter where we compared the different sets of steps of action research and practical theology. However, for our purposes here, we need an even more detailed mapping. An example of a detailed mapping may be seen below in table 3 where Groome seeks to synthesize biblical ways of knowing in his book, *Shared Christian Praxis*. I have created this mapping from his text where he is comparing the models that he has found in the Hebrew Scriptures (i.e., the Old Testament), the Synoptic Gospels (Matthew, Mark, and Luke), Paul's letters in the New Testament, and the writings of the Apostle John in order to illustrate what such a detailed model map can look like.[127]

---

126. Ibid., 79.
127. Groome, *Christian Religious Education*, 141–45.

PART TWO: Methodological Movements

Table 3. A Model Mapping of Groome's Biblical Ways of Knowing

	Hebrew Scriptures	Synoptics	Paul	John
Claims & Definitions	- Hebrew "yada" = knowing by the heart rather than by the mind; knowing by active and intentional engagement in lived experiences; - It is also used to describe lovemaking or a good friend or confidant - "Knowing the Lord" is an activity in which God takes the initiative, which demands acknowledgement of the Lord and obedience to God - It is an experience and response that God is truly known	-"knowing the Lord" = primary meaning is still that of a relationship with, acknowledgment of, and submission to the will of God; it is intended to develop lasting obedience and reflection	-true knowledge of God and of Christ is a dynamic, experienced relationship that must find expression in agape = love of neighbor -knowledge is to be grounded in love and lead to right action	-the one without love has not known God -knowledge and love are grounded in and mutually enriched by each other and do not exist apart -the only way to know God is through a loving relationship -such knowing requires loving action and obedience; faith/belief is a verb directed toward a person -loving actions arise from our knowing that God loves us
Warrants & Worldviews	-learning from experience is important -God is in the midst of history rather than removed from it	-more Jewish than Hellenistic		-The same knowing is to exist between Jesus and his disciples -We are to imitate Jesus -Jesus is our model
Sources & Methods	-for knowing as lovemaking: personal experience & tradition- "Adam 'had knowledge' of Eve"	-Hebrew tradition		-theology: it is because of the love between Jesus and God that Jesus can say that he and God know each other

In essence, this map entails our coming to better understand each of the elements of a model in relation to the others (i.e., their claims/definitions, their sources/methods, and their warrants/worldviews). Such information should be noted of each model and can be represented in tables such as these that list each of the model's elements side by side. The primary goals of such mappings are: (1) for us to gain a better understanding of each model being used, and (2) for us to be better able to make the kinds of comparisons that the next two movements call for.

Seeing and Merging Similarities

Once we have mapped out these basic elements (claims/definitions, etc.) for each of the models we are using, we can then begin to make comparisons between them. In this third movement, we can do this by looking for commonalities and themes that seem to emerge from among them.[128] An example of this may be found in the final chapter of Angie Pears's book, *Doing Contextual Theology*. After having reviewed a range of models related to contextual theology, including feminist and other liberationist approaches, she sets out to summarize some of the common themes from among them. For instance, she writes, "Whilst there is clearly great diversity among liberation theologies, for example, in terms of specific justice concerns and methodologies, there is nevertheless a shared conviction that Christianity is a religion which is inherently concerned with justice."[129] She also notes that these models give a primary emphasis to the "social, cultural, sexual, [and] bodily" contexts of human existence.[130] Pears's overview of these various models is therefore one example of this movement, which is primarily concerned with noting the commonalities and similarities of the models we are considering.

Once we identify these similarities among the models, we can then join them together to be a part of our newly synthesized model. For Pears, this meant asserting a common vision for liberation theologies as being primarily oriented toward both universal justice and local context, which she adapts into her own views of contextual theology with some caveats.[131] We likewise briefly saw how Bill Hull drew connections between Greco-Roman, Jewish, and early Christian roots in formulating his own model of

---

128. Swinton and Mowat, *Practical Theology and Qualitative Research*, 199–200.
129. Pears, *Doing Contextual Theology*, 166.
130. Ibid., 167.
131. Ibid., 179.

Christian discipleship. For our youth group, we might find commonalities between our observations of their bicultural struggles, the youth's own reflections on this, and the identity development resources. An intricate part of synthesizing models therefore entails the merging and harmonizing of common themes that have emerged from among the various models that we are considering.

These similarities and mergings can be related to the claims themselves, or to the sources, warrants, and worldviews that are a part of each model. The primary questions of this step, then, are: What are the themes that emerge as we look at these models? What is the common picture that seems to be coming into focus as we analyze all of them side by side? For our discernment, we might ask, "What is it that God is wanting us to commonly notice here?" It is in this step, then, that we merge such common themes and begin formulating our synthesized model for each of the five core areas.

Noting and Reconciling Differences

The final movement of this step goes hand in hand with the previous one. Here, however, we are no longer looking for the similarities but rather the differences between our models. In the same way that we looked for trends and themes among them, we are now interested in the points of conflict and contention. Do any of the models make conflicting claims? Do any of them draw from similar sources but using different methods? Are the worldviews of each model consonant with each other or in conflict? It is questions such as these that can help to guide our analysis in relation to noting the differences among these various models.

An example of this was seen when we compared the different steps to action research and practical theology in the previous chapter. We noted how these models did not exactly line up in terms of the specific steps that they outlined. We have also heard from Barbour how the claims of biblical literalists and scientific materialists differ so much. Noting such differences is essential when seeking a synthesis.

Once we have identified these differences, we can begin to reconcile them for our synthesized model and these considerations can be the most challenging part of our efforts. It is here that we seek to reconcile the conflicts and discrepancies that exist among the models and resources. Doing so, though, may require our making some very difficult and intentional decisions.

However, it will be helpful to recall that there are at least three kinds of influential relationships that models can have on one another: complimentary, minor modifications, and full integration. We can therefore seek to discern how these conflicts might be reconciled according to these possibilities for synthesis. It may be that some of our models, or parts of them, fit together in a piecemeal and complimentary fashion. Or, perhaps we can see how one model offers a beneficial though minor change to one of the other models. Sometimes, however, two or more models need to be completely overhauled in order to reconcile the differences among them. In addition to these, we can also choose to leave the differences as they stand and then simply note this for our own models.

Turning again to the example of scientific materialists and biblical literalists, as described by Barbour, these two conflicting views need to be modified in major ways in order for Barbour to synthesize their theories into his own.[132] Such changes may need to be made to the worldviews that undergird the model or the model may need to be reconceived in light of the sources and warrants that it is based upon. We saw something like this above when Barbour challenged the inductive claims of scientific materialists.

Overall, then, we can seek to find ways and make changes that reconcile the differences among the models. Again, we may turn to our local contexts for insight and guidance in how to approach such differences. In our Asian American youth group, we might have found that the models of identity development for immigrants differed significantly than those for non-immigrants.[133] If this were the case, given our local context, we would give a heavier weight to the immigrant-oriented models in our synthesis. We would do so because these models more closely match the realities of our local context. Again, the processes by which we reconcile such differences are complicated indeed. We might even be prompted to revisit any of the previous steps in order to help clarify and reconcile some of these differences. We therefore need to engage this step with much care, contextual focus, and discerning deliberation.

---

132. For a discussion on three different models that have sought to do this, see Barbour, *When Science Meets Religion*, 27–36.

133. For a discussion of identity development models for ethnic minorities in relation to mainstream models, see Phinney and Rosenthal, "Ethnic Identity in Adolescence," 145–72.

PART TWO: Methodological Movements

Francis's Neuro-Relational Picture

Based upon these four sources (the contextual data from herself and from Martha, and the two external texts: Dispenza and Barrick), Francis steps back an attempts to develop a more integrated picture of what seems to be emerging. Developing a model mapping table similar to Groome's, she surveys and compares the information that she has gathered to date. Table 4 below shows these sources side by side.

Table 4. Francis's Model Mapping

	Contextual Data			
	Personal Observations & Reflections	*Conversations with Martha & Charles (M & C)*	Dispenza	Barrick
Claims & Definitions	• M & C individualistic and independent M rationalistic thinker, perfectionist • C more introverted and solitary; more so after heart attack • C some temper, some hobbies before; but now more "simple" • Self-differentiation issues? • Less communication b/t them	• Unclear of effects of brain injury • C no strong expressed desires to do things on own since heart attack; less proactive • C more explosive/easily confused now; no hobbies other than TV • M's fears of being "chained down" in the future; yearnings to be active • M mourning the loss of the "old C"	• Frontal lobe's relationship to: willful and purposeful action, planning, personality and identity • Sustained use of the brain leads to changes, particularly via the use of the frontal lobe	• Three parts to a relationship: both partners and the relationship itself • Need to foster both self-realization and the relationship • Men and women differ, but they need to integrate both their "masculine" and "feminine" sides • Relationships = avenue to fulfill our yearnings for union with the Divine • God = source of selfless love and individuation

	Contextual Data		Dispenza	Barrick
	Personal Observations & Reflections	*Conversations with Martha & Charles (M & C)*		
Warrants & Worldviews	• Christian-Theistic perspective	• M: secular scientific; agnostic	• Secular scientific	• Mix of Christian and New Age worldviews
Sources & Methods	• Personal observations and reflections on M & C • Experiences with couples in ministry • DMin education	• M's personal observations and reflections	• Personal experiences • Neuroscience research literature • Chiropractic work	• Experiences as a therapist • Psychodynamic theory

From this mapping, Francis feels that her hunches about the affects of Charles heart attack might be confirmed. Though she knows that she would need to verify them with a healthcare professional, she believes that Charles may have lost some functioning of the frontal lobes of his brain thereby affecting his personality and behavior. She feels that this hunch is at least partly supported by his decrease in purposeful actions and willingness or desires to be more proactive as both she and Martha have observed.

Francis also notes the possible connections between Barrick's claim that we all have deep yearnings for union and relationship and Martha's mourning the decrease in communication and activity that she has with Charles. She also realizes that Martha's fears of becoming "chained down" seem to resonate with Barrick's assertions that each partner in a relationship needs to pursue their own self-realization and fulfillment just as much as they need to foster the intimacy of the relationship. Finally, Francis wonders if Barrick's observations of the differences between men and women and between "masculine" and "feminine" sides might help her to better understand Charles's more general introverted dispositions in relationships. In other words, perhaps Charles does not view the relationship in quite the same way or with the same hopes as does Martha.

One major difference that she notes is in the worldviews and influences that inform each of her sources. For Francis, though, these differences do not seem to result in any significant issues or discrepancies in the claims that are being made. However, in reflecting on this, she realizes that Martha's observations and reflections could very well be influenced by her feelings of loss. She notes that many of Martha's reflections focus on the more negative aspects of Charles's behaviors and their relationship together; they focus more on what he is unable to do rather than on what he can. Realizing this, in addition to her observations of Martha's tendencies toward perfectionism, helps Francis to put Martha's claims into perspective noting that Martha may have the tendency to negatively highlight what isn't there rather than what is.

From all of these synthesizing explorations and analyses, Francis feels that she now has a much better and more unified understanding of the anthropological dynamics of their situation. She feels confident that Charlie's heart attack has influenced his personality and that such alterations may lie in frontal lobe regions. She also affirms, however, that some of Charles's behaviors and lack of communication may not all stem from his heart attack but rather from differences in gender or in his personality type. However, she also notes that the decrease in communication is a change that needs to be addressed. She also now believes that Martha is struggling with at least two issues: the "loss" of the old Charles but also with desires for greater self-realization and fulfillment in some way. Finally, Francis sees that while she will need to continue to dialogue with Martha about their situation, she needs to do so with the realization that Martha may be focusing more on the negative aspects of the situation. Overall, then, Francis feels that she understands their circumstances with much greater depth.

Step Five: Theological Reflections and Translations

Once we have synthesized the models from each of the five core areas, we can then turn to our theological model to help guide our reflections on where we believe God is more and less active in the dynamics of our local context. For instance, if we had synthesized a theory of change model of adolescent identity development that was largely secular, such a model would still not help us to know where and how God is active in our local context according it. We would therefore need to make an effort to reconceive of this model in accordance with our own theistic position.

For example, if our theological position were largely a "panentheistic" one, as is found in edited text on panentheism entitled *In Whom We Live*

Going Deep

and Move and Have Our Being,[134] then we would reflect on how this secular model of identity development might be reformulated in accordance with this theological view. We would therefore seek to discern which parts of our largely secular developmental model appear to be more reflective of God's life and manifestations according to our panentheistic theology. We would also be interested in those parts of the model that do not seem to be all that reflective of God. By turning to our theological model, then, we seek to dramatically recast our anthropologies, cosmologies, and theories of change in light of them. In essence, we are discerningly asking God to help us to more clearly see where and how the Spirit is alive in the core dynamics that we have come to model.

Francis's Process Perspective

With her anthropological understandings of Martha and Charlie's relationship deepening, Francis then seeks to apply her own theological model and location to them. Where, she wonders, does God seem to working in and through these dynamics? Her position is an "incarnational" one and she finds the immanent perspective articulated by process theologians, such as John Cobb, David Ray Griffin, and Marjorie Suchocki, to be helpful ones.[135] God is depicted by these authors as wanting each part (or "actual occasion" in process terminology) of creation to have enjoyment and fulfillment, to work for the greater good, of promoting love, embracing novelty, being inherently related to one another, and of promoting greater peace, unity, complexity, and harmony among all of creation so that the image of God might become more fully manifest.[136] While this general theological model is helpful, Francis seeks to apply it more specifically to the brain physiological and to relational dynamics she has been uncovering.

To help with this, based on the process perspective, Francis creates two categories of goals that she believes the Spirit is actively working toward for every part of creation. The first goal is self-realization and fulfillment. This has to with the enjoyment and fulfillment of the entity or aspect being considered.[137] It is also related to the vitality, health, and

---

134. Clayton and Peacocke, *In Whom We Live and Move and Have Our Being*.

135. Cobb and Griffin, *Process Theology*; Suchocki, *God, Christ, Church*.

136. Cobb and Griffin, *Process Theology*, 51, 56–57, 60, 125. Suchocki, *God, Christ, Church*, 35–36, 45–47, 191.

137. Cobb and Griffin, *Process Theology*, 56.

"livingness" of the aspect or entity.[138] For the brain, this would mean that God is actively working for the full functioning of each of its various parts to extent that they are capable. For relationships, the Divine seeks both the self-realization of each partner as well as the vitality of the relationship as a whole. For her own anthropological model, similar to Barrick's, Francis therefore views the work of both individuation and relational fulfillment as "spiritual" work.

The second category that she creates is harmony, unity, and integration. Here, God's life is seen to be at work in the unifying and joining together of various parts.[139] For the brain, this would mean that the Spirit is active in seeking to integrate its various functions and to help them to work more harmoniously together. In relationships, we would therefore find God to be more fully manifest in those movements that foster greater intimacy, togetherness, and union.

Collectively, these theological reflections help Francis to better understand where it is that the Spirit might be most fully alive and manifesting in Martha and Charlie's relationship. She believes that Martha's self-realization desires to pursue her own vitality and activity are therefore more reflective of God, as may be Charlie's own tendencies toward simplicity, introversion, and quietness. However, she also realizes that the level of communication that has decreased since his heart attack may be less manifesting of God's life as it seems to have had the impact of creating greater distance and frustrations between them.

Francis also better understands that while Charles's frontal lobe functioning may have decreased, it is still very much a part of God's desires—according to her process perspective—to work for its health and restoration. Finally, she acknowledges the mourning that Martha is experiencing and sees God as grieving with her through these difficult times as the Spirit continually works for her enjoyment and fullness of life. With this theologized anthropological model, Francis is better prepared to enter into the design and implementation methods of the next chapter. Not only does this model provide her with deeper insights into Martha's and Charlie's situation, it has also given her ideas about how and where she might begin to intervene and counsel them based upon her theistic location.

---

138. Suchocki, *God, Christ, Church*, 191, 210, 217.

139. Cobb and Griffin, *Process Theology*, 64; Suchocki, *God, Christ, Church*, 9, 33–34, chap 11.

Step Six: Final Observations and Evaluations

Our final step in these practical movements of exploration and analysis involves stepping back and reflecting on the results of the previous steps in relation to the program that we are hoping to develop. In this step, we are now not just looking at a single model that we have synthesized, but all of the core models we have constructed for each of the five areas (ideals, anthropologies, theories of change, cosmologies, and theologies). A central part of this, then, is for us to do so in spiritually discerning ways. In other words, is this the synthesized and unified picture that God is inviting us to work with for our program development? Does it offer the insights and guidance that God needs us to have in order to more effectively partner with the formative movements of the Divine in our local context? More specifically, the following are two sets of reflections that we can discerningly engage in for our newly synthesized core models and the overall picture that has emerged.

Content Reflections

As we look at the core models that have resulted, are there any new understandings that we have from them? Of course, if we have engaged these processes correctly, the answer should always be "yes," otherwise we will essentially have gone through them for nothing. The question really at hand, then, is what these insights are.[140] What do we know more about in relation to our local contexts and the phenomena we are interested in that we did not know before? How have our comprehensions of the dynamics clarified? How have our views and perspectives of our community changed?

As we continue to look back over and reflect on our models, we may also find ourselves with additional questions about it. For instance, is there anything that seems to be missing from the models?[141] Are there aspects of them that still don't seem to be quite right? Is there something more that might further strengthen each one? Do they seem accurately capture the dynamics we are trying to represent with them?[142] Can we rely on them for discerning interventions?[143]

---

140. Britt, *Conceptual Introduction to Modeling*, 132, 162.
141. Sandelowski and Barroso, *Handbook for Synthesizing Qualitative Research*, 81.
142. Britt, *Conceptual Introduction to Modeling*, 171.
143. Ibid., 172.

PART TWO: Methodological Movements

Britt refers to such evaluative criteria as "descriptive" and "predictive" criteria because there should be a sense that our models accurately describe and sometimes predict what we have set out to capture.[144] So, for example, one might feel that their understanding of the bicultural struggles of their youth group is not yet comprehensive enough; that there are still too many questions left unanswered. It is questions such as these that can help to draw our attention to some of the still remaining weaknesses and limitations of our core models.

We also need to ask these same kinds of questions to our local communities. Known as "interpretive" evaluation criteria, here we should be seeking to ensure that the synthesized models are truly representative of the lived experiences of the people we are journeying with.[145] Do they find the models to be helpful? Does it accurately capture their perspectives and lived experiences? Such contextual questions may not apply to every model that we synthesize, but we can nevertheless keep them at the forefront of our minds as we evaluate our theories.

If we do uncover weaknesses, we have a few possibilities. We can return to step one and repeat the process by focusing on the limitations or questionable areas—the parts of the bicultural identity development model, for example, that we feel needs to be elaborated on. Or we may move forward with the model as is keeping the limitations that it has in mind as we proceed. Overall, the purpose of such questions is to help us to better know the limitations of what has been generated.

Process Reflections

Another set of reflections that we can make is in relation to these six methodological steps as a whole.[146] As we set our intensive exploration and analysis efforts aside, we can reflect on it overall. In effect, we applying our discernment processes to all that we have just done. From an Ignatian perspective, for instance, we can look back and ask, how does it sit with us? Were these steps difficult and constricting, feeling like an "uphill battle" the whole way, or was it relatively smooth and easygoing? Does it seem to resonate as having been a "consoling" process or did it strike us as "weak and unstable"?

---

144. Ibid., 133, 137, 137, 140, 153.
145. Britt, *Conceptual Introduction to Modeling*, 133, 143.
146. Ibid., 132.

We are seeking to therefore reflect on not just the outcomes of our work, but also on the overall process. In other words, do we believe that God was guiding us through each one of the steps that we just engaged? If not, why not? Do we need to therefore revisit some of them? As we have heard several times now, spiritual discernment needs to guide the program development journey at every step of the way.

Francis Prayerfully Reflects

Having engaged in these steps for the different core areas, Francis prayerfully looks back and reflects on both the content and process of the journey so far. As it relates to her anthropological model, she generally feels confident in the insights that have been generated and where it is that she believes, following process theology, God is active within it. Francis does, however, still have some reservations in regards to the claims that she making about Charlie's frontal lobe functioning. For this, she desires further confirmation from a healthcare professional who is not only trained in neuro-psychology but is also familiar with his particular case. In response to these concerns, she decides to hold this as being one of the possible interventions that she will suggest to Martha: seeking further healthcare advice for Charlie.

Francis's process reflections are likewise consoling. She feels that she has engaged in each of these steps in a discerning way. However, she wonders whether her brief time with Martha and Charles as well as with the external resources has been enough. Have they really helped her to uncover the essential dynamics that she needs to be aware of in order to proceed to the design and implementation stage? Given the constraints on her time and energy, and the feedback from Martha that has further confirmed the dynamics she has noted, Francis decides that she will continue with the program development but in a more cautious way. As she discerns which interventions to suggest to Martha and Charles, she will continue to explore and analyze their circumstance keeping a look out for any dynamics that she might have misrepresented with her core models or missed altogether. Overall, then, Francis feels consoled and thankful for journey so far.

PART TWO: Methodological Movements

Closing Reflections

In this chapter, we set out to more comprehensively and practically discover some of the major theoretical and methodological movements related to exploration and analysis. Overall, our aim is to synthesize a more coherent understanding of our local contexts, and God's life therein, in order to better enable us to engage in spiritual formation program development. At a minimum, we need to consider the relevant ideals, anthropologies, theories of change, cosmologies, and theologies related to it.

To help us toward these ends, six methodological steps were provided and are shown below in figure 7. These steps are intended to help us to synthesize both contextual observations and external resources just as Francis did for Martha and Charles's situation. They can therefore be applied to the five core areas that will inform our program design and implementation in the next chapter. However, these six steps may also be applied to any set of two or more models that we may seek to synthesize. I have retained such generality so that you may apply them as you discerningly see fit.

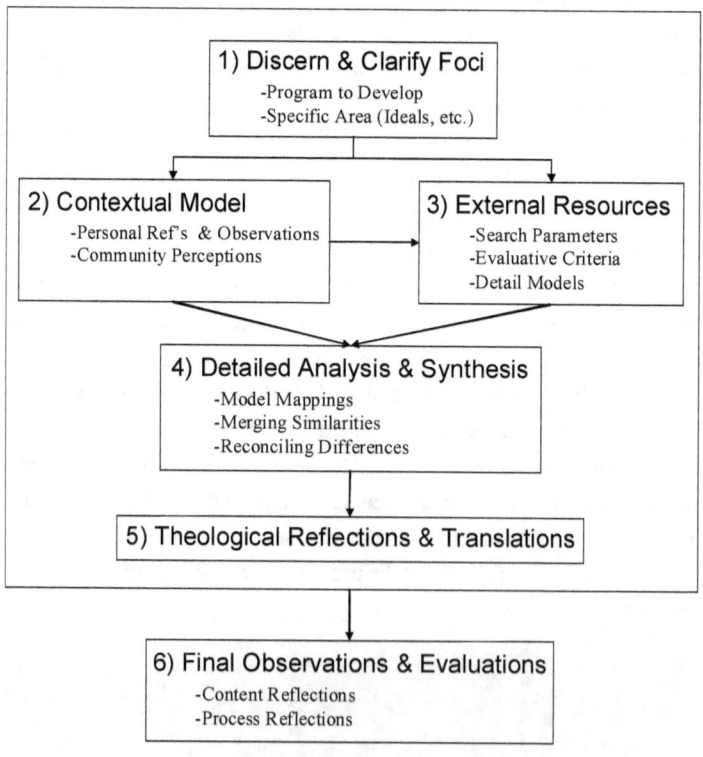

Figure 7. The Six Steps of Exploration and Analysis.

Going Deep

While these steps to synthesizing contextually relevant models may seem somewhat detailed and complex, they can and should also be discerningly tailored to fit with our local contexts and any constraints that we may have in time and energy. For instance, if we are hard pressed for time as Francis was, we can always seek out a single external resource that has already been constructed by someone else. However, we must always remember that the primary KISS purpose of all these efforts is for us to better understand and be able to formatively work with the individuals, close relationships, and communities to which God calls us to. If the models of others are not helping us toward these ends, then we may need to engage in more of the synthesizing steps as outlined in this chapter.

It is therefore in the next chapter that we turn our attention toward applying the result of these efforts. Having now completed the first movement living spiritual praxis, we next turn to considerations of how such synthesized core models might inform the program development design and implementation methodologies that we will utilize in our local ministries.

4

Building a Home
Design and Implementation Methodologies

Before we can build a house, we first need to take the time that is needed to discern all of the different pieces that will be required to be successful in such an endeavor. We need to plan for the foundations that it will rest on. We need to decide on how the house will be laid out and how it will generally look. And, finally, we need to plan for all of the materials and costs that it will require to complete the home.

Spiritual formation program design and implementation is really not much different. Before we can formatively engage with the Spirit in our communities, we must make sure that we have adequately discerned and planned for all of the essentials that are needed. We too need to ensure that the foundations we are basing our program on are solid. We need to take much care in choosing the interventions that we will use. And we need to make sure that our program has all of the necessary resources and supports that it will need.

Design and implementation methodologies are therefore directed toward these ends. They are intended to help guide our program development efforts as we utilize the insights of our deep explorations and analyses for the purposes of moving toward concrete implementation. This chapter will therefore lead us through the necessary theoretical and methodological foundations of these methodologies. In short, we will be learning some of the basics of how to design and implement the formative interventions that our programs will need in order to become the home that our communities can spiritually grow within. As we shall see, we are essentially seeking to discern the approaches through which the Spirit can work to foster the kinds of transformation that God is inviting us toward. This is

Building a Home

our KISS focus for these methodologies. As with the previous chapters, we will begin by laying the theoretical foundations that will be needed before proceeding to the practical steps that we can embody for this second praxis-oriented movement.

Theoretical Foundations

Before we can engage in the actual steps of design and implementation, it will first be helpful to explore a few necessary theoretical considerations. In order to know which interventions to specifically use, for instance, we need to know what the fundamental aims of them are. It will also be helpful to know where we can turn to in order to begin brainstorming the kinds of practices that our specific program might need to use. Specifically, we will be using each of the five core models (ideals, anthropologies, etc.) as contributing sources in helping us to do this.

We also need to consider the interventions themselves. We will find it helpful to briefly survey the landscape of interventions that are commonly used in spiritual formation and it will be helpful to have some set of guidelines to look to in considering which specific approaches are a better fit with our program. In this section, we will therefore spend some time exploring issues such as these in more detail. Overall, these theoretical explorations are intended to be the necessary bases upon which each of the practical steps described in the next section are founded.

Aims of Interventions and Role of Models

Before we can begin exploring how to discern which applications to use for a program, it will first be helpful to better understand the intended purposes of interventions more generally. Once established, we can then begin to discover how the exploration and analysis of our five core areas from the previous chapter might inform our choice and implementation of them. Here, however, we first explore how models in general can help to achieve the aims that all interventions have.

The Aims of Interventions

Organizational change consultant Michael Beitler writes, "An intervention is a set of planned activities with the goal of changing a collaboratively diagnosed problem."[1] It is the assertion that our interventions, the practices and formative approaches that we utilize, have the intended purpose of moving our constituents toward some desirable ends. "The key is that in the end," writes educational researcher Robert Diamond, "your curriculum ensures that each student has the opportunity of reaching the goals and outcomes that you have established."[2] It is therefore the aims of our applications to further the progress of the individuals and communities we are working with.[3]

At their core, interventions are therefore intended to move the people we are working with in our program toward the ideals that we have discerned. Figure 8 below shows this simple relationship. As we come to walk with our constituents through the approaches we have chosen, we should observe them to progress toward our program's horizons.

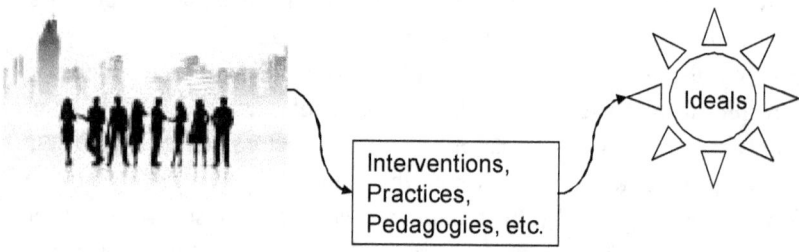

Figure 8. Relationship between Interventions, Our Community, and the Ideals

It is also a relationship, both Beitler and Diamond claim, not only between the ideals that we are striving toward and the interventions we are using, but also the assessments that we make of such progress.[4] We will be addressing such insightful assessments in the next chapter. Hence, what we need to note at this point is that the primary aims of our interventions are to intentionally foster the spiritual growth of those we are called to work with toward the ideals that we have discerned. Stated from a theistic location, then, *our interventions should be the means that enable the Spirit to form our community in accordance with the ideals that God is inviting us toward.* This means intentionally participating with the life of the Spirit in

1. Beitler, *Strategic Organizational Change*, 83.
2. Diamond, *Designing and Assessing Courses and Curricula*, 128.
3. Ibid., 114.
4. Beitler, *Strategic Organizational Change*, 78, 83; Diamond, *Designing and Assessing Courses and Curricula*, 148.

Building a Home

our midst, through our practices, pedagogies, and environment, to move the people we are working with toward our ideals.

Using Models toward These Ends

In order to help ensure that such aims are fulfilled, it will be helpful to have some support and guidance for helping us to choose the specific interventions and practices that we do. Generally, Fordham University Professor John Elias stresses the importance of using theories in the choosing of our interventions when he writes, "It is clear, however, that no matter where one begins in practice, the importance for the development of theory to undergird, explain, and reflect upon practice soon becomes apparent... Theories act as bridges between research foundations and the field of practice."[5] Models, he asserts, should become an intimate and important part of the dialogue that occurs between the interventions we use and the ends toward which we use them.[6]

In effect, models can help to guide the approaches that we use. For instance, Diamond points to the use of psychological developmental models as a basis for helping educators to determine the kinds of approaches that they use.[7] Such theories can help clarify social and institutional contexts, provide structure and coherence, and make explicit some of the inherent assumptions and biases that we have.[8] "The more adult religious educators know," Elias asserts, "about the interests, problems, and issues within the local community, the more they are able to address these in an effective manner."[9] Such insights and understandings are the models and theories that inform our practices. For us, our five areas of exploration and analysis comprise the core models that can undergird the discernment of our formative interventions.

But, we may ask, how does this happen? How do these core models help us in discerning the approaches that we will eventually choose in light of our desired ideals? Once we have our models, we can then more easily reflect on the kinds of applications that the model suggests are needed.

5. Elias, *Foundations and Practice of Adult Religious Education*, 175–76.
6. Ibid., 151–52, 195.
7. Diamond, *Designing and Assessing Courses and Curricula*, 109.
8. Britt, *Conceptual Introduction to Modeling*, 179, 181; Diamond, *Designing and Assessing Courses and Curricula*, 116–18; Elias, *Foundations and Practice of Adult Religious Education*, 152–53.
9. Elias, *Foundations and Practice of Adult Religious Education*, 190.

For instance, psychologist Kurt Lewin's theory of change "assumes that in every situation there are forces to support change and forces to prevent it."[10] Based upon this concept, users of Lewin's theory then seek interventions that strengthened the forces supporting positive change and weaken those that opposed such progress.[11]

If we were to restate Lewin's theory in a theistic way, one of the guiding principles for choosing interventions would be: *support and strengthen those movements that are more manifesting of the Spirit and weaken or oppose those that are less divinely manifesting.* As we shall see in the next section, in fact, this is one of the core principles for the intervention discernment as it comes repeatedly throughout our reflections on each of the five core models. Using this principle, we could then begin searching for interventions that did just this. For example, this might mean Francis finding practices that strengthen Martha's and Charlie's communication skills or Montague seeking to oppose and reform his congregation's racism and sexism.

As we have already heard, the interventions should seek to intentionally foster the kinds of changes that we have discerned God to be inviting us toward. Our five core areas can therefore empower the discernment of such approaches by helping us to see more clearly how to foster such genuinely spiritual growth. In the next section, then, we will be considering how this happens in much greater detail as we explore how each of the five core models can aid us in such discernment.

Looking to the Five Core Models for Guidance

Given these considerations of what the aims of applications are and how our models and theories can generally inform our choosing of them, we can now turn to each our five core models and explore how they might play a role in determining which practices to consider. In this section, we will be looking at how each one of these five areas offers something significant toward these ends. Our purpose here is to consider some of the key theoretical foundations that can inform our discernment of interventions. As we shall presently see, each of these can play a significant role toward these ends.

---

10. Elias, *Foundations and Practice of Adult Religious Education*, 205.

11. Beitler, *Strategic Organizational Change*, 146; Elias, *Foundations and Practice of Adult Religious Education*, 205.

Anthropologies

As we saw, these models give us insights into the current nature and dynamics of the individuals, relationships, and communities that we are working with. Taken with our theological models, as we saw in Francis's case, they can also help us to better know which dynamics the Sacred is more or less present within and through. They can therefore help us to begin to discern which practices might be used to either foster or impede these divine dynamics. The practices we use, therefore, should directly address the elements of our anthropological models that we are intentionally working with.[12] These models can therefore help us to know what kinds of approaches we should be looking to in order to move toward the ideals that God is inviting us toward for each anthropological element.

For example, if we include the heart and affective movements in our anthropology and ideals for an individual, then we should be looking for practices that are asserted to form the heart in these spiritualizing ways.[13] Or if we consider positive relationships and environments to be important interpersonal and communal influences, then we should intentionally seek to foster healthy and formative social and cultural dynamics.[14] In essence, our approaches should address every part of our anthropological models: the elements, their relationships to one another and the environment, and the organism as a whole.

It also depends, however, on what our general views of humanity are and how we address diversity. Are we already made in the image of God or are we fundamentally "stained" with sin and in need of salvation?[15] Depending on which we believe, our practices should reflect these views. We also need to consider such questions as: How does each individual, interpersonal relationship, or whole community differ from others? Are there unique interventions that might be needed in light of these differences? For effective intervention, we need to not only consider such uniqueness

---

12. Dettoni, "What Is Spiritual Formation?," 13; Driskill, "Spirituality and the Formation of Pastoral Counselors," 80; Erasmus, "Handbook of the Militant Christian," 60; O'Connell, *Making Disciples*, 28; Radillo, "Model of Formation in the Multi-Cultural Urban Context," 169.

13. O'Connell, *Making Disciples*, 167.

14. Elias, *Foundations and Practice of Adult Religious Education*, 238; Radillo, "Model of Formation in the Multi-Cultural Urban Context," 169.

15. Lockerbie, "Living and Growing in the Christian Year," 130; Payne, "Personal Healing and Spiritual Formation," 219.

PART TWO: Methodological Movements

but to also tailor our approaches for them.[16] Our anthropologies therefore can provide us with additional approaches when we consider in detail which of its elements we are seeking to work formatively with.

Theories of Change

Our theories of change, as we heard, fundamentally focus on how transformation happens. They therefore can become a more solid bedrock for the approaches we choose. Our approaches should, as we heard in relation to Lewin's change theory, seek to foster or impede these change dynamics depending upon whether or not they support or hinder the spiritual ideals toward which we are being invited.

For instance, contemporary "progressive" education is asserted to look to the Enlightenment for guidance in how to foster educational change among students. As a result, Elias writes, "Natural feelings, reason, and scientific observation became the acceptable ways of arriving at knowledge."[17] These approaches were chosen because these educators viewed them as being able to foster the kinds of growth that they were seeking. Our theories of change can therefore help us to discern which kinds of practices might be more effective; though we must also keep in mind that sustained, progressive growth takes much time and effort as we heard in the last chapter.[18]

Our chosen interventions should also reflect the general nature of change that our communities hold. For instance, there are at least two views of spiritual transformation. The first one holds that our journeys are more of an awakening that happens; one in which we gradually come to greater realizations of God and creation.[19] The other view asserts that all spiritual change comes as a result of a warfare; it asserts that "we must wage war with ourselves."[20] Whereas one holding the former view might gravitate more toward practices that emphasize the quest for peace and

---

16. Beitler, *Strategic Organizational Change*, 84; Diamond, *Designing and Assessing Courses and Curricula*, 119.

17. Elias, *Foundations and Practice of Adult Religious Education*, 161–62.

18. Clark, "Spiritual Formation in Children," 235; Lawrenz, *Dynamics*, 15, 33, 137; McCallum and Lowery, *Organic Disciplemaking*, 269; Wimberly and Parker, "In Search of Wisdom," 17.

19. Jackson, "Forming a Spirituality of Wisdom," 157.

20. Erasmus, "Handbook of the Militant Christian," 40.

joy in this awakening,[21] someone believing in the latter might choose interventions—such as ascetical practices—in preparation for this war.[22] The theories and models that we hold of how transformation transpires can therefore play a very central role in the kinds of approaches that we use.

Cosmologies

How do our views of creation contribute to the discernment of specific actions? How does our local context influence our program? Basically, the idea here is that our approaches should be consistent with what we believe about the more substantial nature of creation. If we believe, for instance, that there is a cosmological war between good and evil, and some formators do, then our approaches should reflect this by working to foster the good while eliminating the evil.[23] However, if we take a more sacramental view of creation as being inherently good, as do some Puritans and panentheists, then our interventions might not reflect a battle/conflict ethos as much as they do an acknowledgement and fostering of the holiness latent within all things.[24] Or if we hold a central place to angelic beings, then our practices might seek to help our communities to rely more heavily on their care and guidance.[25] Our cosmologies about the nature of life can therefore give rise to the kinds of approaches that we use in relation to our program.

Additionally, we must also have some understanding about the contexts in which our approaches will take place because much of our formation happens as a direct result of contextual influences.[26] We saw the central importance of this in the last chapter and we must continue to give a central place to such considerations as we begin to look to the practices that we consider. For instance, we might ask such questions as: What is

21. Jackson, "Forming a Spirituality of Wisdom," 154.

22. Erasmus, "Handbook of the Militant Christian," 30, 54, 65.

23. Hull, *Complete Book of Discipleship*, 292–93; Lawrenz, *Dynamics*, 49; McCallum and Lowery, *Organic Disciplemaking*, 136.

24. Gregersen, "Three Varieties of Panentheism," 21, 27, 31; Knight, *God of Nature*, 94; Ryken, "Puritan Model," 50–51.

25. *John Cassian: The Conferences*, 514; Law, "Serious Call to a Devout and Holy Life," 91, 100, 159.

26. Radillo, "Model of Formation in the Multi-Cultural Urban Context," 168; Van Kaam, *Fundamental Formation*, 57.

the context for our program? Is it hospitable or toxic?[27] What are the cultural values and influences that are present within it?[28] What resources are available for our constituents? What they think of the environment? Similar to our transformation models, our interventions can intentionally seek to nurture positive contextual influences while simultaneously seeking to minimize the more negative and detrimental effects. Our cosmological models can therefore help to further guide our discernment of approaches.

Theologies

As we have already seen, what we think about God impacts how we will engage our programs. The main emphasis here is for us to choose practices that partner with the work that we and our constituents believe God is doing in our midst. As theists, those who seek to see and be with God in all that we are and do, we can consider our spiritually formative endeavors as ultimately the work of God in our midst, as many formators do.[29] As a result, our theological propositions should inform and guide the kinds of actions that we turn to.[30] In essence, then, our interventions should—similar to Lewin's change theory, though with our theistic bent—strengthen those movements we deem to be more in alignment with God's work in our midst and weaken and/or modify those that appear not to be.[31]

For instance, as we noted in the introduction, a central ideal for Christians is imitating Christ's life.[32] It is a matter of partnering with the work of the Holy Spirit "which conforms the child of God more and more to the image of Christ."[33] Our approaches, as Christians, should therefore intentionally seek to foster both the imitation of and partnership with

---

27. Hull, *Complete Book of Discipleship*, 154.

28. Graham, "Race and Ethnicity in the Formation of Pastoral Counselors"; Marshall, "Gender Identity, Sexual Orientation, and Pastoral Formation"; Mucherera, "Pastoral Formation of Counselors in Intercultural Studies"; O'Connell, *Making Disciples*, 85–86.

29. Dettoni, "What Is Spiritual Formation?," 11; Erasmus, "Handbook of the Militant Christian," 40; Lawrenz, *Dynamics*, 142; Wimberly and Parker, "In Search of Wisdom," 13.

30. Elias, *Foundations and Practice of Adult Religious Education*, 210; Lawrenz, *Dynamics*, 109.

31. Lawrenz, *Dynamics*, 145–46.

32. Hull, *Complete Book of Discipleship*, 114.

33. Lightner, "Salvation and Spiritual Formation," 39.

Christ's life in our midst.[34] As Erasmus writes, "Whatever things you find Christ's image in, join yourself to them."[35] For some, Christ is theologically understood to play a guiding role in our mind's perceptions and inner life.[36] For others, he is active in the church and its traditions.[37] As a result, our approaches should seek to help us to tune into these inner and outer movements of the Spirit, for that is the KISS-centered essence and nature of spiritual formation as we have heard many times now. The point to draw from all of this is that our theologies can and should be a key source for the kinds of interventions that we use in our formative programs.

Ideals

Finally, we have already seen how the approaches we use must be linked with the horizons toward which we are seeking to journey with our communities. As a result, our ideals should be stated as clearly and succinctly as possible in order to clarify our objectives and help us to better know how to evaluate progress toward them.[38] These goals should be both challenging and attainable, and they should inspire vision and hope for the people we are working with.[39] For Christians, these ideals are again often rooted in the life and teachings of Jesus, though other goals, such as the educational aim of "critical thinking," can also be considered.[40]

Once these ideals are clearly defined, we can then begin the processes of brainstorming some of the approaches that might lead toward them.[41] Specifically, we can think about the skills, experiences, knowledge, and even attitudes that might be needed in order to achieve these ends and

---

34. Hull, *Complete Book of Discipleship*, 28.

35. Erasmus, "Handbook of the Militant Christian," 92.

36. Au and Au, *Discerning Heart*, 5; O'Connell, *Making Disciples*, 15–16; Payne, "Personal Healing and Spiritual Formation," 213.

37. Schreck, "Principles of Church Renewal," 154.

38. Beitler, *Strategic Organizational Change*, 100; Diamond, *Designing and Assessing Courses and Curricula*, 152; Elias, *Foundations and Practice of Adult Religious Education*, 224.

39. Beitler, *Strategic Organizational Change*, 84; Hull, *Complete Book of Discipleship*, 30; McCallum and Lowery, *Organic Disciplemaking*, 57–58.

40. Dettoni, "What Is Spiritual Formation?," 16; Diamond, *Designing and Assessing Courses and Curricula*, 149; Elias, *Foundations and Practice of Adult Religious Education*, 177–78, 213–17; Felder, "Counsel from Wise Others," 94; O'Connell, *Making Disciples*, 128.

41. Elias, *Foundations and Practice of Adult Religious Education*, 229.

our interventions should intentionally foster these needs.[42] For instance, Diamond writes for teachers, "If the major focus of the course is on information dissemination, lectures and independent study become the obvious instructional models."[43] Alternatively, if the intention is to nurture "black personhood, hope, and liberative action," then the interventions should do this, asserts Yale professor of Christian Education Yolanda Smith, "by bringing about their critical consciousness of wisdom inherent in the black cultural heritage."[44] The ideals that we therefore hold can be yet a further source of potential applications to consider when we begin to think about what is needed in order to partner with the Spirit's efforts to move us toward these ends in more concrete ways.

Landscape and Guideline Considerations

Before moving on to the concrete steps by which to pull all of these foundations together into a more practically applicable set of steps, there is one last set of theoretical issues to discuss. Namely, the interventions themselves. If we are hoping to design and implement a set of practical approaches, it will be helpful to address two sets of considerations. The first is related to the general and specific kinds of interventions that are available to us. In other words, what does the wider landscape of possible approaches look like? What is the fuller range of approaches that we might begin to draw from? Are there specific practices that formators in the Western Christian tradition have generally turned to? Knowing this larger landscape will help us to know what is available to us as we begin to think more concretely about the specific interventions that we might use.

The second set of considerations is related to the kinds of information that we need to have in mind when considering specific interventions. What is it that we need to know about a particular spiritual practice, for instance, in order to decide if it will be helpful for our community or not? Are there a set of guidelines that we can turn to in the selection of actual interventions? The first set of considerations is therefore intended to help us to know the broader range of interventions that are available to us to draw from while the second should help us to better know if a specific intervention might be more or less useful for our program. Overall, these

---

42. Diamond, *Designing and Assessing Courses and Curricula*, 149.
43. Ibid., 135.
44. Smith, "Forming Wisdom through Cultural Rootedness," 40.

are the final foundations that we will need to know in order to engage in the practical steps detailed below.

Landscapes: A Survey of Available Approaches

As you might be able to guess, one cannot speak about spiritual formation without giving some attention to the approaches, practices, and influences that can help us to enact the kinds of formative movements that we are seeking to be a part of with God. Western Christian literature on the various kinds of available approaches, both historically and contemporarily, is voluminous. In essence, these various approaches comprise the materials that our program can choose from when considering how to build our spiritually forming home with God.

In an effort to simplify things, following the KISS principle, I will briefly outline five core kinds of approaches that are commonly asserted as being a part of our work according to a smaller subset of what is out there. Following this, I will then discuss four specialized practices that this literature addresses repeatedly. Together, these reflections are intended to provide us with a brief overview of the kinds of general and specific approaches to consider in the discernment of our interventions. Once we know what is available, we are in a better position to choose from among this broader landscape.

Five Core Approaches

As mentioned, there seem to be five core categories of approaches that spiritual formators regularly consider for their craft. These five categories are depicted in figure 9 below. We can see that each general category of approaches represents a sort of flow in an individual's, relationship's, and/or community's life that completes a cycle from outer to inner and back to outer again.

PART TWO: Methodological Movements

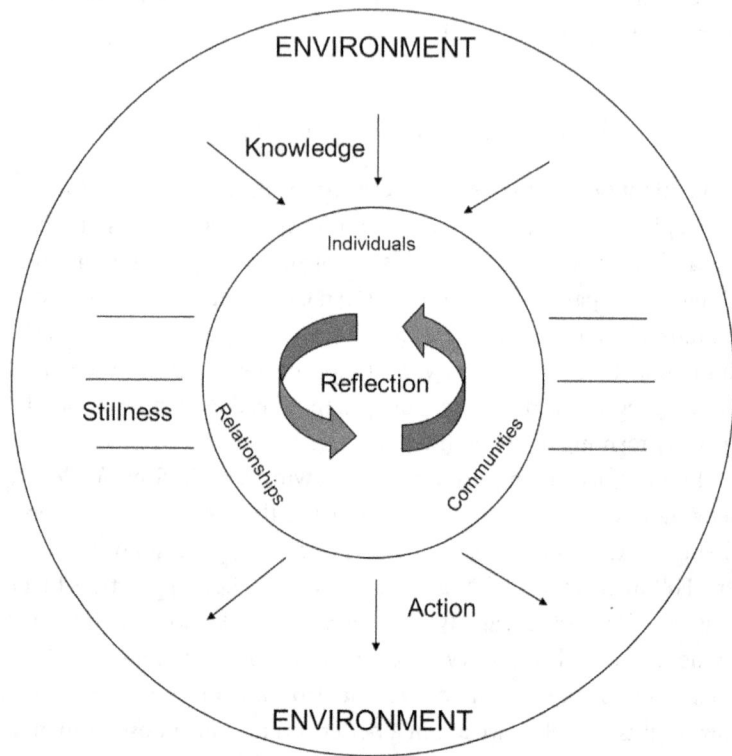

Figure 9. Five Core Categories of Approaches.

The first broad category are approaches that foster the acquisition of knowledge. These approaches, as we can see in the diagram, are primarily oriented toward introducing information and insights into people's life from outside. A primary emphasis in the Christian tradition is given to the role of Scripture as being one such source.[45] It is intended to transform the person's life through regularly attending to its insights and teachings.[46] In addition to this, the acquisition of knowledge more generally is considered to be a staple of a growing disciple.[47] "Knowledge, or learning,"

45. Hull, *Complete Book of Discipleship*, 190; Law, "Serious Call to a Devout and Holy Life," 91, 115, 121, 206; Piper, "God Is Most Glorified in Us," 83; Wimberly and Parker, "In Search of Wisdom," 13.

46. Clark, "Spiritual Formation in Children," 242; Erasmus, "Handbook of the Militant Christian," 92; McCallum and Lowery, *Organic Disciplemaking*, 108; Whitney, "Teaching Scripture Intake," 164.

47. *John Cassian: The Conferences*, 163, 373, 511–12, 515; Erasmus, "Handbook

Erasmus teaches us, "fortifies the mind with salutary precepts and keeps virtue ever before us."[48] Such learning is ultimately intended to educate and invite each person into an ever deepening relationship with God as well as empower them to more fully live out their spiritual lives.[49]

A second set of core approaches are those associated with intentional reflection. As one comes to gain greater knowledge and insights, there needs to be some intentional effort to further internalize and absorb this new information, values, et cetera, into one's life.[50] Journaling is one specific example of such a reflection practice.[51] These practices can deepen self-knowledge—for the individual, relationship, or community—which is considered to be a cornerstone of spiritual growth, strengthening one's identity.[52] "We all travel through life experiencing events and circumstances that shape us," Hull writes, "How we interpret them determines how God forms and transforms our inner person."[53] Such transformations and interpretations, in these approaches, often come about by our cultivating a critical and reasoned consciousness toward the influences of our lives.[54] The result is a life that thinks and acts differently in the world.[55] Such reflection approaches therefore comprise a second set of core approaches to spiritual formation.

A third set of approaches are those that invite us to act outwardly on the newer life in God that we are cultivating; often in the form of service.[56]

---

of the Militant Christian," 35; Jackson, "Forming a Spirituality of Wisdom," 163; Law, "Serious Call to a Devout and Holy Life," 49, 93; Lawrenz, *Dynamics of Spiritual Formation*, 19, 57; O'Connell, *Making Disciples*, 148–49; Ryken, "Puritan Model," 57.

48. Erasmus, "Handbook of the Militant Christian," 35.

49. Graham and Whitehead, "Role of Pastoral Theology," 9; Greider et al., *Formation of Pastoral Counselors*, 178; Law, "Serious Call to a Devout and Holy Life," 50, 127–28, 179, 184, 193, 240, 250, 258, 300; O'Connell, *Making Disciples*, 142; Radillo, "Model of Formation in the Multi-Cultural Urban Context," 170.

50. Law, "Serious Call to a Devout and Holy Life," 68, 339–40; Wimberly and Parker, "In Search of Wisdom," 14.

51. Wimberly and Parker, "In Search of Wisdom," 13.

52. Bidwell, "Formation through Parallel Charting"; Felder, "Counsel from Wise Others," 101; Radillo, "Model of Formation in the Multi-Cultural Urban Context," 174.

53. Hull, *Complete Book of Discipleship*, 191.

54. Erasmus, "Handbook of the Militant Christian," 45; Graham and Whitehead, "Role of Pastoral Theology," 22; Law, "Serious Call to a Devout and Holy Life," 92–93, 95, 345, 351; Smith, "Forming Wisdom through Cultural Rootedness," 40, 53.

55. Cooper-White, "Thick Theory," 47, 62.

56. Law, "Serious Call to a Devout and Holy Life," 91, 115, 117, 272; Lawrenz, *Dynamics of Spiritual Formation*, 19; O'Connell, *Making Disciples*, 180.

PART TWO: Methodological Movements

It is by serving that each of us "lives out the very meaning of grace."[57] Not only is such service intended to be a means by which we journey, but it is also an ideal toward which we continually strive.[58] Such desires to give, it is claimed, are a natural outgrowth of a growing life in God.[59] The primary purpose of such actions are that they help to form us more fully into the image of Christ, and it is in doing that we ultimately come to find more of God.[60] Action, then, constitutes a third set of approaches that are considered to be foundational to fostering spiritual growth.

While these first three approaches may seem somewhat obvious, the fourth one can be a bit more confusing. Some practitioners hold that stillness and solitude are a necessary set of approaches that disciples should regularly engage in.[61] Such approaches are categorically different than the one's above because these previous ones were more concerned with the tangible things that individuals, small groups, and communities can do: we can read, we can journal and reflect together, we can serve at a soup kitchens, et cetera. This fourth set of core approaches, however, is not concerned with action at all. It is, in fact, quite the opposite. It is primarily about being still in one's self knowing that God is alive in such motionlessness.[62] It is also about letting the soils of our souls and our communal work to lie fallow for a time and thereby gain the needed rest that it requires in the pursuit of its ideals. Stillness and solitude, being categorically different from the first three, therefore comprises another set of core approaches to be used in spiritual formation.

The fifth and final set of approaches are those related to intentionally shaping the environments in which our program is taking place. While it has been noted that humans have the tremendous capacity to adapt and survive in even the most inhospitable places, the more ideal environment

---

57. Greider et al., "Formation for Care of Souls," 178; Lawrenz, *Dynamics of Spiritual Formation*, 128.

58. Erasmus, "Handbook of the Militant Christian," 68; Hull, *Complete Book of Discipleship*, 28; Lawrenz, *Dynamics of Spiritual Formation*, 9; McCallum and Lowery, *Organic Disciplemaking*, 241; Ryken, "Puritan Model," 50.

59. McCallum and Lowery, *Organic Disciplemaking*, 207.

60. Hull, *Complete Book of Discipleship*, 191; Law, "Serious Call to a Devout and Holy Life," 90, 95, 121, 193, 225, 287–88, 344; Lawrenz, *Dynamics of Spiritual Formation*, 133.

61. *John Cassian: The Conferences*, 45, 345–46, 375, 386, 512; Law, "Serious Call to a Devout and Holy Life," ch. 15.

62. *John Cassian: The Conferences*, 345–46.

Building a Home

is one that embodies trust, grace, humility, submission, affirmation.[63] In quest to nurture such environments, and to guard against the more inhospitable ones, it necessary that we give consideration to the cultural, racial, gender, biological, and other dynamics that are at work within and around our programs.[64] Our formation approaches must therefore take such environmental influences into consideration and we must seek to intentionally form them as well. Each of these five sets of core approaches should be a central and regular part of a formator's repertoire in the development of her or his program.

Four Specific Practices

In addition to these five foundational approaches, there were specific sets of practices that are also mentioned repeatedly in the literature. While these practices usually embody more than one of the core approaches above, they have the same primary purposes of all interventions: to foster a growing spiritual life. As formators, we can therefore draw from and use the wisdom that has been handed on in relation to each of these four very specific practices.

The first set of practices is related to prayer. Prayer, like reading Scripture, has long been considered an absolute necessity in Christian, as well as in other religious traditions.[65] "The constant emphasis that Paul and Jesus placed on prayer," write pastors Dennis McCallum and Jessica Lowery, "clearly suggests that you should make prayer a central emphasis in your discipleship ministry."[66] As any trip to a bookstore will attest, there are many methods, kinds, and ways to pray.[67] Prayer is therefore considered a primary means by which "to be satisfied with God's love."[68]

---

63. Hull, *Complete Book of Discipleship*, ch. 5.

64. Graham, "Race and Ethnicity in the Formation of Pastoral Counselors"; Marshall, "Gender Identity, Sexual Orientation, and Pastoral Formation"; Mucherera, "Pastoral Formation of Counselors in Intercultural Studies."

65. Driskill, "Spirituality and the Formation of Pastoral Counselors," 81; Erasmus, "Handbook of the Militant Christian," 35; Law, "Serious Call to a Devout and Holy Life," 280; Lawrenz, *Dynamics of Spiritual Formation*, 19, 69; Wimberly and Parker, "In Search of Wisdom," 13.

66. McCallum and Lowery, *Organic Disciplemaking*, 122.

67. For examples, see: *John Cassian: The Conferences*, 336–38; Hunt, "Teaching People to Pray"; Law, "Serious Call to a Devout and Holy Life," ch. 15; McCallum and Lowery, *Organic Disciplemaking*, 131; Wilhoit, "Following the Lord's Pattern of Prayer."

68. *John Cassian: The Conferences*, 340; Erasmus, "Handbook of the Militant

Not only, then, should spiritual formators themselves engage in prayer, but they also need to be knowledgeable in the forms of prayer appropriate to their tradition and community.

A second set of specific practices are just as commonly discussed as the first, and they are those related to worship.[69] Worship is primarily intended to orient us toward God and can have many different styles and elements to it, such as: music, ritual, liturgies, prayers, et cetera.[70] As with prayer, there are many resources available and each formator must be familiar with those of their local context.

The third set of specific practices that are commonly noted, are those related to the use of metaphors, stories, and symbols. The imagination, it is asserted, is a powerful mode through which formation can happen.[71] Eramsus, for instance, regularly encourages his readers to use their imaginations to challenge and transform temptations when they arise.[72] In spiritual formation, then, we can access the imagination through use of stories, analogies, and contemplative practices for the purpose of more deeply transforming our communities.[73] It is through such narratives and symbols that new values and meanings are shaped more deeply within us.[74] Narrative and metaphorical approaches to spiritual formation are therefore seen as being a necessary part of a formator's tool belt.

The fourth and final set of specific practices are those that are intended to form the spiritualizing habits in some part of a person's life. An example of these are the mindfulness habits that some formators, such as the early desert monastics, assert are essential to a growing spiritual life.[75] Another example is the practice of virtues in our life such as truthfulness,

---

Christian," 35; Piper, "God Is Most Glorified in Us," 81.

69. Bauman, "Spiritual Formation Through the Liturgy," 99; Gangel, "Spiritual Formation Through Public Worship," 111; Lawrenz, *Dynamics of Spiritual Formation*, 19; Wimberly and Parker, "In Search of Wisdom," 13.

70. Lawrenz, *Dynamics of Spiritual Formation*, 82, 88–89, 113–14, 116; O'Connell, *Making Disciples*, 133–35, 155; Parker, "Singing Hope in the Key of Wisdom"; Smith, "Forming Wisdom through Cultural Rootedness," 53.

71. O'Connell, *Making Disciples*, 105; Payne, "Personal Healing and Spiritual Formation," 219–20; Van Kaam, *Fundamental Formation*, 245.

72. Erasmus, "Handbook of the Militant Christian," 81, 84, 89.

73. *John Cassian: The Conferences*, 415; Jackson, "Forming a Spirituality of Wisdom," 162; Law, "Serious Call to a Devout and Holy Life," 174; O'Connell, *Making Disciples*, 4, 111–14, 117; Wimberly and Parker, "In Search of Wisdom," 15.

74. Graham and Whitehead, "Role of Pastoral Theology," 23.

75. *John Cassian: The Conferences*, 43, 46, 50, 162, 377; Erasmus, "Handbook of the Militant Christian," 39, 46, 78; Law, "Serious Call to a Devout and Holy Life," 306.

Building a Home

humility, forgiveness, and other ethical standards.[76] Still another example of these are the ascetical practices, such as fasting, that we may embody as ongoing part of our discipleship.[77] These practices all have the primary purpose of cultivating habits that are more imitating and manifesting of God in our own lives. They are therefore considered to be yet another integral part of the approaches that we can draw from.

Guidelines: Criteria to Consider When Selecting Interventions

Okay, so if we are looking at this huge landscape of potential practices that we might consider, we can ask: What details do we need to know about each intervention in order to help us to narrow down the range of choices? What are some criteria and guidelines for helping us to decide which specific approaches might best fit with our particular program and local context? While it is true that each of the five core models discussed above can help us to gain a better idea of the kinds of interventions that we might generally consider, we also need to reflect on the details of each specific practice. In general, there are six guidelines to consider in the discernment of whether a specific intervention is more or less ideal for our specific program. Each of these criteria are essentially intended to help us to select the materials that our programs will need in order for it to become the spiritually nurturing home that we are working to build.

GUIDELINE #1: HISTORICAL CONSIDERATIONS

The first guideline is related to how the particular approach has been used in the past and what its reported effects have been. Our religious and cultural traditions have many practices that have been commonly utilized for generations, if not for hundreds of years,[78] as we have seen above. By looking into this history of an intervention's uses and what its spiritually

---

76. Erasmus, "Handbook of the Militant Christian," 91; Felder, "Counsel from Wise Others," 106; Law, "Serious Call to a Devout and Holy Life," 85–86, 91, 101, 274; O'Connell, *Making Disciples*, 42, 45, 176.

77. *John Cassian: The Conferences*, 163, 247, 265; Erasmus, "Handbook of the Militant Christian," 86; Law, "Serious Call to a Devout and Holy Life," 78, 91, 112, 128, 219; Wimberly and Parker, "In Search of Wisdom," 13.

78. Bauman, "Spiritual Formation Through the Liturgy," 99; Lawrenz, *Dynamics*, 19, 57; McCallum and Lowery, *Organic Disciplemaking*, 122; Ryken, "Puritan Model," 57.

formative influences have been, we can better understand the potential that the specific practice might have for our own ministries. For instance, if centering prayer has been traditionally used in a quiet setting with little distractions, then we need to know this if we are thinking of using it with our youth group at Grand Central Station in New York City during peak commuter hours.

We must therefore realize that how each specific practice will be implemented in our own context might be different than how it has been historically utilized. Practices, like plants, have grown up in particular environments and we need to be aware of these when deciding whether a particular one might be a good fit for our purposes or not. This first guideline is therefore related to historical roots and applications and it can help us to further find and discern which practices we might adopt for our current and local needs.

Guideline #2: Intended Aims

The second set of guidelines that we can use when considering a specific practice are its intended aims. Here we can note what the intended purpose of the practice is and how it might relate to the ideals of our program.[79] For instance, is its intention to clearly "present information in an organized manner," as a lecture is intended to?[80] Or are its ends meant to be oriented toward helping people to "become a powerful force for God in this world" by regularly reading scriptures?[81] As formators, we must be explicit about the intended aims of the specific practices in relation to the overall ideals of our program.[82]

In essence, the particular practice should help our communities to move toward these ideals. For instance, if one of Francis's hopes is to help Charles to improve his communication and openness with Martha and others, then she needs to choose interventions that are oriented toward these aims. She might have him to begin journaling, or encourage Martha to enroll him in an art or writing class. Since these practices are geared toward self-expression they are potential candidates for Francis to consider.

---

79. Beitler, *Strategic Organizational Change*, 84.
80. Elias, *Foundations and Practice of Adult Religious Education*, 248.
81. McCallum and Lowery, *Organic Disciplemaking*, 108.
82. Clark, "Spiritual Formation in Children," 242; Cooper-White, "Thick Theory," 62; Graham and Whitehead, "Role of Pastoral Theology," 9; Jackson, "Forming a Spirituality of Wisdom," 163; O'Connell, *Making Disciples*, 142.

She would probably be less likely to suggest, however, that Charles take up contemplative practices that are more silent and solitary because these approaches are not immediately oriented toward his actually engaging in communication with others. This second guideline is therefore related to our understanding what the intended aims of an intervention are in comparison with the ideals of our program.

Guideline #3: Anthropological Foci

We can also consider what the approach is intended to be anthropologically directed toward. Is it meant to be applied to individuals, as mentoring and teaching efforts sometimes are?[83] Toward interpersonal relationships as in the case of small group ministries?[84] Or are they meant to be engaged for the benefit of whole communities and cultures, as do social-interaction and congregational development approaches?[85] Here, our goal is to better understand which specific area the practice is intended to be focused on.

For instance, at the level of the individual, some practices focus on the fostering of the mind through information-processing pedagogies, critical analysis exercises, and mindfulness practices.[86] If our program had the expressed intention of seeking to develop the mind, then we might consider such approaches. However, if our only focus was to nurture physical health and vitality, as physical therapists and personal trainers do, then these mind-focused interventions would not be very helpful for us. As formators considering any given intervention, we therefore need to be aware of anthropological aspects that it is intended to be focused on.

Guideline #4: Practice Theology

We should also reflect on how God is asserted to be an intimate part of the specific practice, for our approaches are considered to be the means

---

83. Dettoni, "What Is Spiritual Formation?," 17; Felder, "Counsel from Wise Others," 104.

84. Deison, "Spiritual Formation through Small Groups," 270.

85. Elias, *Foundations and Practice of Adult Religious Education*, 235; Wimberly and Parker, "In Search of Wisdom," 17.

86. Elias, *Foundations and Practice of Adult Religious Education*, 234; Erasmus, "Handbook of the Militant Christian," 92; Smith, "Forming Wisdom through Cultural Rootedness," 53.

through which God can work more effectively in our lives and our world.[87] For instance, some practices, such as reading or hearing scripture as well as prayer, are asserted to be the direct means through which to be in relationship with God.[88] Similarly, our vocations and missions are understood to be the ways that we not only give back to God but also how God gives to our world through us.[89]

Noting the theology of the specific practice can therefore help us to know whether it is a good avenue to choose for our program based upon where we believe God is more or less active in our communities. This guideline is essentially the core one mentioned above: we should seek to foster those movements that are more embodying of God and discourage/transform those that are less manifesting of the Divine. Knowing the theology of each practice, then, can help us to better discern if it will fulfill these aims. Will it foster the godly movements and alter the non-godly ones? Such theological considerations are therefore a help guideline.

Guideline #5: The Changes That It Fosters

Next, we can also reflect on how the specific intervention is understood to foster change in the people that we are working with. For instance, using real-life simulations—such as case examples and drama scenarios—are asserted to foster change by closely approximating actual experiences.[90] Similarly, some narrative theologians and ethicists look to the use of stories as an important practice because they "rekindle experiences, allowing them to live in our imaginations."[91] Many other practices—such as imitation, prayers, acquisition of knowledge, self-reflection, and service—have all been discussed in terms of the formative changes that they foster among their practitioners.[92]

87. Dettoni, "What Is Spiritual Formation?," 18.

88. Hull, *Complete Book of Discipleship*, 47; Whitney, "Teaching Scripture Intake," 165.

89. Hull, *Complete Book of Discipleship*, 191; Ryken, "Puritan Model," 50.

90. Elias, *Foundations and Practice of Adult Religious Education*, 253.

91. O'Connell, *Making Disciples*, 174.

92. Erasmus, "Handbook of the Militant Christian," 35; Hull, *Complete Book of Discipleship*, 191; Lawrenz, *Dynamics of Spiritual Formation*, 88–89, 133; McCallum and Lowery, *Organic Disciplemaking*, 207; Meye, "Imitation of Christ," 199; O'Connell, *Making Disciples*, 144–45; Payne, "Personal Healing and Spiritual Formation," 219–20; Piper, "God Is Most Glorified in Us," 81; Wimberly and Parker, "In Search of Wisdom," 14.

Building a Home

For our own programs, we have deeply explored and analyzed the theories of change related to our community. The interventions that we choose should therefore align with the kinds of changes that we are seeing as they are the means by which to foster such transformations. For instance, if we have discerned that Gilligan's model of moral development accurately capture the kinds of growth that our seniors group is transitioning through, then we need to choose approaches that are asserted to foster them. Such change dynamics therefore need to be considered by us as we reflect on the effects of specific practices.

Guideline #6: Necessary Resources and Supports

Finally, we can also consider the resources and supports that any given intervention needs in order to be effectively implemented. It would not be very helpful for us to choose a particular practice and show up to our congregation and realize that we do not have the adequate materials, support, or experiences needed to facilitate it. Any consideration of an approach must therefore account for these necessary supports for they can dramatically impact not only whether or not the intervention will be used, but also how it is engaged if implemented.[93] We must also consider whether or not our community has the capabilities to engage in the practice being considered.[94] For instance, attempting to lead a group of three-year-olds through a thirty-minute-long centering prayer session would not be advisable because they do not have the developmental capacities or attention spans to sit silently and motionless for that length of time. Many practitioners have therefore discussed the appropriate methods and means that are commonly needed to use particular practices such as prayer, rituals, music, combating temptations, imaginative and narrative-based approaches, and the like.[95]

Additionally, we should not only consider the resources and capacities that are needed for each practice, but also the amount of support that it will need in order to be implemented.[96] For instance, we might reflect

---

93. Diamond, *Designing and Assessing Courses and Curricula*, 131.
94. Ibid., 200.
95. Erasmus, "Handbook of the Militant Christian," 81; Hunt, "Teaching People to Pray"; McCallum and Lowery, *Organic Disciplemaking*, 131; O'Connell, *Making Disciples*, 4, 133–35, 176; Parker, "Singing Hope in the Key of Wisdom"; Wilhoit, "Following the Lord's Pattern of Prayer."
96. Beitler, *Strategic Organizational Change*, 101.

PART TWO: Methodological Movements

on whether our local community is able to support the intervention: What are the limits to their time and energies? Do they really support the practice that we are considering? What about the structure and organization of the community, is it well suited to incorporate the intervention?[97] Also, we might wonder whether we have or need adequate guidance from a mentor who is experienced with the practice. Each of these resource and support details therefore needs to be explored when considering each specific practice.

Overall, then, any methodology for choosing a set of approaches needs to review at least these six sets of guidelines for each of the specific practices that they are considering. Generally, it is a matter of thinking about where the intervention came from, what its potential impact might be anthropologically, theologically, and transformationally, and the resources that are needed to embody it. These six guidelines will therefore become a central part of the practical steps that we will now explore.

Methodological Movements

Our theoretical foundations have helped to better understand what the core aims of our interventions are: to be the means through which the Spirit moves us and our communities toward the ideals that we have discerned. To help in the choosing of such practices, we have also seen how models—particularly our five core areas (anthropologies, etc.)—can help us have a better idea of which specific kinds of approaches to begin considering. We have seen a brief sketch of the broad landscape of core and specific interventions that are available to us in the Western Christian tradition and we have learned of some of the guidelines that we need to consider in the choosing of specific approaches.

We are now able to turn our attention to drawing all of these foundations together and assert a series of practical steps for using models as an integral part of our spiritual formation program development. It is through these steps that we actually design and build the nurturing home that God is working with us to create. As with the exploration and analysis methodologies, these five steps represent some of the major movements that we can look to for guidance when discerning a set of interventions to use in our formative contexts. You may find that your own use of them may vary from situation to situation both in the extent to which you use them and in the order in which they are presented. As always, returning

---

97. Ibid., 107.

our spiritually centered KISS principle, the most important thing is for our approaches to further foster the life of the Spirit who ever seeks to move us toward the horizons that we have discerned.

As a part of helping us to more fully understand how these steps might be embodied, we will be looking to one representative case example of how these steps have been used. We will be following the work of Min, a pastor of religious education and spiritual formation.[98] She has been asked by her denomination to develop a fifteen-week program to teach local lay leaders about the basics of religious education and spiritual formation ministry. The overall hopes of this program are to introduce them to the theoretical and practical foundations of these kinds of ministry. In what follows, we will see how Min uses these steps to help her to design and implement the educational interventions that she ultimately does for this program. Overall, they are intended to provide us with practical insights into each of the five steps.

Step One: Brainstorming with the Five Core Models

We can begin our design and implementation methodologies by turning to the possibilities that our five core models can generate. As we may recall, the purpose of our interventions is to move our communities from where they currently are—anthropologically, cosmologically, and developmentally—toward the ideals that we have come to discern. Our five core areas can therefore be used to help us to brainstorm what the broader range of possible approaches might be that we can and should be considering.[99]

For instance, let us assume that we seeking to formatively address the "mind, body, and heart" of a group of seniors that we are working with. Each of these anthropological elements can then become the basis for our brainstorming all of the different ways that we can engage them. We might pair them up in dyads and have them share with each other how their lives are going in order to help address their emotional health and vitality. We might travel with them to the Holy Land to help increase their knowledge and experiential bases. And we might invite a yoga instructor to help them

---

98. As with the previous case examples, the names, details, and locations of all information herein have been changed for confidentiality reasons. All details relating to "Min's" case have been taken from notes, files, and reflections that she generated in preparation for this course.

99. Elias, *Foundations and Practice of Adult Religious Education*, 227; O'Connell, *Making Disciples*, 15–16; Radillo, "Model of Formation in the Multi-Cultural Urban Context," 169.

with physical strength and resilience. Depending on what our ideals are for each of these anthropological areas, we can therefore use each of its elements to help us brainstorm all the different interventions to consider.

We can also think about the specific goals for our program and look at how our interventions tangibly support and foster these goals. "If, for example," Diamond reflects on curriculum development for schools, "speaking skills are identified as a basic competency that every student must have by graduation, public speaking must be initially taught and then reinforced, and no student should be able to graduate without receiving appropriate instruction and practice in this skill."[100] The goals we have can therefore further help us to think about the kinds of interventions that our program will need to achieve its desired ends.

We find another example of this kind of brainstorming in Valerie Isenhower and Judith Todd's book on spiritual discernment, *Living into the Answers*. The core ideal they note for discernment is "listening to God, walking in God's way, and choosing life and possibilities."[101] It requires, they assert, that we "become skilled in listening for God and paying attention to the ways God speaks to us." A possible approach stemming directly from this ideal is for us to therefore be centered on listening for what we believe "God's longings" are for us in relation to each decision.[102] Also, they explore how our childhood and past experiences can contribute to our images of God; images that can profoundly influence how we approach discernment.[103] As a result, they recommend that we critically reflect on these images.[104]

We can begin to see from this how our five core models can lead to our considering various approaches. In this way, we can turn to each of them as a source for such brainstorming. We might also find, through these brainstorms, that we need to return to the previous methodologies and modify our core models in order to have the greater depth of understanding that such reflections need. Or, we might realize that we need to modify a part of one of our models. We must therefore be open to such promptings, in spiritually discerning ways, for they can help to further strengthen our program development.

---

100. Diamond, *Designing and Assessing Courses and Curricula*, 85.
101. Isenhower and Todd, *Living into the Answers*, 17.
102. Ibid., 16.
103. Ibid., 29.
104. Ibid., 37.

The people we are working with should, whenever possible and where appropriate, also be a part of these brainstorming sessions. What are their ideas for what we should collectively be doing? What have they done in the past to help with the kinds of spiritual formation we are hoping to foster in the program that we are trying to design and build? As formators, our work should be collaborative, and brainstorming is yet another way to include our communities in our program development.

We can also look back to the general and specific approaches that were briefly outlined above. Or we can also look to the practices that our specific communities and religious traditions are already using. Do any of these seem to resonate for us? Which ones appear to address one or more of our five core models? These landscape and communal resources can therefore be additional fuel for our brainstorming sessions.

At this point in the process, it is not yet important to closely critique the interventions that emerge. Approaching this step in a spiritually discerning way, we should rather list as many as we think are viably possible. What is the fuller range of interventions that we believe God is inviting us to consider? It is then in the coming steps that we will be compiling, refining, and ultimately choosing the specific interventions to finally implement. In this step, however, we are only seeking to uncover the fuller range of possible approaches that we might consider.

Min's Big Brainstorm

Following the exploration and analysis steps detailed in the last chapter, Min took some time to develop her understandings of each of the five core areas. She then sat down to brainstorm what some of the possible approaches might be to help her lay leader course to achieve the ideals that it has set out. Table 5 below shows the results of this brainstorming session and all of the potential interventions that it yielded.

PART TWO: Methodological Movements

Table 5. Min's Five Core Model Brainstorming Results

Five Areas	Descriptions	Possible Approaches
Ideals	<ul><li>Overall<ul><li>The primary purposes of this course are to introduce you to the theoretical and practical foundations of religious education and spiritual formation</li></ul></li><li>Subject<ul><li>Shows knowledge and understanding of the core theoretical foundations of Christian education and formation</li><li>Demonstrates understanding and appropriate uses of formation pedagogies</li><li>Follows God's movements as the subject unfolds</li></ul></li><li>Individual<ul><li>Demonstrates critical thinking, analysis, reflection skills</li><li>Demonstrates clear communication</li><li>Demonstrates the ability to design, implement, and reflect on a formation program in accordance with one's unique calling</li><li>Shows willingness to encounter and engage with diversity</li><li>Shows commitment to serving wider community and world</li><li>Demonstrates adequate self-care and tending to one's own formation</li><li>Ability to integrate the material into one's own life</li></ul></li><li>Interpersonal<ul><li>Teamwork, collegiality</li><li>Friendships</li></ul></li><li>Whole Class<ul><li>Open, supportive, safe environment</li><li>Is inclusive of diversity, particularly: learning styles, cultural, and theological/religious</li></ul></li></ul>	<ul><li>Readings</li><li>Lectures</li><li>Experiencing pedagogies in class for each level—should experience all four kinds (knowledge, reflection, action, stillness) for each one</li><li>Doing pedagogies on their own</li><li>Reflection papers/practices = linking with local ministries as well as with personal vocation/interests</li><li>Small groups and dyads</li><li>Classroom discussions = modeling inclusivity, openness</li></ul>

Five Areas	Descriptions	Possible Approaches

Anthropologies	• Kinds of students expected
	  ▫ Mix of experiences in RE/SF ministry—some new, some longtime educators/formators
	• Diverse backgrounds
	  ▫ Theological
	  ▫ Cultural, ethnic
	  ▫ Life stages
	  ▫ Learning styles (multiple intelligences?), personality types (MBTI—sensing, intuiting, feeling, thinking; artists, rationals, guardians, idealists)
	• Subject Itself = Introduction/Overview of Formation
	  ▫ Theory and Pedagogies
	  ▫ Have to experience it to understand
	  ▫ Need experiences in using it = praxis-oriented
	  ▫ More of a didactic course, a passing on of knowledge
		• Need to apply the theories
		• Draw on life experiences
		• Foster sharing of diversity and viewpoints in formation
		• Need to have multiple kinds of pedagogies for different learning styles
		• Need for more knowledge intensive approaches:
		• Readings
		• Lectures
		• Handouts
		• PowerPoints
		• Websites
		• Biblio lists

Theologies	• God as the author and finisher of Formation
	  ▫ Need to detail this out for all three levels:
	    ▪ God as Transcendent
	    ▪ God as Immanent
	    ▪ God as Personal
	• God as working in this course via:
	  ▫ Development of the subject from class to class
	  ▫ In the student's past and current formation experiences
	  ▫ In the student's relationships
	  ▫ In the class as a whole
		• Communal discernment and listening approaches
		• Allowing the subject to develop in me, the students, and in the class as a whole
		• Watching and sitting with "God's movements" in student's sharing, in dyads/Small Groups (SGs), and in class dynamics as a whole

PART TWO: Methodological Movements

Five Areas	Descriptions	Possible Approaches
Theories of Change	• Perry's model of diversity development = from dualistic thinking to self-differentiation in the midst of paradoxes • Subject forming in the students; cognitive development = initial exposure, then growing out branches, then adding details • Relationships/Teamwork = forming, norming, storming, performing • Class as a whole (much more minor for this subject/course)	• Introducing various positions and working with them to explore them and locate self • Repetitiveness with increasing complexity • Discern if forming set SGs/Dyads is desirable, then build relationships in these
Cosmologies	• Creation is pregnant with Your life => fundamentally good • Ministry context => very busy, high expectations/stress • Political/Theological stance of region	• Look for/nurture positive movements • Lower course requirements if needed • Diversity exposure • Need to address formation of the formator = "self-care"

We can see from this that each of the five core models are given in some detail. The ideals and anthropological explorations included not only the students, their relationships with one another, and the class as a whole, but also the subject that they were to be exploring itself. The theologies sought to briefly detail some of the ways that she considered God to be an intimate part of the course, while the cosmologies and theories of change reflections drew on external models as well as the ethnographic observations and experiences of Min.

Based upon these models, Min brainstormed approaches in relation to each area. For instance, it was observed in the cosmological reflections that the work of the lay leaders is sometimes a place of high stress and expectations for students because of their having to juggle their church ministry along with their regular jobs. One of the possible approaches that resulted from these reflections, as we can see in the right column, was the need for this class to intentionally address self-care and "formation of the formator." We can also see in the anthropological reflections how the potential diversity of the class raised the need for approaches that intentionally integrate this aspect into the course. Each one of the five core models that Min developed therefore became a source for to begin brainstorming the kinds of approaches that her course might need.

In addition to these reflections, Min also additionally considered some of the core approaches that are available. These reflections are shown

Building a Home

below in table 6. These explorations sought to do so in light of the traditions of the courses that her denomination regularly offers to lay leaders, seeking to better outline and understand their possible contributions to her particular class. This therefore provides us with a concrete example of how each of the five core models, and the landscape of possible approaches from ones own tradition, can help us to brainstorm the range of interventions that our programs might draw from.

Table 6. Min's Core Approaches Brainstorming

Five Areas	Descriptions	Possible Approaches

Core Approaches	• Knowledge
	  ▫ Nature of these classes = cultivating wisdom => seeking experiential/practical/intuitive wisdom of formation
	• Reflection
	  ▫ Personal: To help internalize and relate material to own life
	  ▫ Vocation: Synthesis and integration with ministry vocation
	• Action
	  ▫ To experience the material
	  ▫ To actualize in one's own personal/unique ways
	  ▫ To praxis-learning from actions
	• Stillness
	  ▫ To let the material soak in and gel on its own
	  ▫ To rest and rejuvenate so that we might be fresher for more material
	• End of class projects/papers
	  ▫ Common in these classes
		• Knowledge
		  ▫ Lectures
		  ▫ Readings
		  ▫ Sharing
		• Reflection
		  ▫ Reflection papers
		  ▫ Journaling
		  ▫ Use of arts—drawing, music, videos, collages, movements, stories
		• Action
		  ▫ Project
		  ▫ Class practices/pedagogies
		  ▫ Visiting formative sites different from one's own background
		• Stillness
		  ▫ Contemplative practices
		  ▫ Sabbath practices
		  ▫ Trips to holy, restful, sacred sites
		  ▫ Rituals with materials

We may also recall from above that these reflections can be as detailed or sparse as we have the time or energy for. Min could have conducted much more extensive research and made many more detailed observations in relation to each of the five core models for her class. For some of our formative endeavors, such detail may be required, while for other applications only a brief sketch is needed. We must therefore be very discerning in how much time and energy to invest into these core model reflections.

PART TWO: Methodological Movements

Step Two: Compiling and Reducing the Possible Approaches

Due to the extensive amount of information that the previous step can result in, it can seem like a sort of explosion of data as it did for Min. This step is therefore directed more toward weeding through, pruning down, organizing, and compiling this knowledge so that it can be more useful for us in our final discernment of which interventions to actually implement. There are two movements to this step that will be very helpful for reducing this mass amount of possibilities. Overall, our spiritually discerning question is: What are the more narrow range of possible approaches that God is wanting us to focus on right now?

Compilation Categories

To help us toward these ends, we can categorize all of the possible approaches that we have brainstormed so far in various ways. For instance, we can look to the general and specific landscape of interventions that was sketched above. Using these as categories, we can compile all of the possible interventions that we have just brainstormed according to them. With our senior group, for example, we might be considering a Bible study, watching a movie, and traveling to the Holy Land. All of these could be grouped together under the knowledge category of core approaches.

Or, we might categorize each of the brainstormed applications according to our ideals. If we will remember, the primary aims of our interventions are to help our communities to move toward these ends. We might therefore find it helpful to link the interventions that we are now considering with one or more of these goals. Regardless of which method of categorizing we may choose, doing this can help us to see where there may be overlap and redundancy among these many interventions.

Reducing the Possibilities

Once we have this compiled list, we can then begin to eliminate and merge our possibilities. Our intentions here are to reduce the number of possible approaches so that we can better choose from among the more viable interventions in the coming steps. At this point, however, we do not want to drop approaches just for the sake of reducing their numbers. Instead, we are seeking to: (1) merge together those approaches that are essentially the same; and (2) eliminate those interventions that are redundant.

Building a Home

If we were seeking to help an administrative committee in church to engage in their tasks in more spiritually discerning ways according to Isenhower and Todd's book, for example, we might have brainstormed a number of practices that are intended to foster the kinds of deep listening that they assert are needed. The approaches we brainstormed might have been: having members to practice listening to one another; having them meditate on scripture passages; or encouraging them to take time to reflect on what is stirring within themselves. Being grouped under the reflection category, we might then seek to further merge these practices into one by having members meditate on a passage, listen for what stirs within them, and then pairing them up to share with each other their experiences. In this way, we can seek to decrease the larger number of possible approaches that our brainstorming session has generated.

Min Simplifies Her Possibilities

Table 7 below shows the approaches that Min compiled as a result of her five core model reflections. She has chosen to list them along side the course ideals, because she has chosen to categorize them according to both of the suggestions that were made above, as we shall see. In this first format, we can see the range of approaches being categorized according to four of the five core areas of our landscape. We can see that she has compiled and reduced most of the approaches she brainstormed into only one of these categories with none of the practices repeating across them. This has allowed her to see more clearly both the number of approaches she is considering as well as how well each of these categories of core approaches is covered. Immediately, we can notice that the knowledge and reflection categories have the most number of approaches. Min affirms this because the overall aim of the course is one primary of introducing her students to religious education and spiritual formation ministry and then reflecting on and integrating it into their ministries. With such an ideal being inherently one of education and reflection, we would therefore expect the interventions to favor these two categories.

PART TWO: Methodological Movements

Table 7. Compiled Goals and Approaches for an Introductory TSF Class

	Ideals for Each Area	Compiled Approaches
Course Goals & Compiled Approaches from Above	<ul><li>Subject<ul><li>Shows knowledge and understanding of the core theoretical foundations of Formation</li><li>Demonstrates understanding and appropriate uses of formation pedagogies</li><li>Follows God's movements as the subject unfolds</li><li>Demonstrates critical thinking, analysis, reflection skills</li></ul></li><li>Individual<ul><li>Demonstrates critical thinking, analysis, reflection skills</li><li>Demonstrates clear communication</li><li>Practitioner: Demonstrates ability to design, implement, and reflect on a formation program in accordance with one's unique calling</li><li>Academic: Demonstrates knowledge and use of research methods according to one's own vocation and interests</li><li>Shows willingness to encounter and engage with diversity (Perry/Cog. developmental model)</li><li>Shows commitment to serving wider community and world</li><li>Demonstrates adequate self-care and tending to one's own formation</li><li>Ability to integrate the material into one's own life</li></ul></li><li>Interpersonal<ul><li>Teamwork, collegiality</li><li>Friendships</li></ul></li><li>Whole Class<ul><li>Open, supportive, safe environment</li><li>Is inclusive of diversity, particularly: learning styles, cultural, and theological/religious</li></ul></li></ul>	<ul><li>Knowledge<ul><li>Readings</li><li>Lectures</li><li>Handouts</li><li>Observations of a formative community</li><li>Exposure to diverse views in class and course materials</li><li>Diverse pedagogies for diverse learning styles</li><li>Own research</li><li>Increasing repetitiveness & complexity as course develops</li><li>Defining methods and sources for final projects/papers</li><li>Detail importance of formative work</li></ul></li><li>Reflection<ul><li>Self-reflection/ location papers</li><li>Final project/paper</li><li>Small groups/dyads</li><li>Class discussions</li><li>Discernment processes: individual, interpersonal, communal</li><li>Students applying material to their own life = create a mini-formative program?</li><li>Use of narrative pedagogies</li></ul></li><li>Action/Experience<ul><li>Subject's pedagogies engaged in class</li><li>Doing pedagogies on own</li></ul></li><li>Stillness<ul><li>Contemplative practices and classroom environment</li></ul></li></ul>

In addition to compiling these approaches according these categories, Min also decided to use her ideals in a like manner. Shown below in table 8, we can clearly see which approaches appear to Min to foster each specific goal that she has for the course. Categorizing them in this way is useful because it can help Min to ensure that her program is intentionally seeking to address each one of the ideals that she has discerned. It can also help her, as we shall see in a moment, to see which approaches may be redundant. One of the drawbacks to this approach, however, is that approaches—such as lecture—are listed across multiple goals making it difficult to know how many practices she is really considering. Nevertheless, both ways of categorizing our brainstormed interventions can be helpful in our quest to reduce the number that we have.

In this performing this step, Min also reduces and compiles some of the approaches from her first list above. For instance, looking at the knowledge interventions, she has combined "lecture," "diverse pedagogies for diverse learning styles," and "increasing repetitiveness and complexity as course develops" all into just "lecture." Min therefore plans on ensuring that her lectures address these concerns in intentional ways. Merging these together has therefore helped her to better understand the kind of lectures that she will need to give. They have helped her to gain a better sense of the kinds of interactions that she will need to have with our students in order for her course to be more successful. In short, these compilations and reductions are helping Min to clarify what her class should like when it is concretely enacted.

PART TWO: Methodological Movements

Table 8. Min's Course Goals and Their Supporting Interventions

Level	Goals	Approaches	Evaluate/ Assessment Tools
Subject	Shows knowledge and understanding of the core theoretical foundations of Formation	• Lecture • Readings • Handouts	• Self-reflection papers • Final Proj/Prog
	Demonstrates understanding and appropriate uses of formation pedagogies	• All: Individual mini-formation project • Practitioners: Final Program	• mini-formation reflection paper • final prog reflection report

	Follows God's movements as the subject unfolds	• Prof:
		  ▫ Ignatian Disc
		  ▫ Following the consoling movements of life
		  ▫ Adherence to ethics of justice, peace, truth, care
		• Students/Class:
		  ▫ Individual/Communal Discernment processes
			• mid/end course eval's
			• prof observations

Level	Goals	Approaches	Evaluate/ Assessment Tools
Individual	Demonstrates critical thinking, analysis, reflection skills	• Lecture • Group/Class discussions and questions	• Self-reflection papers • Final proj/prog
	Demonstrates clear communication	• Discussions	• Self-reflection papers • Group/class discussions
	Demonstrates ability to design, implement, and reflect on a formation program in accordance with one unique calling	• Rubric for final formation project	• Class Project—formation program
	Shows willingness to encounter and engage with diversity; Perry/Cog. development	• Visiting a formation site different from one's own religious/theological tradition • Participation and active listening in small groups and class discussions in positive, open, and supportive ways/behaviors	• Site visit reflection paper • Self-reflection and location assignments
	Shows commitment to serving wider community and world	• Lecture • Class/group discussions	• Choice of project/program done in connection with underserved populations or under addressed research areas
	Demonstrates adequate self-care and tending to one's own formation	• Individual mini-formation project	• Self-reflection paper on mini-proj and self-care
	Ability to integrate the material into one's own life	• Lecture • Class discussions • Reflection assignments	• Final proj/prog • self-reflection papers
Interpersonal	Teamwork, collegiality Friendships	• Practices of getting to know and work with one another • Small groups/dyads	• mid/end-course evaluations • prof observations

PART TWO: Methodological Movements

Level	Goals	Approaches	Evaluate/ Assessment Tools
Class	Open, supportive, safe environment	• Lecture • Readings • Group/class discussions	• mid/end course evals • prof observations
	Is inclusive of diversity, particularly: learning styles, cultural, and theological/religious	• Use of varied pedagogies = "praxis" pedagogies • Use of diverse materials: culturally, theology/religious	• mid/end course evals • prof observations

In light of these two sets of categorization and reduction, Min finally compiles the remaining approaches that she is considering. In particular, she decides to focus on the following:

- Knowledge
  - Lecture
  - Readings—draw from diverse materials: culturally and theologically/religiously
  - Small group/class discussions (active listening)
- Reflection
  - Professor, student, and class discernment processes
  - Self-reflection papers:
    - Student background and "What is formation?" reflection paper
    - Site visit reflection paper = Site Visit to a Formational community different from one's own tradition
    - Mini-formation/self-care reflection paper
- Action/Experience
  - Final Formation Project
- Stillness
  - (active/contemplative listening)
  - (self-care paper)

We can see that she has managed to narrow the range of potential approaches down to just six interventions that she will use in her course: lecture, readings, discussions, discernment, reflection paper, and the final project. Looking back at her course goals, she feels not only that these interventions will help her and her students to journey toward the ideals but also that they are realistically manageable (i.e., there are not too many of them). She therefore decides to move onto the next step and detail each one of these.

Step Three: Detail Each Intervention

Once we have narrowed down the possibilities of approaches to use, we can begin looking at each one of them in greater detail. As we noted in the theoretical section on guidelines above for the specific practices that we are considering, we can and should note the histories, intended aims, anthropological foci, theologies, theories of change, and resources that are needed in relation to each one.[105] Overall, our spiritually discerning question is: What is it that God wants to know about each practice in order to discern if and how it will be used?

While this may seem like a lot to do, we must remember that we can always discerningly adapt it to fit with our time and energy constraints. For instance, if we are considering practices that we know very well and use on a regular basis, then these kinds of reflections will likely not be necessary. At any rate, the purposes of considering these six guidelines in this step are twofold.

Exploring Potentials

First, this information will help us to more clearly determine the extent to which each of these interventions might formatively influence our communities. We are interested in the potential that each one has for helping our program to attain the ideals that we have discerned. For example, if one of the ideals that we have for our seniors group is to increase their scriptural knowledge, we can ask whether a bible study, a movie, or a trip to the Holy Land might be most effective toward achieving these ends. If some of our members could not afford to travel, then that option might be eliminated unless additional funding resources were available. Also,

---

105. See page 190.

we might come to find, in reflecting on a practice's history in relation to our community, that our group has done numerous bible studies over the years and are now yearning for different ways of engaging with Scripture. Knowing the guidelines for each of these possibilities can therefore help us to better see the potential that each intervention might have toward helping us to achieve our program's ideals.

Anticipating Adaptations

The second purpose for using the guidelines to explore each approach is to help us to know what kinds of adaptations may be needed in order to use each of them. For instance, if we were considering using centering prayer with our youth group, knowing the details about this practice can help us to better adapt and apply it to this particular community. In essence, this step therefore entails our beginning to think more concretely about what will be needed to actually implement our program.

Min's Details

Since Min has facilitated many educational programs in the past that have used similar sorts of interventions, she did not spend too much time exploring each one in relation to the guidelines. However, she did briefly reflect on them as they related to this particular application. Table 9 below shows the results of her reflections.

Table 9. Min's Guideline Reflections

Practice	History (local)	Intended Aims	Anthro. Foci	Theology	Theory of Change	Supports
Lecture	Commonly used/expected in these courses	Passing knowledge via words, images, music, videos, stories, etc	Subject itself Mind, cognitive Sometimes affective	God is active in through this medium; Ex: sermons	Hearing → Doing → Being	Multimedia as needed
Readings	Commonly used/expected in these courses	Passing knowledge via written text and images	Subject itself Mind, cognitive Sometimes affective	We can encounter God while we read; Ex: Lectio	Reading → Doing → Being	Photocopies
Discussions	Commonly used/expected in these courses	Passing knowledge via conversation Self-reflection Communication skills Diversity exposure Class environment	Subject itself Mind, cognitive Sometimes affective Relationships: small groups and class-wide	"Wherever two or more are gathered …" God is active in the ideas that develop via our conversations	Perry's = exposure to diversity leads to less dualistic thinking	Room set-up to facilitate such conversations = "round table" type of set-up
Dscrnmnt	Not explicitly engaged in courses → will need to be explained	Individually and collectively following God's lead in our class	Individuals Dyads, small groups Class as a whole	God guides us in our discernment of him	Abiding in and following Christ → spiritual growth/maturity	Willingness on the student's part to engage in this both individually and collectively
Reflection Papers	Commonly used/expected in these courses	Self-reflection Experiential engagement with the material Critical thinking Integrating material into one's life/ministries	Cognitive Affective Vocational	God is active in our reflections, yearnings, insights, etc.	Reflecting → Doing → Being	Student willingness

PART TWO: Methodological Movements

Practice	History (local)	Intended Aims	Anthro. Foci	Theology	Theory of Change	Supports
Final Project	Commonly used/expected in these courses	Experiential engagement with the material Critical thinking Integration of the material into one's life/ministries	Cognitive Affective Vocational	God is active in our actions	Doing → Being	Student willingness

We can see that these reflections help her to further ensure that these particular interventions will cover the specific and unique needs of her particular program. Not only do they help her to note the history of each as they have been commonly used in courses such as the one she will be facilitating, but they also help her to further confirm that they will address the ideals and anthropological areas she has discerned. For instance, she more deeply sees how lectures, readings, and discussions are intended to help the students to not only learn more about the subject, but also that they can additionally impact the affective side of her students. Reflecting on this helps Min to remember that using stories, images, and metaphors—one of our four specific practices—should be a cornerstone of her lectures.

These reflections have also prompted her to reflect, briefly at least, on where and how God can formatively act in her program if she does decide to use them. Min takes care to ensure that each of the theological areas she outlined with her core model are being addressed by these interventions. If we recall from above, for her God was active in the subject itself, in each student's formational experiences, in their relationships, as well as in the class as a whole. Looking at the theology column above, she confirms that each one of these areas is being addressed by one or more of the interventions that she is considering.

She has also taken care to make sure that these specific approaches foster the kinds of transformation her program is seeking and that their practical implementation is possible in terms of the resources and supports that they need. These guidelines, as we can see more clearly through Min's case, can therefore help us to ensure that each of the needs of our program are being intentionally met by the specific practices that we are considering. So, with the strong and thorough foundations that these first three steps, Min is now in a position to discern whether she will use all of these, part of them, or whether others are additionally needed.

Step Four: Choose the Interventions to Use

Having used our guidelines as a set of lenses through which to detail each of the interventions we are considering, we are now in a position to decide upon which ones we will actually be implementing. In effect, our core discernment question here is which of these interventions is God inviting us to formatively participate with the Spirit's life in our midst. Through which means does the Sacred want to transform our constituents? Which of these interventions do we believe are going to be most effective in helping us to achieve the ideals that we have set before us? This step is therefore directly oriented toward engaging in our spiritual discernment processes, in light of the three previous steps, and choosing the interventions to use.

As guidelines for such discernment, as we have seen, the interventions should be directed toward anthropological areas we are interested in engaging. They should foster the kinds of transformations that we anticipate with our theories of change. They should intentionally work to nurture the movements that are more manifesting of God and eliminate/decrease those that are lesser so. We should have the resources and capacities to implement them, and, ultimately, they must move us toward the ideals that we are working toward. As we look back over the details that the previous step has generated, we should therefore have a much clearer idea of which of the interventions we are considering are best suited for the needs of our program.

Min Finalizes Her Syllabus

With so much work having gone into Min's detailed design and reflection work, she feels that the basic interventions that she has come to focus on will fulfill the needs and aims of her course. Confirming these with her own discernment process, she comes to realize that the primary focus of this step lies in more clearly deciding how each of these approaches will be implemented in her class. In reviewing the content of the course material, she comes to finalize her syllabus. The following is an excerpt from this syllabus showing the final interventions she has chosen to utilize:

PART TWO: Methodological Movements

- "There are three sets of assignments that will be used to both help you grow in this material and help me to evaluate the progress of this course:

  - Class Presence & Participation (10%)—Attendance in class is important for a number of reasons. First, many of the formative pedagogies that we will be exploring will be experienced during our class time together. Second, because all of us have a lifetime of formation experience, much of the learning in our class will also come via our small group and classroom discussions. Participation in these experiences/discussions is therefore a central component to our praxis learning.

  - Reflection Papers (20%)—Throughout the coming weeks, you will be asked to write three short reflection papers. The intention of these papers is for you to further reflect on how the material/experiences of this class connect with your own life and vocation as well as our wider world. Each of these must be between 2 and 5 pages, double spaced. They are the following:

    1. *Introductory Reflection*—For this first paper, you will be answering the question: "What does 'formation' mean to me?" This paper should include a discussion of how your understanding is linked to your cultural and religious background as well as to any significant formative experiences that you have had. The purpose of this paper is to provide me with a better understanding of you in relation to our class material.

    2. *Site Visit Reflection*—You will be expected to attend one formative "event" (e.g., scriptural study, worship service, lecture, service project, etc.) in a religious tradition other than your own and reflect on how you see some of the theories and pedagogies of our class present in this community. The purpose of this is to expose you to diversity and to help you to begin practicing the art of reflecting on how different communities embody formation.

    3. *Self-Care/Formation Reflection*—"How do you personally embody these theories and pedagogies in your own life? How can you do this more deliberately? How has this class changed your own formative journey? What kind of self-care do you currently engage in?" The goal of this paper is for you to reflect on how you might integrate the course material into your own life.

- Final Project (70%)—The primary purposes of the final project are for you to demonstrate your understanding of the course material and to further integrate this class into your vocational development. Using the theories and formative pedagogies of this course, design and implement a formation program that may be used either in your own personal life or in the community in which you are ministering. In your report (10–15 pages), you will discuss the theoretical bases for your program, how the program was carried out and evaluated, and what the results were."

We can see from her syllabus that Min's discernment of which interventions to use have not changed significantly. She is still planning on using lectures, discussions, readings, reflection papers, and a final project. The final intervention, "discernment," is one that she has decided to facilitate in class. What has changed in this fourth step for her, however, is the level of detail that each of these approaches now has. She therefore not only knows what the general interventions will be for her course, but also how they will be concretely implemented throughout the fifteen-week class.

Step Five: Final Planning and Implementation

Once we have considered all of the possibilities for our discernment and made a decision about which applications to engage, we next begin the task of working out the details for what it will take to implement them. This step therefore essentially entails the logistics and planning that is needed in order to ensure a successful and more spiritually formative program. Once we know what it is that our house will look like, and the materials that will be needed, we next need to begin gathering them together and start our construction. Toward these ends, there are two final considerations to make before actually implementing the program.

Steps to Achieve Progress?

Termed "tactics," by Beitler, these are the "steps that must be taken to execute the strategic plan."[106] Here, we need to think about all of the movements that will be needed in order for our interventions to be imple-

---

106. Beitler, *Strategic Organizational Change*, 101.

mented. How will they be introduced? Carried out? Is there any follow up that may be needed after our program is finished? Questions such as these can help to guide this last phase of planning. The general discernment question here is one of details: What are the specific and concrete steps that will be needed in order to carry out the program?

For instance, if we did finally decide to travel with our seniors to the Holy Land, what are all of the "nuts and bolts" kinds of details that will be needed actually go there? Which flights will we take to travel there and back? Where will we stay? Where will we eat each one of our meals? Et cetera. It is this level of detail that we must consider before our program can be implemented.

Resources/Support Needed?

A second major consideration for the logistics of our applications are the resources and support that are needed in relation to them. In the third step above, we considered these supports for each of the practices we were looking at. In this final step, we therefore return to these concerns and actually begin pulling these resources together so that we may start our program. Not only do we need to consider this for the specific practices we have discerned, but also for the program as a whole. In other words, we might ask, do we and our communities have the supplies, space, time, staff, et cetera, necessary to support the program that we have discerned? Now is the time to ensure that we have everything we need to move to the final phase of this step: implementation.

Go for It! But First . . .

The last part of this step really needs no explanation, for it is the obvious one of doing what we have been preparing for all this time. Having potentially engaged in eleven distinctive steps between our exploration and analysis methodologies and the ones discussed in this chapter, we can finally implement our program. With so much spiritually discerning preparations, we can hoist our sails and let the winds of the Spirit move us and our communities toward the heavenly horizons that we have been joyfully invited. In other words, now is the time for us to go for it!

Before doing this, though, it would be wise to engage in the kinds of final reflections that our last set of methodologies, as well as some of our spiritual discernment authors, encouraged us to engage in. Specifically, we

Building a Home

should first step back for a "holy pause" and reflect on both the content and process of what has just transpired. As we look at the whole of the interventions we have just discerned and our program as it is about to be embodied, how we feel? What do we notice? Do we really believe that this program is as God wants it to be? Do we really feel that we were tracking the Spirit's movements throughout? Such final content and process discernment reflections should be just as integral to this methodology as they were for the previous one.

Finally, monitoring and evaluating the progress of our programs is also an important part of our implementations. The purpose of this ongoing data is to help us to continually update and modify our practices such that our formative interventions improve as we go.[107] Such considerations, however, are left for our final praxis-based set of methodologies discussed in the next chapter.

Min Prepares and Performs

Min spends the final weeks before the start of her course preparing for its kickoff. She finalizes her lecture notes and materials. She makes copies for her students. She contacts the location where the class will be held to ensure that the room is ready and that she has all of the multimedia equipment that she needs. In short, Min finalizes the details and gathers all of the resources that her class needs to be successful. After she has completed all of this, Min spends the remainder of her time praying for her soon-to-be students, reflecting on the processes she has just engaged, and enjoying what little Sabbath and stillness time she had before the first class.

Closing Reflections

In this chapter, we have sought to explore some of the methodologies for how to design and implement our program. To help us toward these ends, we explored the more fundamental aims of interventions, which were to the means through the Spirit moves us toward the ideals we have discerned. We then turned to our five core models in an effort to help us to better understand the details and dynamics of our formative program and what some of the possible approaches might subsequently be. Using each

---

107. Beitler, *Strategic Organizational Change*, 85; Diamond, *Designing and Assessing Courses and Curricula*, 107; Elias, *Foundations and Practice of Adult Religious Education*, 152, 195–96.

PART TWO: Methodological Movements

one of them as the basis for a fruitful brainstorming session, we therefore had an array of interventions to choose from.

However, in case we were not sure of the kinds of approaches that are available to us, we also briefly surveyed the landscape of interventions—both general and specific—commonly found in the Western Christian tradition. To help us further understand these and any practice that we might be considering, we then reviewed six guidelines. These are intended to help us to better know if a specific practice fits well with the needs of our particular program.

Based upon these theoretical foundations, we then walked through the five methodological steps of program design and implementation. Figure 10 below these steps as they have been presented herein. We can see that their general trend is a movement from the larger array of approaches that our initial brainstorming step generated toward a smaller and more effective set of interventions. In the end, these steps culminate in the concrete set of approaches that we actually implement in our local context.

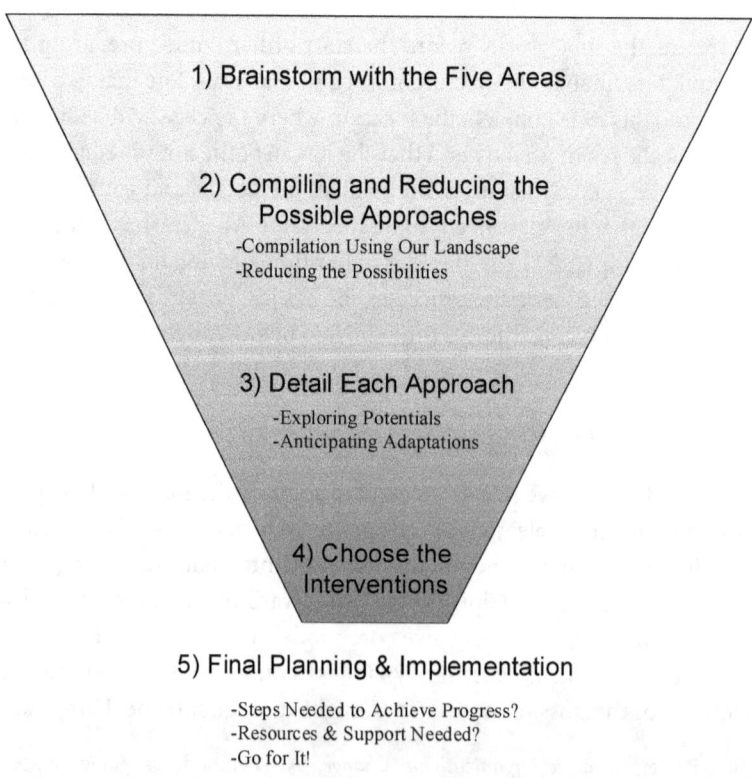

Figure 10. The Five Steps of Design and Implementation

Our program development methodologies, however, are not finished. In fact, as we shall see next, they should not be completed until our program is. For as we implement our interventions, we will inevitably encounter obstacles, changes, and unexpected events that will prompt us to modify what we have just designed. If we were to actually begin to build a house, we might find that the soil upon which it sits is weaker in some areas than in others. Realizations and unforeseen encounters such as these can prompt to modify what we have designed and how we are going about building it. In our final set of methodologies, then, we will see how to engage with these unexpected events as we continually assess and modify our program.

5

The Cycles of Ministry
Assessment and Modification Methodologies

LIFE... sometimes it seems like it goes round and round and round. Life is born, it lives, it dies, and new life is born again. Seasons come and go and come again. The sun rises, faithfully traverses the sky, and sets only to rise once again. Ministry itself can also be seen to have such a cyclical nature as weeks come and go, programs begin and end and begin again, and as the ups and downs of religious living endlessly wash upon us like waves on the beach.

We have now seen how the deep foundations that undergird our programs can help to lead to their design and implementation. As we begin to put all of our intensive planning and preparations into practice, we might be tempted to think that the bulk of our program development is finished. However, as we shall currently see, such is not the case because of the cyclical and ongoing nature these praxis-oriented movements. For as we implement or programs, there inevitably will be changes and adaptations that we will need to make to them as they unfold. These changes can therefore lead us to reconsider our deep explorations and analyses which can then prompt us to modify the interventions we are using, and the cycles of praxis, program development, and ministry continue on and on...

But how will we know if such changes are happening in our programs? How might we assess whether we need to revisit our foundations and modify our interventions? It is therefore the purpose of this chapter to explore these questions. We will be reviewing some of the ways that we can monitor, assess, and modify our programs as they are being implemented. Overall, our aims are to continually ensure that our program is heading in the directions that the Spirit is leading us in step by step. As these directions can change at any time, we need to continually assess and modify both deep foundations as well as our practical interventions. Just as with the previous chapters, we will be exploring such issues both theoretically and methodologically. Not only will we learn of the nature and basis of such assessments and modifications, but also some of the practical steps for embodying them in our spiritual formation program development.

Theoretical Foundations

As our spiritual formation KISS goal is to continually follow after the life and movements of the Spirit as we implement our programs, we must therefore have some ways of tracking these movements. We will therefore begin our theoretical explorations by briefly exploring some of the essentials of monitoring and evaluating our programs as they unfold. However, merely tracking our progress is not enough, for if we begin to see that our programs are developing in ways that we did not anticipate, then we additionally need to understand how modify the five core models of our explorations and analyses as well as the interventions that we discerned based on them. It is therefore in the sections below that we investigate these: how we might revisit and refine our models of our five core areas, and how we can reassess and modify the interventions that we have been using. These theoretical foundations will then become the basis for the practical steps to assessment and modification that are presented below.

Reflecting on Feedback: Basics of Monitoring and Evaluation

At the end of the last chapter, we heard of the importance of being able to observe and assess the formative work that we are have come to implement. Doing so is a central part of a praxis-oriented way of enacting spiritual formation. This is because if praxis entails critical reflection on experience and practice, as we heard in the second chapter, then we must have some ways of both gathering the experiential data that we will be reflecting on and assessing its relevance for our program and its progress. This section, then, offers a brief introduction and overview to these all important techniques of monitoring and evaluating our programs.

PART TWO: Methodological Movements

Why Monitor and Evaluate?

There are four basic reasons for why such data gathering and assessments are important. First, monitoring and evaluating allows for accountability to exist in relation to our programs. Being particularly important when resources are limited, assessments can help both us and the organizations we are a part of to more clearly know the extent to which our formative endeavors are successful.[1] Such evaluations can be made by comparing the ideals that were set from the beginning with the measured progress that our communities are observed to be making.[2] For instance, if one of our ideals was for our youth group to learn some of the commonly referred to stories from our religious and cultural traditions, then this can be evaluated by engaging them in discussions that ask them not only what they know about these stories but also what they think about them.[3] Assessments are therefore important because they can help to hold us accountable to the ideals that we had discerned through our exploration and analysis methodologies.

A second reason for monitoring and evaluating our programs is to help us to stay on track as it unfolds. Articulated clearly by Diamond, he writes, "The ongoing collection of good information will give you a clear sense of what is and is not working, and thus you'll have the opportunity to make adjustments immediately as problems occur."[4] The basic idea here is that such data can better help us to know how our interventions are working (or not) as we are engaging them. Rather than waiting until the very end of our program and then looking back to reflect, a well instituted monitoring and evaluation system can help our efforts to stay more on track toward the ends we have set ahead of us.[5] Such *in vivo* feedback can not only help us with unexpected situations that arise,[6] but it can also help us to be more sensitive and discerning of God's movements. In other words, such ongoing feedback should be an integral part of our continually discerning approaches to spiritual formation.

---

1. Elias, *Foundations and Practice of Adult Religious Education*, 270, 273.
2. Diamond, *Designing and Assessing Courses and Curricula*, 176–77; Schmuck, *Practical Action Research for Change*, 36.
3. For an example of these kinds of programs, see such authors as Wimberly, *Soul Stories*.
4. Diamond, *Designing and Assessing Courses and Curricula*, 176.
5. Ibid., 176–77.
6. Ibid., 164, 313.

The Cycles of Ministry

A third important reason, which is closely related to the second, is that such assessments help us to improve our interventions both now and in the future.[7] As our program comes to an end, we can look at the overall effectiveness of it and how it went.[8] Such reflections should help us to improve such things as a program's content, sequence, and pacing the next time such a program—or one like it—is implemented.[9] These reflections can also help us to decide whether or not to continue with specific interventions that we have used.[10] Monitoring and evaluating our programs can therefore help us to improve the interventions and programs that we are engaging.

The fourth and final reason for using systematic assessments is to provide vital feedback to both the formator and the people who are a part of the program. For formators, success can be understood as the extent to which the goals of the program have been realized and how our communities have been impacted.[11] For a theist, this means reflecting on how well we were a part of God's formative movements with the individuals and communities we were working with. These formative movements will have already been articulated in terms of the ideals, so it is to the goals that we can turn in helping us to discern our formative success.

For our constituents, such feedback has the purpose of helping both them and us to assess their progress as they participate in our programs.[12] It can aid them in better discerning how they are doing and where their growing edges may still lie.[13] This data can help them to see more clearly what has been changing for them and where they may be headed next.[14] Some people may need additional support and attention, and our monitoring and evaluation approaches should be able to identify these needs early on.[15] For instance, some of the youth in our group may not know the religious and cultural stories as well as they would like to, so we may need to spend extra time and create additional interventions to help them

---

7. Elias, *Foundations and Practice of Adult Religious Education*, 270.

8. Diamond, *Designing and Assessing Courses and Curricula*, 175–76.

9. Ibid., 297.

10. Beitler, *Strategic Organizational Change*, 189; Elias, *Foundations and Practice of Adult Religious Education*, 273; Erasmus, "Handbook," 58.

11. Diamond, *Designing and Assessing Courses and Curricula*, 182.

12. Ibid., 162, 175–76.

13. Erasmus, "Handbook," 32.

14. Diamond, *Designing and Assessing Courses and Curricula*, 176–77.

15. Ibid., 98–99, 176–77.

with this. Such support can therefore further inspire and empower our communities toward greater spiritual growth.[16] It is because of these four reasons that intentional monitoring and evaluation approaches should be a systematic part of all spiritual formation programs.

What to Assess?

This is a complex and difficult question because of the many possibilities and differences that each program embodies. However, there basically two sets of considerations when thinking about what to monitor and evaluate in relation to our own programs. The overall aim here is for us to assess those aspects of our programs that will help us to adequately discern how well our interventions are working.

The first set of considerations that we can assess are the specific elements of our program. For instance, if fostering teamwork and collegiality were an important ideal for our program, then we should define what this means in "measurable"[17] ways and track its progression.[18] Similarly, there may be specific skills or competencies that we want the people we are working with to have—such as Min's lay leaders to know how to develop a Bible study program from start to finish. If this were the case, then we could monitor how well these lay leaders are able to explore and analyze, design and implement, and assess and modify such an educational endeavor. We can also evaluate each of the specific practices we are utilizing in order to help us to better know the kinds of impact that they are having.[19] We can also monitor both student learning and attitudes as we engage with them.[20] This first set of evaluative foci is therefore related to specific aspects of our programs: the ideals, the interventions, the competencies of our communities, et cetera.

The second set of considerations to assess is more general in nature. These have to do with the overall strengths and weaknesses of our

---

16. McCallum and Lowery, *Organic Disciplemaking*, 270.

17. Here, "measurable" is understood as all the various ways that we can track the progress of a program, both qualitatively as well as quantitatively. For discussions on different ways to do this, see research method texts such as Cohen et al., *Research Methods in Education*; Moberg, "Guidelines for Research and Evaluation."

18. Diamond, *Designing and Assessing Courses and Curricula*, 178.

19. Schmuck, *Practical Action Research for Change*, 65.

20. Ibid., 37.

The Cycles of Ministry

program.[21] Here, the focus lies in assessing which parts of our program are going well and which parts we are struggling with. These general considerations are also related to the overall processes and outcomes of our interventions. Not only can we be concerned with the content of our programs but also with how they are being implemented.[22]

For instance, we may have discerned that centering prayer is an intervention that our youth group could greatly benefit from. However, trying to teach this practice while waiting for a subway in Grand Central Station during peak hours may not be the best place to introduce it to them. These kinds of assessments are related more to the process of how we are implementing this practice than it is to the practice itself. We can therefore monitor how we are implementing our programs as much as we can evaluate what we are putting into action.

Finally, general comparisons and contrasts can also be made between our programs and others that are like it.[23] For our youth group, we might compare how we are teaching centering prayer along side of other similar kinds of programs that have done this. Again, the goal of these specific and generally assessments is for us to be able to gauge the success of our program in relation to the ideals that we have discerned. As a result, what we assess should be directly related to these ideals.

How to Evaluate?

The approaches to monitoring and evaluation are quite broad and diverse. Nevertheless, there are guidelines that can help us to construct and go about our own ways of assessing our programs. Here, I will briefly mention how our ideals, outside resources, and specific assessment tools can help us in these endeavors.

The ideals that we have discerned not only provide us with the standards against which to evaluate success, but they also provide us with insights into what we should be assessing.[24] Overall, the primary question we are trying to assess is: How do we know if our programs are really working? As a result, our goals should be stated clearly and succinctly. We saw an example of this above where Min used her clearly stated ideals to help her categorize the interventions that she was considering.

---

21. Beitler, *Strategic Organizational Change*, 100–101.
22. Ibid., 189–90; Diamond, *Designing and Assessing Courses and Curricula*, 152.
23. Diamond, *Designing and Assessing Courses and Curricula*, 298.
24. Elias, *Foundations and Practice of Adult Religious Education*, 271.

PART TWO: Methodological Movements

Our ideals should therefore be articulated in ways that can be evaluated by the assessment measures we are using.[25] For instance, the goal of having our youth group know and engage with common religious and cultural stories is verifiable because we can check to see how well they know them. However, what some religious educators such as Elias caution us against, are ideals that are too precise and constricting thereby leading to "a loss of freedom and spontaneity" on the part of the participants.[26] For our youth, we would not want them to be solely locked into these aims to the complete ignorance of their own passions. Like our ideals, our assessments should be constructed in consultation with our communities whenever possible.[27]

In constructing assessments, we can also turn to outside support in the form of experts, already existing assessment tools, and programs that are similar to our own, as we have heard. Those who have some expertise in assessing the specific kind of formative program that we are implementing can be a valuable resource. "Not only can they assist you in developing and field testing your own assessment plans," Diamond claims, "but they can also help you locate other materials that may be of use."[28] For instance, we might ask a minister who has many years of experience facilitating programs similar to our own to be a mentor for us. To help us locate such mentors, we can seek them out online, through our own religious organizations, or via the resources that we have turned to in the exploration and analysis movement.[29]

Already existing assessment tools can also aid us with our evaluative efforts. More common in the field of secular education, if we are able to find such tools they can save us a tremendous amount of time and energy in trying to develop our own.[30] When these types of resources do not seem to be available, we can also turn to the mentors that we have just identified above for guidance on this.[31]

Just as the range of what we can monitor and assess is quite broad, so too are the specific evaluative approaches that are available. The use of

---

25. Elias, *Foundations and Practice of Adult Religious Education*, 276.

26. Ibid., 275.

27. Beitler, *Strategic Organizational Change*, 189, 191.

28. Diamond, *Designing and Assessing Courses and Curricula*, 162–63.

29. Elias, *Foundations and Practice of Adult Religious Education*, 263; Schmuck, *Practical Action Research for Change*, 64.

30. Diamond, *Designing and Assessing Courses and Curricula*, 165, 312.

31. Ibid., 298–99.

simulations, interviews, questionnaires, tests, discussion groups, observations made by facilitators and peers, et cetera, are all potential possibilities.[32] These approaches can be used not only by the formator, but also by the individuals, groups, and communities that we are working with.[33] As we can see, constructing an assessments system for our formative efforts is no easy task. However, we can and should look to each of these resources for help and guidance in preparing our own.

One Final Note: Challenges to Assessing "Spiritual" Progress

One final comment needs to be in relation to monitoring and evaluating theistic spiritual formation programs, and that is related to our views of God's work in our midst. When it comes to assessing such work, some resistance has been noted in the field of religious education by some, such as Elias. Specifically, there are worldviews which assert "that faith and the working of the Spirit cannot be measured."[34] If this is accurate, then our monitoring and evaluation approaches are really being carried out for nothing, since "the aims of education [are] otherworldly and divine."[35] Hence, there is no need for assessment tools because we cannot really measure and evaluate "spiritual" progress.

Such resistances to assessment are also challenging for the formative field of spiritual care and counseling. David Moberg, a longtime scientific researcher in this area, notes the difficulties of such views for his work because they depict spirituality to be "very complicated, seemingly ineffable, ephemeral, inscrutable, invisible, diffusely interwoven into all human beings and their behavior, and so transcendent that we cannot observe it directly with the human senses upon which all sciences rely."[36] Again, this worldview makes any observations or evaluations of the Spirit's work in our midst to be inaccessible.

How are we to respond to such claims? If it is true that God is too "otherworldly," too "transcendent and ineffable," then isn't it impossible to track God's work in our midst? I respond to these claims by asserting

---

32. Diamond, *Designing and Assessing Courses and Curricula*, 179–80; Elias, *Foundations and Practice of Adult Religious Education*, 275–76; Schmuck, *Practical Action Research for Change*, ch. 4.

33. Elias, *Foundations and Practice of Adult Religious Education*, 276.

34. Ibid., 271.

35. Ibid., 272.

36. Moberg, "Guidelines for Research and Evaluation," 213.

that regardless of one's theological views, there is something tangible that God is seeking to do in this world. If not, then what is the purpose of any spiritually formative endeavor or any spiritual discernment process? If our interactions and participations with God do not result in any tangible transformation in our lives or our world, then why are we pursuing it? It is possible to consider spiritual formation as solely an inward and therefore outwardly unobservable journey. However, it is the position of the praxis-based view of spiritual formation that has been presented herein to assert that this is not solely the case.

Such a theological position is that God's action in creation results in tangible and observable transformations in our midst. The Spirit longs and works for the concrete liberation—both internally as well as externally—of the individuals, relationships, and communities we are called to journey with. If this is a more accurate depiction of God's manifesting life in creation than the alternative and "otherworldly" view presented above, then monitoring and evaluating becomes possible. This is because our ideals can be used to articulate what the Spirit's concrete movements look like in our midst, as we saw in our chapter on spiritual discernment. Freedom from political and economic oppression, positive self-identities, and open and mutually sharing relationships, to name a few, all represent spiritual goals that we can walk toward and assess as we go.

The core issue here for each formator, then, lies in clarifying what you believe about the nature of God's manifesting life within and to creation and whether or not you can articulate it in such a way that it can be assessed in your spiritual formation programs. While my own position is "yes," yours may differ. If it does, then you must still wrestle with whether or not your programs are "effective" and, if you believe they are, how do you know that they are? How will know whether or not your practices and interventions are really "spiritually forming" and how will you know if and how they can be improved and adapted for different contexts and circumstances? Indeed, when it comes to monitoring and evaluating our efforts, these are important questions and challenges to consider.

Reflecting on Theory: Revisiting Our Five Core Models

Now that we have a better understanding of what our assessment approaches are intended to do and some beginning understandings for how they might be carried out, we are in a position to begin considering how we might use their feedback to further inform and modify our program. As we shall see now, this vital feedback can be used to alter the core models of our five areas resulting in a more accurate representation of what is actually occurring in our local contexts. We will begin by generally looking at how these core models might change for each of the fundamental aspects of a model that we considered in our chapter on exploration and analysis: claims/definitions, sources/methods, and warrants/worldviews. As we heard above, practical experience can influence the understandings that we have and it is in this section that we will see more clearly how this is.

The Need to Revisit Our Models

With all models having descriptive and predictive aims,[37] they are intended to help us better understand what is actually transpiring in our local ministerial contexts.[38] In the chapter on exploration and analysis, we saw how we might initially construct such representations with as much accuracy as we were able to at that time. However, we have heard many times now that these model building processes must be an ongoing affair.[39] Even if our core models were precisely accurate when they were first constructed, which is unlikely, they will still need to be continually updated as the dynamics of our local contexts change.

As we shall now see, such contextual variations can impact our models at each of the three levels discussed below. In considering these variations, we may need to revisit both our contextually constructed models as well as the external resources we originally drew upon. In effect, we are returning to our exploration and analysis methodologies and reengaging them thereby embodying the cyclical nature of these praxis-oriented movements.

Claims/Definitions

The claims that the core models of our five areas make need to be continually reevaluated in light of our ongoing experiences. There are at least four sets of questions that we can ask of these models as we reflect on their

---

37. See Appendix B.

38. Britt, *Conceptual Introduction to Modeling*, 187.

39. Ibid., 179; Diamond, *Designing and Assessing Courses and Curricula*, 107; Pears, *Doing Contextual Theology*, 46.

usefulness and applications. Each of these is intended to provide us with the necessary sets of lenses for further refining these core models.

First, we ask of them as to whether or not they accurately represent the dynamics of our contexts.[40] For instance, do the ideals that we have set really reflect the directions that God seems to be leading us in now, each step of the way?[41] Do the anthropologies closely depict the dynamics we originally expected to encounter?[42] Are our theological formulations challenged by what is emerging as we journey forward?[43] All of these are necessary questions that we can ask of each model in relation to their accuracy.

So, for instance, on the first day of class, Min might realize that some of her students have special needs that she did not anticipate. She would therefore need to update her anthropological models to reflect this new contextual data. Or Francis, as she begins to work more closely with Martha and Charles, realizes that the hopes for their relationship—which have informed the ideals that she discerned—might be changing as Martha comes to accept Charlie more for who he is now than what he was like in the past. What we expect to be and what actually becomes do not always match up. We must therefore continually reflect on and assess these five sets of core models.

Second, we can also inquire into the nature of the relationships that our models depict both between the model's components and with the context.[44] For example, is the mind really related to body in the ways that we originally thought they were? How is the community influencing the individuals we are working with?[45] Are our interventions having the kinds of effects that we thought they would have on the body?[46] As these relationships are highlighted, our core models should better fit with our circumstances.

---

40. Britt, *Conceptual Introduction to Modeling*, 166.

41. Beitler, *Strategic Organizational Change*, 189; Elias, *Foundations and Practice of Adult Religious Education*, 276; Greenwood and Levin, *Introduction to Action Research*, 96–97.

42. Elaine Graham, *Transforming Practice*, 134.

43. Ibid., 137; Graham, Walton, and Ward, *Theological Reflection*, 202.

44. Britt, *Conceptual Introduction to Modeling*, 111–12, 156.

45. Pears, *Doing Contextual Theology*, 74.

46. Swinton and Mowat, *Practical Theology and Qualitative Research*, 255.

Variations with time and circumstances can be a third source for evaluating and modifying our models.[47] If one of our core models describes the identity or group development of our constituents, then is the progression depicted by this model really reflective of the changes that we are actually seeing in our local contexts?[48] How have the attitudes of our students changed throughout the course of our program and did we expect these sorts of changes?[49] Time and changing conditions can therefore prompt us to refine the theories that we are turning to.

Finally, we can reflect on whether our models are too simplistic or complex for our purposes.[50] Sometimes, our theological assertions turn out to be in conflict with the theologies that are emerging in our contexts.[51] For instance, we can recall the two theological categories that Francis created in light of Martha and Charlie's situation: (1) self-realization and fulfillment; and (2) harmony, unity, and integration. However, as she continues to journey with them, she might come to realize that there is a third additional way that God seems to be active in their relationship and that is to help both Charles and Martha to move toward greater transcendence, which is also considered to be an integral part of process theology.[52]

In such cases, we may therefore need to either construct simpler versions of our original claims, or we may need to add to their complexities as Francis might. Another example of this is found in the efforts of contextual theologians who strive to find "Christ within the exiting culture rather than importing or bringing Christ into that culture."[53] The point we want to draw out here is that our local contextual experiences may necessitate that we either simplify or complexify our models.

Overall, then, our *in vivo* experiences may give us cause to revisit each of our five core models and ask questions such as these. In doing this, we can turn to both the contextually constructed and external models, upon which our finally synthesized models were based, and ask these very same questions. It may turn out that we must reconstruct and modify our

---

47. Britt, *Conceptual Introduction to Modeling*, 112.

48. Duncan-Andrade and Morrell, *Art of Critical Pedagogy*, 126; Schmuck, *Practical Action Research for Change*, 70.

49. Diamond, *Designing and Assessing Courses and Curricula*, 176–77.

50. Britt, *Conceptual Introduction to Modeling*, 114, 186–87.

51. Swinton and Mowat, *Practical Theology and Qualitative Research*, 96.

52. Cobb and Griffin, *Process Theology*, 47, 57; Suchocki, *God, Christ, Church*, 43–44.

53. Pears, *Doing Contextual Theology*, 18.

original contextual models as well as turn to alternative external resources in order to help us to utilize models that are more representative of our local contexts and all that we perceive God to be doing therein. As we shall see in the methodological steps below, each of these—the contextually constructed models, the external resources, and our resulting synthesized models—can therefore be a significant source of assessment and modification.

Sources/Methods

Since "data gathering should be an on-going process,"[54] we can also revisit the sources and methods that our five core models were originally founded upon. In Christianity, there is a strong emphasis on turning to its tradition as a central source for the theories that we utilize.[55] However, our experiences may prompt us to question some of these sources and their validity for our local applications.

Liberation theologians such as Gustavo Gutierrez, we learned in chapter 3,[56] have found this to be the case in their work with the poor and oppressed in South America. Their ministries caused them to question the sources of their models and to subsequently look to alternative models—such as Marxism—that were more representative of their local needs. Our own reflections can therefore be focused on reevaluating the sources and methods that our five core models are based upon in light of our ongoing contextual experiences. Are these sources still valid? Do we need to change the methods by which we are accessing these sources? As with liberationists, we may also determine that our models need to look for additional, if not alternative, foundations than the ones that we initially based our claims upon.

Warrants/Worldviews

"Practical activity," Elias writes, "with its successes and failures, leads to a questioning of assumptions, an awareness of limitations in present theories and models, and a search for new theories and models."[57] In revisiting

---

54. Beitler, *Strategic Organizational Change*, 85.
55. Graham, *Transforming Practice*, 112; Pears, *Doing Contextual Theology*, 20, 42.
56. See p. 143.
57. Elias, *Foundations and Practice of Adult Religious Education*, 152.

The Cycles of Ministry

our core models, we may very well find that many of our supporting assumptions, and the justifications that we originally had for constructing the models, do not hold up. We may therefore also have to return to the warrants that we used in our exploration and analysis methodologies and refine them since such assumptions are likewise asserted to be context bound.[58]

For instance, contextual theologians such as Angie Pears note the limitations of using "Western theological tools and methods" as the basis for engaging in such theological reflection in non-Western contexts.[59] The claim is that such tools still contain the perspectives of Western theologians and therefore may be limited in their abilities to help construct theologies that are more representative of local contexts. Our own local experiences may therefore give us cause to question the underlying warrants of our own core models.

Closely paralleling this discussion, we might finally reevaluate the worldviews and interpretations that are embodied by the theories we are using.[60] Gutierrez did this when he challenged "traditional Christian understandings or theologies which stress the inner development and liberation to the exclusion or expense of any external, social factor."[61] The goal here is to bring to the surface any underlying and previously unseen assumptions and to question their validity and applicability in light of our ongoing local experiences.

For example, Montague's initial assumptions were that he was being sent to his urban church not only to discern its future but also to begin attempting a revitalization, which he experimented with on a number of occasions. He also came with the desires and expectations of leading the church to be more actively engaged in their local community. These initial perceptions, we heard in our chapter on spiritual discernment, skewed how he viewed his congregation. As we worked with them, however, his views of his reasons for being there changed. In the final processes of discernment, he ultimately came to realize that God had sent him there to close this church with much care and compassion for the members who were still there. This realization then shifted how he viewed them (i.e., it

---

58. Greenwood and Levin, *Introduction to Action Research*, 104; Pears, *Doing Contextual Theology*, 70.

59. Pears, *Doing Contextual Theology*, 16.

60. Greenwood and Levin, *Introduction to Action Research*, 104; Pears, *Doing Contextual Theology*, 22.

61. Pears, *Doing Contextual Theology*, 70.

changed his anthropological model of them) and therefore how he ministered to them for the remainder of their time together. We therefore need to continually monitor and assess the both the worldviews and warrants that undergird our five core models.

In summary, revisiting our five core exploration and analysis areas needs to be an integral part of these final methodologies. Not only should these critical evaluations address the claims of our core models, but also each of the foundations upon which these claims are made. Doing so might lead us to further revisit the contextually constructed and external resources that we originally turned and refine them as well. Overall, the purpose of these efforts is to allow our ongoing monitoring and evaluations to help us to refine our core models. We will then be able to better reassess the interventions that were at least partly based upon each of them.

Reflecting on Practice: Reassessing Our Interventions

As we heard in chapter 2, the praxis way of being involves a cyclical "quadri-lectic" between theory, practice, reflection, and transformation. We have already seen how our monitoring and evaluation techniques can be a valuable source of reflecting on our programs, and some of the key considerations that we can address in revisiting the core models that undergird them. In this section, we will now look more closely at how the interventions we discerned using the design and implementation methodologies of the last chapter might be reassessed in light of our monitoring and evaluation feedback.

How Well Are They Working?

The basis of such evaluations of our practices essentially revolves around two considerations. First, as we may recall, some of our interventions will have been chosen because they were intended to help our constituents to move toward a specific ideal. If our assessments show that our progress toward that particular goal is not as we expected, we may then turn to its interventions and begin exploring each of them more closely.[62] In the example of trying to help our youth group to learn and integrate the stories of their cultural and religious traditions, for instance, we may have found

---

62. Diamond, *Designing and Assessing Courses and Curricula*, 176, 183; Schmuck, *Practical Action Research for Change*, 36.

that they are having difficulty making connections between these stories and their own lives. We could then turn to our interventions that were seeking to help them to do this and begin to question why they are not have the intended effects that they are.

However, our discernment processes may have also generated interventions that are not specifically connected with any particular objective. An example would be our community engaging in specific spiritual practices—such as prayer or worship—that have been handed down for generations, but either they do not seem to be directly connected with any of our ideals or they address many of them simultaneously. In these instances, we might need to develop specialized assessments that help us to better understand what role(s) these interventions are playing and what their effects have been to date. Some intervention theorists, such as organizational development consultant Michael Beitler, assert that each of our interventions should be closely monitored and evaluated in these ways.[63]

We can therefore see that there are at least two ways to evaluate and reassess our interventions: based on the whether or not our ideals are being realized as we expected, and based on how well each intervention is impacting our community in the ways that we had expected it to. Both of these represent different guides and bases for gauging the value of each intervention. We should therefore look to both of them in such reassessments.

What Can Be Changed?

If our assessments reveal that some of our specific approaches are not working as well as they could or were expected to, what then? What can we modify? Basically, there are two different kinds of modifications that we can make to our applications.

The first is related to the specific interventions themselves. For each of them, we can look to the particulars for how each one is being implemented. Specifically, Diamond writes, "You will use this data to identify the changes you should make in procedures, in content, and in sequence to improve the quality and effectiveness of your course or curriculum."[64] By studying the details of how our approaches are being used, we can alter them in any one of these ways: their content, their order, and the procedures for how they are engaged. We can also reassess the resources

---

63. Beitler, *Strategic Organizational Change*, 189–90.
64. Diamond, *Designing and Assessing Courses and Curricula*, 297.

that each intervention requires,[65] since it may turn out that a particular practice is under resourced and therefore not as effective as it should be. Overall, this first set of modifications is geared toward the efficiency and effectiveness of each intervention.[66]

The second category of changes that we might make are the additions and subtractions that we can make to them.[67] In these cases, we would be looking for interventions that are extraneous (i.e., ones that are really not doing very much). For instance, Min may come to learn that her students do not have the time to complete all of the readings and that she is able to cover all of the material during class. In this case, she might consider dropping these readings altogether, or making them optional. Deleting interventions from our program may not only bring a needed simplicity but it might also free up resources that can be reallocated more effectively elsewhere.

There might also be new interventions that we need to add. An example of this is found in educational settings when the prerequisite knowledge that a student is expected to have is lacking. For example, this may be a youth's first time visiting the group and therefore has never been exposed to the congregation's religious and cultural stories. In these instances, we may need to institute remedial interventions so that participants in this situation have the adequate support that they need in order to meet our program's objectives.[68]

There may also be instances when unforeseeable events and feedback prompts us to add approaches that we did not anticipate. For instance, if Charles had another heart attack, Francis might suggest additional formative approaches for both he and Martha. Both of these kinds of changes—in how the interventions are implemented and in the addition/subtraction of approaches—can result from the reassessments of our applications.

"KISS"-ing the Transformative Bottom Line

As a final word before continuing on to the steps below, in line with the KISS principle, we seek to return to the ultimate aim of these praxis-based movements, and that is transformation.[69] We must remember that

65. Beitler, *Strategic Organizational Change*, 189–90.
66. Diamond, *Designing and Assessing Courses and Curricula*, 176–77.
67. Elias, *Foundations and Practice of Adult Religious Education*, 273.
68. Diamond, *Designing and Assessing Courses and Curricula*, 98–99, 176–77.
69. Ibid., 91; Elias, *Foundations and Practice of Adult Religious Education*, 195–96;

The Cycles of Ministry

our ongoing goal is to be ever more fully a part of God's unfolding and ever-manifesting work in our ministerial contexts.[70] A core assumption of praxis and spiritual formation, as we saw repeatedly in our theoretical chapters, is that this work of God is ever oriented toward tangibly and positively transforming the people we are called to work with.[71] It is therefore the final goal of all of these assessments and modifications that we be directed toward these spiritually forming changes of the Divine. With this as our KISS focus, the very heartbeat of a theistic approach praxis formation, we now turn to the practical steps that can help us to more concretely journey toward these never-ending spiritualizing horizons.

Methodological Movements

As we can see, when spiritual formation is conceived of as praxis it is a cyclical lifestyle that stands at the intersection of theory, practice, and reflection for the explicit purposes of fostering spiritual transformation. It is one that continues the dance between these various aspects of our formative craft as we continue to live and work with the people and communities we are called to. If this is the case, then, what are some of the concrete movements that can help us to embody such assessments and modifications? As we shall presently see, there are five steps to this methodology. As with the other two, each of these may actually be engaged differently by each of us depending on the work that we discern the Spirit to be doing in our local contexts. Nevertheless, these five movements represent the major beats that we can be conscious of in our work of pursuing such a living spiritual praxis.

To help us to further see how each of these steps concretely looks in an actual context, as we have before, we turn to a case example. For this methodology, I have chosen a brief example that is described in Richard Schmuck's book. In chapter 6, Schmuck describes the steps of a particular approach to action research known as responsive action research.[72] As an illustration of these steps, he shares a story of "Matt Reardon," an English literature public school teacher at Rosemont High School. Frustrated with the realization that his students, "some of the brightest" at Rosemont, are not engaging very deeply with the course material, Matt intentionally

---

Greenwood and Levin, *Introduction to Action Research*, 3.

70. Graham et al., *Theological Reflection*, 192.

71. Ibid., 171; Pears, *Doing Contextual Theology*, 27.

72. Schmuck, *Practical Action Research for Change*, 92–95.

applies the responsive action research steps with transformative results.[73] As we explore these five steps, we will be following Matt's assessment and modification story as it unfolds in accordance with these praxis-oriented methodologies. I have chosen to present this example of a public school teacher because we must remember from our introductory chapter that formators work in a variety of contexts. While it is not presented from a theistic perspective, this story still embodies the essential steps of these assessment and modification methodologies.

Step One: Gather, Evaluate, and Analyze Data

In order for us to embody spiritual praxis, we must have some way of knowing how it is going in our local contexts. The first step of these assessment and modification methods is therefore for us to develop and put into practice our monitoring and evaluating system, which we can draw from for analysis purposes. These represent three essential components to the feedback that we will need to work in praxis-oriented ways: monitoring, evaluating, and analyzing.

Monitoring

Monitoring, as we have seen, begins with our determining what it is that we need to be tracking in order to more fully assess how our programs and interventions are working. At a minimum, we should be monitoring the parts of our programs that have specific objectives. For instance, if we are interested in nurturing teamwork among the small group we are formatively working with, then we need to clearly define what this might look like in measurable ways and begin watching for these developments.[74]

Again, we can track both the specific outcomes, such as the extent to which teamwork is being engaged, and the processes by which such teamwork is being developed. The goal here is for us to be very clear about what we, in partnership with our communities, are seeking to formatively work with and to then be very intentional about tracking each of these parts. As always, spiritual discernment is an intentional part of this as we seek to know what it is that God would have us track at every step of the way.

---

73. Ibid., 82.

74. Diamond, *Designing and Assessing Courses and Curricula*, 178.

Evaluating

Once we have instituted a monitoring system, we can then begin the process of reflecting on the data that it generates. Such reflections need to be evaluative in nature, meaning that we should be critically appraising what this data is telling us. In other words, we can think about the meaning of our observations for the current and future directions of our interventions. Overall, we are interested in how well our programs are working. Our evaluative criteria should therefore help us to assess these kinds of questions. In the case of teamwork, for instance, we can ask whether the small group is moving in the directions that we have set out as goals or not.

Our ideals should therefore be the basis for these comparisons, but so might some of our other core models such as our theories of change. For instance, we might compare how the team is progressing in relation to group developmental models that we are using.[75] In developing these evaluative criteria, we can therefore also look to our other core models at times.

The purpose of these evaluations is therefore to aid us in reflecting on the data that our monitoring system has generated and its significance for our interventions (i.e., whether they are working or not and to what extent). This information will, as we shall see, become a further part of our ongoing discernment processes. This first step therefore entails discerning and implementing this monitoring and evaluating system.

Analysis

This next phase is merely an extension of the previous one. Once we have gathered the feedback data and have a set of evaluative standards against which to compare it, then we are ready to discerningly analyze it. We are encouraged in this step to engage spiritual practices from our traditions that will better enable us to know what the Spirit is trying to show us through this gathered data in relation to the evaluative measures and ideals that we have set.

While the next two steps will have us analyze this data in relation to our five core models and the interventions we are using, this initial step entails our looking at the data in more preliminary and less specific ways. In doing so, we ask such questions as: What themes seem to emerge as we compare where we are with where we are hoping to go? What trends seem

---

75. Schmuck, *Practical Action Research for Change*, 70.

PART TWO: Methodological Movements

to emerge as we look at the data? Does it show progression or regression? What does the data seem to be saying overall? This step therefore would have us reflectively sit with the feedback that is being generated and reflect on the data in more general ways.

Matt Interviews His Students and Reflects

In response to his frustrations with his student's lack of engagement with the course, Matt hosts a session with his students in which he asks them how his teaching is impacting them. To help guide this feedback, "He tells students to print a plus sign on one side of a piece of blank paper and a minus sign on the other. He has them list the helpful things he does on the plus side and the unhelpful things he does on the minus side."[76]

Matt is utilizing input from the people he is formatively working with to gain better insights into how his own interventions, in this case this teaching pedagogies, are working. He has already determined that one of the goals for his teaching is to have a positive impact on his students. In order to help him assess this goal, he decides to interview and obtain feedback directly from each person. His monitoring approach is the questions he asks his students, while the evaluating system is the ideals that Matt has in mind in relation to what is "helpful" and "unhelpful" for them. Given both of these, Matt is therefore in a place to assess the ideals that he is striving for in his class.

Compiling the feedback that his students give to him, Matt takes the next few days to consider what they had to say. Overall, "He thinks that while the students appreciate his expertise in literature and find his information helpful, they also think he talks too much and doesn't facilitate discussion."[77] Matt also begins to realize that the ways he talks to his class during discussion times is intimidating for them and therefore doesn't foster the kind of openness that he was hoping for. He also sees that the amount of information they are trying to cover is too much for his students, who really want to engage some of the material more deeply over longer periods of time. Matt therefore learns much from the process of taking a step back to generally reflect on the overall and initial impressions that his data seems to be telling him.

---

76. Ibid., 83.
77. Ibid., 83–84.

Step Two: Revisit the Five Core Models

While these general reflections can reveal much to us, we can also be more specific with them as well. Since praxis involves reflection on both theory and practice, our reflections can engage both of these aspects of our craft. In this step, we therefore take the time to revisit the core models from our exploration and analysis methodologies to see if any revisions need to be made in order to improve the accuracy of their descriptive and predictive representations. Our guiding discernment question here is: What shifts in understanding is God inviting us to make?

Modifying Model Details

Regardless of which of the models we are looking at, we can use the feedback we have gathered and preliminarily analyzed to think about each of the details of that specific model: claims/definitions, sources/methods, and warrants/worldviews. This essentially involves our reflecting on the extent to which our models match with the ongoing experiences and feedback that we are assessing. As we explored in detail above, do the claims still seem to hold? Are the warrants and worldviews still valid? Do the sources that the model was built upon still relate to our context? This step is therefore essentially a process of returning to each of our five core models and reflecting on just how valid they still are in light of our ongoing experiences.

For instance, let us assume that our theology depicts God as more rationalistic, individualistic, linear, and domineering in relation to our work. However, perhaps we are working with people who continually report that their experiences of God are more "holistic, corporate, ecological and cyclical" in nature.[78] If this is the case, it might prompt us to revisit our own theological presumptions and modify them in light of this feedback. Not only might we change our theological claims about the Spirit, but we might also question the assumptions that they are based upon and where they originally came from. For each of our core models, then, we can continually ask how the data that our monitoring and evaluation system is generating confirms or challenges their claims/definitions, warrants/worldviews, and/or sources/methods.

78. Graham, *Transforming Practice*, 134.

PART TWO: Methodological Movements

Returning to the Exploration and Analysis Methodologies

For this step, we will often only need to return to the models that we originally synthesized via the steps presented in chapter 3. However, there may be times when these core models are so inaccurate—so misrepresentative of the dynamics of our local contexts—that we need to take two steps back and revisit the contextually constructed models and externally utilized resources as well. If this is the case, then our task essentially becomes one of returning to the steps that were outlined in the chapter on exploration and analysis and possibly restarting from square one.

The new information that we are gathering will then become a part of the original data that we used to create our contextually constructed models as well as being a part of the basis for possibly choosing different external resources to use in our new synthesis. An example of this will be detailed in the next chapter when we consider Tom's case where he had to revisit the external resources he was using and modify these as a direct result of the feedback that he received during his program.

Matt's Changing Anthropology

In Schmuck's descriptions of Matt's case, he does not seem to explicitly address this step. However, we do see traces of these kinds of reflections and model evaluations happening for Matt. For instance, Matt initially views his seemingly disinterested students as having a hunger for things other than what Matt has to offer. "They're hungry, Matt thinks, but only for food, not great drama, novels, and poetry."[79] In essence, Matt has—consciously or unconsciously—formed an anthropological view of his students as having motivations and passions for things other than the content of his class. These views therefore formed part of the basis for the core models that inherently influenced and guided his initial design and implementation.

However, this view of his students was then challenged by the feedback he received directly from them. In his discussions with them, many stated that they would like more opportunities to learn about the readings from one another through small group discussions. They also would like to interview Matt about the authors who wrote the stories and they have an interest in spending more time with each text so that they can

---

79. Schmuck, *Practical Action Research for Change*, 82.

The Cycles of Ministry

understand them in a deeper way.[80] In short, Matt is learning from them that it is not just food that they hunger for but also a more focused and intensive engagement with the course's material.

As a result, Matt's anthropological views of his students changed as he worked in close consultation with them. The results of these modified views, we shall see, come to completely transform not only what will he taught in the coming months, but also how the class went about engaging with the material.[81] We can therefore see how the data that our monitoring and evaluation system creates can play an integral part of helping us to continually reassess and alter the core models that undergird and help guide our formative programs.

Step Three: Reassess Each Specific Intervention

Our assessments and modifications, of course, cannot stop with our five core models. If transformation is truly our praxis-directed horizon, then we also need to reassess the actual interventions that we are using. Here, our goal is to use the feedback data to help us evaluate how each of the specific practices we are using is impacting our communities. These evaluations can be made in relation to each intervention's content, sequence, or order.

For instance, Schmuck also shares a case example of another educator, named Marilyn, who reassesses one of her specific classroom interventions.[82] In this case, Marilyn had her students write a biography about someone else. However, the reports did not meet her expectations for the assignment; "many were too short, some were poorly written, and few were inaccurate."[83] After gaining feedback from the students, a mentoring teacher, and her principal, she finds that this practice could have been engaged in very different ways. Specifically, Schmuck notes, "Marilyn realizes that she should have helped students generate a standard list of interview questions and that the whole class should have created a standard outline for the biographies."[84]

We can see in this brief example how intervention assessment can generally proceed. Marilyn realizes based upon her own evaluations of

80. Ibid., 84.
81. Ibid.
82. Ibid., 65.
83. Schmuck, *Practical Action Research for Change*, 65.
84. Ibid.

the student's work that one of her practices is not working quite as she had originally anticipated. After exploring this specific interventions in detail with both the community she is working with as well as outside consultants (i.e., her mentor and principal), she makes plans for how it will be engaged differently next time around.

Generally, then, our data should be such that it is not only able to tell us about the impact that each intervention is having but also about the mechanics of how it is working. Only then will we be in a position to modify the content and processes associated with our approaches in the next step. Here, we are therefore seeking to theistically discern what the Spirit would have us notice in relation to each of the means that God is formatively working through. This third step, however, is one of assessing and reflecting on each one of the specific interventions that we are using in our program.

Matt Assesses His Pedagogy

As we have already heard, Matt realizes that there are a number of shortcomings for some of the interventions that he is using in his literature class. For example, he realizes that his methods of questioning are too scary and the amount of information he is trying to cover is too much in too short of a time period.[85] Matt's reflections on these specific interventions come directly from the feedback that his students give to him. This therefore shows us that our monitoring and evaluation systems should include data that is centered directly on each of the specific practices that we are utilizing. Matt's response to this information is, we shall see next, to modify his pedagogies in consultation with his students.

Step Four: Discern and Implement the Modified Approaches

Having now spent the previous three steps gathering and reflecting on the significance and implications of our feedback data, we are now in a position to return to the practical mechanics of how our programs are being operated. It is therefore in this step that we modify our ongoing applications for the purposes of improving the transformative impact of our interventions. Following our design and implementation methodologies, there are two basic movements to this step: reassess and decide, and

---

85. Ibid., 83–84.

then implement. From a discernment perspective, we are interested in the changes that God is prompting us to make as our program continues to unfold.

Reassess and Decide: Revisiting Our Design and Implementation Methods

From our reflections, we may now have not only a modified set of core models, but also a better idea of how each of our specific interventions is being engaged. Both of these can therefore become a part of the basis for further rethinking our overall program. In essence, this can involve returning to the design and implementation steps of the previous chapter and again thinking through how our newly modified core models might give rise to new or different interventions. The feedback on how effective our approaches seem to be from the previous step will also help us know whether some of them need to be slightly modified, added to, or eliminated altogether. This step therefore entails bringing all of this information together to reassess and spiritually discern how our current formative approaches might be altered in light of all of this feedback.

For example, perhaps one is leading a Bible study in a fashion similar to Matt's: covering too much material too quickly. Discussions with this group and reflections on how the class is facilitated should reveal this and suggest that maybe the class needs to continue at a much slower pace. Additionally, the facilitator may have originally designed this study for a specific group of young adults in her/his congregation but a number of stroke victims with learning disabilities are now also in attendance. She/he would therefore need to revisit the theories of learning that they originally synthesized and possibly do additional research in order to better understand how certain kinds of strokes can impact not only cognition but faith development as well.

It is in this step that the practitioner would therefore bring all of this research and information together to begin the process of reflecting on what their possible implications are for the applications she/he has been engaging. Again, the details for how go about doing this are found in the previous chapter. In line with these design and implementation steps, we would finally come to a decision as to how to modify our program. Overall, the goal here is for us to reassess the current applications we are using in light of this input and decide how to proceed from here.

PART TWO: Methodological Movements

Implement

Once discerned, we then modify our interventions. If the changes are significant, then we may need to reconsider the resources and supports that are needed for each of the interventions as well as for the program as a whole. What additional help and guidance might we need in order to introduce and facilitate these modifications? Do resources need to be reallocated in order to support the quality and effectiveness of the program? How will the people/communities I am working with respond to the changes I am thinking about making? Questions such as these can help us to further plan for and effectively implement the alterations we have discerned. Again, returning to the design and implementation steps can help us toward these ends.

Major Overhaul to Matt's Class

After deciding that his general pedagogies and some of his specific interventions needed to be modified, Matt returned to his own hopes as well as to those of his students in his efforts to help him reassess and redesign both the structure and the content of the course. Turning to the class, Matt asked them to suggest new and different ways for how he might teach the class.[86] Together, they generated sixteen ideas and then chose six from among them, which included suggestions such as: "Spend more class time in student groups to learn about the readings;" "Students come up with questions to ask Mr. Reardon about authors, their ideas, and literary themes;" and "Focus on just a few authors."[87]

Also, as a part of his assessments, Matt took the time to outline his modified hopes and concerns for the class. As an educator, he wanted his students to both enjoy and deeply engage with the course material.[88] However, he was also concerned that allowing his students to work in small groups more often would allow for some students to "hitchhike" and allow others to do the work for them.[89] In the end, however, Matt decides to try out the changes that his students selected, adding his modifications to help address his concerns and further realize his hopes for them. They

---

86. Ibid., 84.
87. Ibid.
88. Ibid., 85.
89. Ibid., 86.

started working in small groups, asking Matt questions about each author's background, and covered fewer texts but with greater depth.

We can therefore see how Matt's reflections on the data that was fed back to him via his monitoring and evaluation systems helped him, in consultation with his students, to majorly overhaul the course. Not only did his core models, such as his anthropological views of his students as well as his hopes and concerns for them, inform this process, but so did the feedback that he received directly from the class. Taking these together, Matt and his class were able to redesign not only what would be covered in class, but also how they would go about engaging it. Matt then implemented these changes with his students.

Step Five: Continue on Living Spiritual Praxis

The title of this chapter is "The Cycles of Ministry," and it is in this final step that we see why. Living spiritual praxis is not something that happens one time and is finished; it is not an end goal that we achieve and we're done with it. Rather, spiritual praxis is a way of life. It is one that only finds its fulfillment in its continual unfolding.

This final step, then, is really a continuation of the work that has already been initiated with the two previous methodologies. Here, monitoring and evaluation are ongoing, models and interventions are continually revisited and reassessed, and our spiritual formation programs cycle along as the interpenetration of theory, practice, and reflection lead—with God's ever guiding care—toward greater liberation and transformation of the people and communities we are called to work with. This final step is therefore the embodiment of the cyclical nature of living spiritual praxis to which we are being invited through each of these three methodologies.

Matt's Class Continues

Returning to one of the major texts for their class, *King Lear*, Matt and the class collectively try out the newly discerned interventions. Right away, Matt is pleased with how the class proceeds. Summarizing, Schmuck writes, "Matt notes that those students who have not spoken up in class are now speaking in the small groups and to the whole class. He is impressed with the quality of the group reports and thinks that the interviewers [with him] did an adequate job."[90]

As their class continues on, Matt remains attentive and responsive to the unfolding of their time and progress together. Not only does he continue to observe the students as they work in small groups and engage in class discussions, but he also interviews his students once per week to hear their feedback for how his teaching approaches are going.[91] Matt also continually consults with a mentor who offers both advice for him and critical observations of his class. We therefore see Matt embodying the cyclical praxis way as his class continues to move toward the ideals that they have collectively discerned.

Closing Reflections

In their book on spiritual discernment, entitled *The Discerning Heart*, Wilkie and Noreen Cannon Au write, "Living with a discerning heart entails a commitment to stay in ongoing conversation with this mobile God, who walks with us in all the seasons of our lives."[92] It is a view that a life with God is one of a never-ending conversation as we take each step in spiritually discerning ways.

These assessment and modification methodologies, shown below in figure 11, have sought to provide some of the details for what such a discernment-centered way of life might look like in relation to monitoring and evaluating our spiritual formation program. This does not only happen via reflections on the five core models that we have, but also in conversation with the specific interventions that we are using. Ultimately, as we have seen, these final methodologies can help us to further embody a discernment-centered vocation that leads us and our communities, step by step, toward the transformations to which we are ever being invited. Our hopes, through each of these methodologies, are that God will ever more fully be able to lead us through the cyclical seasons of our lives.

---

90. Schmuck, *Practical Action Research for Change*, 86.
91. Ibid., 86.
92. Au and Au, *Discerning Heart*, 21.

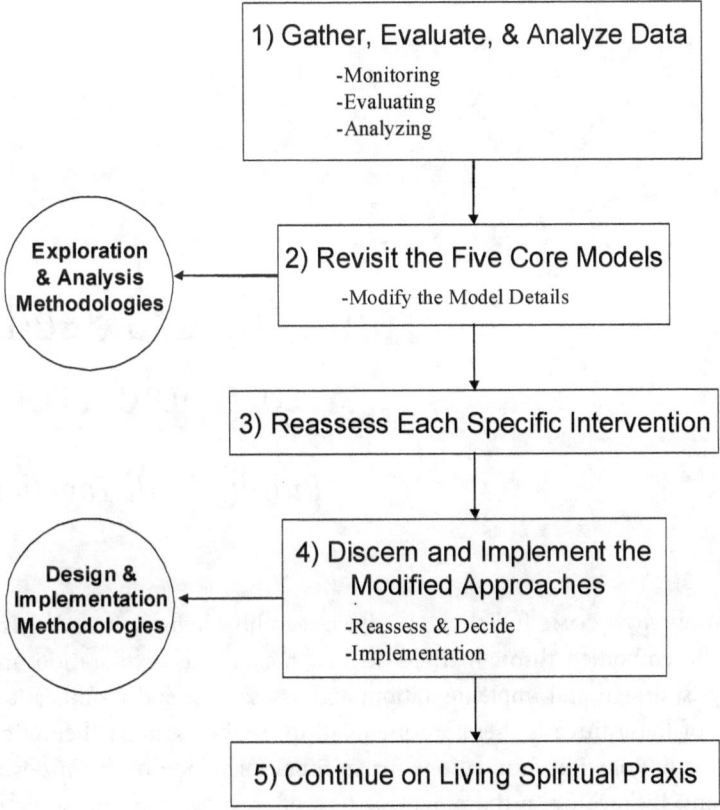

Figure 11. The Five Steps of Assessment and Modification.

6

From Mustard Seeds to Apple Trees

Pulling It All Together

WE HAVE NOW COME full circle. We have seen how living spiritual praxis may be embodied through three distinct movements: exploration and analysis; design and implementation; and assessment and modification. Each of these three is therefore intended to be the essential theoretical and methodological foundations for spiritual formation program development. By turning to the practical steps of each, we can find some of the necessary steps that can help to guide our formative work with our communities.

In this final chapter, we will be taking a step back and considering one complete case example where we will see each of these methods being utilized in a formative program. We will be following Tom as he develops his contemplative spiritual formation program for the retreatants that he will be engaging. First, however, we will briefly compile the all of the steps that we have covered thus far. Overall, the purpose of this chapter is to help us to better see how the many theories and methods of this book might apply to our own work in more integrative ways. In the end, we hope to see more clearly how we can live spiritual praxis.

The Methodological Steps at a Glance

Before journeying with Tom, it will first be helpful to compile the steps that we have seen from each of the three previous chapters. Again, it is important to highlight that not every program we prepare for and engage will necessarily need each one of these steps, or even each one of the methodologies. The ultimate KISS goal that we are working toward at all times is to better partner with the formative work that the Spirit is doing in our local ministerial contexts. Just like the design of the very complex 747 airplane, all other decisions and components flow out of this core spiritually formative focus. Hence, as long as we are moving toward this ultimate ideal, we are doing what is most appropriate for our constituents, regardless of whether we engage with each of these steps or not.

As they have been presented in this book, the following are the steps that have been outlined for each of the three praxis-oriented methodologies:

- Exploration and Analysis Steps
    1. Discern and Clarify Foci
    2. Construct a Contextual Model
    3. Search, Select, and Detail External Resources
    4. Perform a Detailed Analysis and Synthesis
    5. Theological Translations and Reflections
    6. Final Observations and Evaluations
- Design and Implementation Steps
    1. Brainstorming with the Five Core Models
    2. Compiling and Reducing Possible Approaches
    3. Detail Each Intervention
    4. Choose the Interventions to Use
    5. Final Planning and Implementation
- Assessment and Modification Steps
    1. Gather, Evaluate, and Analyze Data
    2. Revisit the Five Core Models
    3. Reassess Each Specific Intervention
    4. Discern and Implement the Modified Applications
    5. Continue on Living Spiritual Praxis

PART TWO: Methodological Movements

As we can see, these processes can be quite detailed and time consuming. Whether we engage with each of these steps or not will depend on the specific program we are developing. For instance, if we were seeking to discern an intervention for something smaller, say an attempt to address a minor food addiction that we have such as chocolate or sodas, then our planning and preparations might not be as involved as if we were seeking to develop a holistic spiritual formation program for the children and youth of a large congregation. In using these methodologies, then, the hopes are that we will be able to adapt them for the purposes of the specific situations that we are confronted with.

We have also noted throughout that these three methodologies are not completely separate from one another. For instance, ongoing contextual feedback is an inherent part of our exploration and analysis methods: the more we know about our local situations and our communities, the better our models will be. Also, we have seen how our assessment and modification steps are intimately linked with the other two methodologies. Finally, our design and implementation steps are ones that may need to be repeatedly engaged as our knowledge and assessments of our programs unfolds. As a result, none of these methods are completely independent and this eventually leads to the mutually interactive way of being that the term "spiritual praxis," at least as it has been used throughout this book, is intended to capture.

What is important to remember in relation to these steps, then, is that we must engage each one while simultaneously thinking ahead to what the other methods might entail. Doing so, will help to ensure a more successful program development process from the beginning. It is therefore recommended that we think through each of the three methodologies as we begin to plan and prepare for any formative program we are discerning. It is such tightly interconnected relationships that comprise a central part of spiritual formation. However, even when we do approach program development with this awareness, our journey may take us in unexpected directions as we are about to see.

Tom's Changing Contemplative Program: A Case Example

As we have heard repeatedly, these methodologies should have the flexibility to be implemented in real-world applications in various ways. So, how do they look for a complete program? We have already considered smaller case examples for each of the three methodologies, such as we did for Francis, Min, and Matt, but we still have yet to see how they might be implemented when put altogether.

In this section we will be walking with Tom, our seminary student from the introductory chapter,[1] as he seeks to engage with these methods for the contemplative program that he designed for his local context. As we shall see, Tom's embodiment of these methods is as unique as was his local context. The hope of presenting this case is to provide one example of how these methods might be applied to the development of an entire program.

From Soil, to Seeds, to Sprouts: Exploration and Analysis

Tom engages in the first of our three methodologies by beginning with his own personal reflections and observations of his local context at the seminary he attends. From here, the idea for his program germinates and he then moves through the steps outlined by our exploration and analysis methodologies. These preparations, as we shall see, become the foundations for his program.

Surveying the Soil and Small Mustard Seeds: Tom's Idea for the Program

Tom is a young student at a small seminary located in a large and very diverse metropolitan city. During his own time at the school, Tom experienced periods of confusion and questioning as a result of being exposed to so much diversity on the campus and in his classes. Tom also noticed, through classes and small group discussions, that many of his classmates seemed to be experiencing similar struggles. In particular, questions for Tom and his peers centered on such issues as: who they are, what they believe, and why they are with their current religious, or nonreligious, communities. Tom also believes, given the diversity of the large metropolis, that these sorts of questions might also be common for others in the local community just beyond the seminary walls. As a result, Tom decides to develop a program for one of his classes that will engage with person's

---

1. The names and locations of this case example have been altered in order to maintain confidentiality, just as they have been in each of the previous ones. All quotations from Tom are taken from the proposal, journaling notes, and final report that Tom generated.

who are currently wrestling these questions of personal identity and faith development.

As it relates to our many steps above, he has discerned and clarified the initial intentions of the program he will develop (i.e., step one of the exploration and analysis methods). We can also see here that Tom has already begun the process of developing a contextually constructed model. By reflecting on his own experiences and those that he has observed of his classmates and the surrounding area, he has begun to clarify some of the anthropological and cosmological dynamics that his program will be seeking to engage. These are important considerations for Tom as he continues in its development.

The Mustard Seed Becomes a Bush: Tom and the Five Core Models

Tom took the time to look at each of the five core models that were outlined in this first methodology. From these, Tom was able to gain greater insights into both the heartbeat of his program as well as into some of the particulars that it might need in order to ensure success. As we shall presently see, Tom's engagement with the exploration and analysis and the design and implementation methods was intermixed, sometimes simultaneously engaging steps from both. We therefore follow Tom as he develops his own synthesized core models and the interventions that he began brainstorming based on them.

Program Goals & Ideals

Tom's stated purpose for the program is: "To help participants to come to learn more about themselves in the midst of this [pluralistic] context so that they may live their lives more closely with God." It is a goal of attempting to partner with the Spirit as it works to help individuals to learn more about themselves. It is also one of seeking to help the participants to do so in the context of much diversity and plurality of worldviews. Tom also holds an underlying assumption that accompanies this goal: there is a direct correlation between our own individuality and the unique ways that we will live our life with God. In other words, Tom hopes that by helping people to learn more about themselves, he will simultaneously be helping them to life a closer relationship with God.

In his efforts to be more specific, Tom lists three objectives for the program: (1) Creating a safe, affirming, and supportive environment where each of the participants can learn more about themselves in conversation with the material that they will be engaging with; (2) To actually learn some of the material that is related to personal spiritual growth and development for better working with themselves as well as with others; and (3) For each participant to grow in their own intrapersonal development, specifically in the area of their "spiritual identity."

For these goals, we can see that Tom has a clear focus that derives directly from his own contextual experiences. Tom is seeking to nurture a group environment that is open to diversity, individuality, and hospitality. Tom is also seeking to help the participants to learn and deeply engage with the identity-related material that he is planning on drawing from. What we do not see Tom doing here in relation to our exploration and analysis steps, however, is turning to external resources for additional insights and input. Instead, Tom opts for more simply choosing to use his own contextually constructed ideals for his program.

Tom's "Anthro-Cosmological" Models

For these reflections, Tom combines the anthropological and cosmological models and seeks a theory that can provide him with greater insights into the participants that he foresees working with. Unlike the ideals, however, Tom does turn to external resources for additional help and guidance. Specifically, he considers the developmental theories of William Perry in his book, *Forms of Intellectual and Ethical Development in the College Years*, James Fowler and his *Stages of Faith* text, and Robert Kegan's *The Evolving Self*.[2]

However, after reviewing these resources, rather than seeking a synthesis between each of them and his own contextually constructed understandings, Tom finds it most fitting to focus on Perry's model and the stages of development that it describes for college students in a liberal/pluralistic environment similar to his own. Tom makes this decision because his program is interested on exploring such questions as: Who am I as a child of God? How can I more closely follow and be with God in my life? What are some of my gifts and how might they best be used in service to God and creation? And, with so many different ways of living a life with God, which way might I be better suited for and called to? Given these foci, Tom believes that Perry's model, which generally tracks

---

2. Fowler, *Stages of Faith*; Kegan, *Evolving Self*; Perry, *Forms of Intellectual and Ethical Development in the College Years*.

the progress of students as they move from more dualistic positions (i.e., "black or white" thinking) to more committed positions in the midst of pluralism, is an adequate description of the kinds of dynamics that he anticipates his participants to be experiencing based on his own contextual experiences and observations. He therefore decides to primarily focus on Perry's model.

More specifically, Tom believes that he needs to be seeking to design this program for individuals who are in Perry's stages 4–5 and are seeking to move toward stages 6–9. Stages 4–5 of Perry's model represents those individuals who have come to see and accept a diversity of ideas and ways of approaching life.[3] Stages 6–9, alternatively, are when one comes to affirm one's own position in light of the diversity of choices available all around them.[4] Tom also notes of Perry's model that such developmental progress is alleged to involve at least four considerations: (1) affirmations in the midst of relativism; (2) coming to terms with one's past and with who they are in light of their contexts; (3) balancing various internal and external tensions; and (4) leading one to a greater understanding and formation of one's self-proclaimed identity.[5]

This external resource has therefore helped Tom to gain greater insights into some of the anthropological and cosmological dynamics that he believes his program will be engaging. Specifically, Tom's own personal experiences, the reflections he has heard from his classmates, and Perry's model have all helped him to realize that two fundamental dynamics seem to be at work here: (1) "the further development of one's spiritual identity"; and (2) "the relationship of that identity to the larger contexts of which one is a part." In other words, Tom's "anthro-cosmological" explorations have helped him to see more clearly that his program needs to address how each participant sees themselves in relation to the larger histories and contexts of which they have been and are currently a part of. Hence, while not as explicit or detailed as Francis's synthesis, discussed in chapter 3, Tom has engaged with the synthesizing steps for this core model.

These reflections have also provided Tom with beginning insights into the kinds of interventions that may be needed in order for his program to move toward the ideals that he has set forth. Tom realizes now that he will not only need to help his participants to reflect on who they are and how they currently see themselves, but also to help them to do so in

---

3. Perry, *Forms of Intellectual and Ethical Development*, 119, 128.
4. Ibid., 150.
5. Ibid., 151–52.

light of the experiences, cultures, and contexts that they have been a part of. Again, we can see here that our methodologies are tightly interrelated; as we engage one, we can also simultaneously engage the others. In this case, as we develop our core models, we can simultaneously begin our brainstorming for possible interventions to consider.

Theories of Change

To help him further clarify the theories of change that may be most accurate for his program, Tom returns to Perry's developmental theory. In addition to the developmental trajectory described above, Tom also notes in Perry's model four different factors that influence change in the ways that Perry describes it. The first is the obvious exposure to the liberal education and the "pluralistic environment" that Perry's students found themselves within.[6] Second, the college students in Perry's research were critically reflective of their experiences and education. A third element that seemed to emerge for Tom in Perry's model was the intentional choices and commitments that students made in each stage of their unfolding development.[7] A fourth and final element of growth that Tom noted in Perry's model were the simultaneous and competing internal urges to both progress and conserve.[8]

We can see here that in addition to trying to understand a core underlying theory of what change is according to Perry's model, Tom was also seeking to understand the factors that seemed to contribute to the kinds of transformation that were embedded in this theory. Tom's explorations here have therefore led him to declare the need for "praxis" approaches: "ones in which the participants will hopefully engage in intrapersonal transformation and learning through education, reflection, and experience." As he did with his anthro-cosmology, Tom is taking note of which practices might be helpful based upon each of this theory of change. Not only does this save time, it also allows Tom to be thinking ahead as he works. The results of these theories of change reflections are a core set of approaches that Tom will increasingly focus in on as he continues to move toward implementation.

6. Ibid., 4–5.
7. Ibid., 42.
8. Ibid., 58.

PART TWO: Methodological Movements

The Bush Burns, but Is Not Consumed: Theological Translations

Theologically, Tom sets forth what he describes as an "incarnational" view of God. It is one, he asserts, in which God is seen as being "incarnated within and through every part of creation." He then goes on to relate this incarnational view to this particular program. Specifically, Tom sets forth a definition of "spiritual identity" as being "those parts of one's self that God is seen/experienced to be most alive and fully manifesting through."

For Tom, this is a significant theological translation because it means that a central part of his program will be focused on helping the participants to reflect on their own lives and identities from this theistic perspective. In other words, Tom will seek to help them to reflect on which parts of their lives seem to be more reflective of God, according to their religious traditions, and which do not. Tom's theology has therefore not only helped him to engage in theological reflection (i.e., the fifth step of our exploration and analysis methods) in relation to this program, it has also provided him with insights into the kinds of reflective practices that he might engage with.

The Mustard Bush Blossoms: Design and Implementation

With these deep explorations and analyses in place, Tom then turns his attention to task of discerning which interventions his program might utilize. His hopes in this phase are to come to a concrete decision as to which specific approaches his program will use to help his participants to move toward the ideals that he foresees. The following is the progression that Tom made as he discerningly moved toward these ends.

Branches: The Results of Tom's Brainstorming So Far

We have already seen each of the core models above prompted Tom to begin brainstorming potential interventions. Table 10 below are the results of these possibilities. We can already see that, as in Min's case, some of these practices overlap and repeat across these areas. However, we can also see that the focus of Tom's program is further clarifying as it begins to take a more concrete form. It is becoming clear to him that much of his time with the participants will be spent in personal and contextual reflections and explorations. As Tom looks back over his hopes and ideas for his program, this resonates with him as being the type of contemplatively formative interactions that he longs to engage in with others. These brainstorms have therefore helped Tom not only to begin giving actual shape to his program, they have also helped him to further clarify and discern his hopes for it.

Table 10. Tom's Brainstormed Interventions

Five Core Areas	Potential Interventions
Ideals	• Personal reflections • Reflecting on and exploring one's life with God • Education of personal spiritual growth • Group sharing
"Anthro-Cosmology"	• Exploring own life in relation to one's context • Balancing internal and external tensions • Identity development reflections • Explorations of one's past and culture
Theories of Change	• Exposure to diversity • Critical reflection on experiences • Making intentional choices about one's identity • Praxis approaches: education, reflection, experience • Discerning between what to hold on to and what to let go of
Theological Considerations	• Theological/Spiritual reflections on identity

Twigs: Tom Narrows the Range of Possibilities

From these reflections, Tom narrows down the number of possible interventions. He identifies and describes the details of four specific practices, which embody the range of approaches listed above. The first practice is exposure to knowledge and education, specifically to: "autobiographies, personality types, developmental theories, depth psychology, various approaches to spirituality, and religious charisms." His theory of change for this approach is that by exposing participants these external resources, it will help them to better understand themselves and the journeys of their lives. Asserting that one of the ways that the Spirit forms individuals is through such education, Tom outlines the theology of this intervention.

Second, Tom plans to spend a significant amount of time in reflection with the group as well as providing them with reflection exercises to do on their own. As one of the core approaches that has been used throughout

Western Christianity, as we heard in our chapter on design and implementation, Tom feels confident that such practices are very much in alignment with the ideals that he has discerned and is coming to feel more assured in. Looking directly to the insights that he has gleaned from Perry's change theory, he believes that these practices should not only form the core of his program but that they will help to foster the kinds of transformation he is interested in.

A third central part of this program will be the small group community that Tom hopes to nurture to become a "supportive, encouraging, and listening community." These interventions are intended to be focused on both nurturing the community as a whole as well as exposing the participants to the diversity of the group. Seeing God as being active through both of these movements, Tom believes that they are supported by Perry's change theory wherein students develop when intentionally engaging with one another in supportive and reflective ways.

Finally, given the contemplative orientation of the program, which he now believes is appropriate for the ideals that he is aiming for, he is planning on leading the class through a diverse set of guided contemplative practices that will help them to deepen their personal and contextual reflections. With their primary aim being to help practitioners to "take a long loving look at the real,"[9] Tom is confident that a contemplative focus is well suited for this kind of spiritual formation program. Not only will these practices provide additional reflection tools for his participants to draw from, but they will also help this group to develop the kinds of focus and intentionality that his own experiences and Perry's model suggest are necessary for such transformation. With these reflections, Tom has essentially compiled, reduced and detailed the specific interventions that he is considering for his program (i.e., steps 2–4 of our design and implementation methodologies).

Blossoms: Tom's Final Planning and Implementation

Based upon these all of this, Tom then proposes a basic structure and curriculum for his program. "The content," he writes in his proposal, "will more intentionally be focused on exploring one's self: our autobiographies, how our lives compare to various stage developmental theories, our personality type structures and traits, and some of the psychodynamic parts of our psyches." Again, the primary focus of the program for him is to

9. Burghardt, "Contemplation," 14–18.

help participants to gain a better understanding of who they are as unique individuals and where they are in their life's journey with God.

For this program, Tom begins by proposing a basic format for each session that he will facilitate with his participants; one that embodies each of the four sets of approaches that he has discerned above. This structure, Tom believes, will not only allow the participants to engage with the material in both didactic, reflective, and experiential ways, but it will also enable Tom to gain the feedback that he will need in order to more adequately employ his own discernment processes, which will be discussed in greater detail below. The following is this format:

- Greetings & Group Sharing (30–45 minutes)
- Content to Be Presented (30 minutes)
- Introduce Reflective Exercise for the Coming Week (5–10 minutes)
- Contemplative Practice (5–20 minutes)

With this basic format in place, Tom next prepares a syllabus. Appendix C shows this very detailed plan that he constructed for each session. We can see that his program seeks to pursue the ideals that it sets out in accordance with the core models that he has synthesized and used to aid him in the discernment of his program's content.

As we can see in this appendix, Tom has decided to divide his program into six distinctive parts. With the opening and closing sessions being two of these, the other four parts are centered on the content that he wants to reflectively walk with his participants through. The first of these four areas is autobiographies. Here, Tom seeks to directly address one of his ideals by having his group intentionally reflect on the full journey of their own lives. Providing different contemplative practices and enough group sharing time to support these personal explorations, Tom seeks to help members deepen their self-knowledge in relation to the contexts and cultures they have grown up in.

Turning next to stage theories, his program takes a more educationally oriented focus from this point onward. Based upon the assertion that educating participants about the dynamics of human development will better enable them to understand themselves more deeply, Tom will seek to explore two such stage theories. We can see how each of the reflective and contemplative practices that he has chosen is intended to support and experientially deepen these explorations.

Following this format and these intentions, the final two phases of program focus on personality type systems and one psychodynamic theory that has been articulated in a book by Tom Holmes. Again, his program is seeking to help his participants to deepen their self-understandings in relation these models of human development and psychological dynamics. And, again, we can see that the reflective exercises he assigns and the contemplative practices that Tom plans on facilitating, are intended to further foster these transformations.

Finally, we can also see level of detail that such an extensive program can require. In a sense, each one of Tom's sessions is a mini-program to discerningly develop. However, we can also note that their development is made easier by all of the work that Tom has already done for the program as a whole: he already knows the general direction that each session should be helping to foster; he knows the format that each one will have; and he knows the content that they will generally engage. Nevertheless, as we can see more clearly with Tom's case, each one still needs some level of intentional discernment in order to ensure the success of the overall program.

From Mustard Bush to Apple Tree: Assessment and Modification

With this syllabus completed, Tom has effectively completed both of the first two praxis-based methodologies. However, before Tom can actually implement his program, he first needs to discern the monitoring and evaluation system that he will be using to help him track the program's progress and unfolding. Once this is in place, Tom can then move forward and bring all his hard work to fruition by kicking off his program. However, as we shall currently see, things can change in dramatic and unexpected ways when we implement our programs.

Watching the Grass Grow: Tom's Monitoring and Discernment System

Tom's final preparations now turn to the monitoring and evaluation system that he will use to help him track the progress of his program once it begins. As we heard in the last chapter, these are essential components to assessing and modifying our spiritually formative endeavors. Here, we briefly walk with Tom as he considers both of these elements: monitoring and evaluation.

Tom's Monitoring Techniques

Tom details the means through which he will track the progress of his program. Using his own observations, small group reflections, and through his own personal interactions with participants, Tom plans on gaining the valuable knowledge and insights that he will need in order to engage in the discernment process outlined below. In addition to identifying these sources of monitoring, Tom also begins to think about how he will actually go about engaging them. For instance, Tom realizes that in order to have access to the knowledge that personal interactions can provide, he will need to make himself available both before and after class as well as in between sessions. By doing this, Tom hopes to have additional time through which to talk with participants one-on-one and here how the program is progressing for them. The bulk of his monitoring approaches are therefore centered on the observations that he makes and the feedback that he receives from the group.

Evaluation: Tom's Spiritual Discernment Process

Rather than viewing evaluation as more of a mechanical-like comparing of observations with expectations, Tom instead decides to focus on the discernment process that he is planning on utilizing in order to help him follow the "Spirit's lead" as the program unfolds. Calling it "integrative discernment," Tom asserts that by monitoring what he understands to be God's movements in specific parts of the program, he will be able to collectively and integratively discern where it is that God is leading the group from session to session. Returning to our chapter on spiritual discernment, we can see here that Tom is choosing to follow the "integrating" rather than "emerging" path for making decisions.[10]

In choosing to view his evaluation process as discernment, however, Tom still creates evaluative criteria, in the form of sets of questions, to help guide him. His hopes in doing this are to help him better know the extent to which his program is successful in relation to the ideals that he has discerned. He categorizes these questions according to the four areas that he sees his program as focusing on:

- "Material: Are we really learning and understanding the material that is being offered? We will retain enough of it and know how to

---

10. See fig. 4 on p. 52.

use this material after the program is over in our own lives as well to help others?

- Spiritual Identity: Are we incorporating this material into our self understandings? Is our life being changed in some way through such engagement? Is this change, as challenging as it may be, generally in a positive and progressive direction? What is coming up in our weekly conversations? What do we, as a group, seem to be collectively saying?

- Community: How are we treating, receiving, responding, and interacting with one another? Is there a general environment of compassion, affirmation, support, and encouragement?

- More Generally: I will also be reflecting on my own internal movements in relation to this program as well as any contextual factors that either seem relevant or influential on our program."

We can see that these align with the objectives that Tom outlined when he discussed his ideals for the program. By reflecting "contemplatively" on each of these areas, Tom asserts, he will be able to gain better idea of the overall directions that the Spirit is attempting to lead his program. To help support him in these discerning reflections, Tom also plans to meet with a group of fellow classmates and professors with whom he can discuss the progress of his program and receive vital feedback and mentoring. So rather than creating evaluative criteria to be rigidly followed for his program, Tom instead chooses to use them to define and clarify the discernment process that he will be engaging for the duration of the program. With his monitoring and evaluation system in place, Tom now moves forward and actually implements his program.

The Death of the Mustard Bush: Tom Implements His Program

With even the best laid plans . . . Spirit happens! Tom has now spent a considerable amount of time planning and preparing for his program. He has discerned the foci that his program will have, the interventions and path that he believes will lead them there, and he has a monitoring and discernment system ready to be put into action. Unfortunately for Tom, as we shall currently see, God had other plans for his program. In this section, we will continue to follow Tom as he moves from his prayer closet and the pages of his planning to the real-world implementation of his program. In this section, then, we will not only see how the assessment and modification methodologies can be embodied, but also why spiritual discernment is so central to our craft and what can sometimes happen in the context of our ministries.

THE BUSH GETS SHOCKED: TOM'S FIRST SESSION

Tom advertised his program extensively on his seminary campus. He also sent flyers and made personal contact with four local churches and communities. Tom also worked to further clarify his monitoring approaches by refining the kinds of questions he would have the group reflect on and the information he would record as the course progressed. The stage was set, the first session was scheduled, and Tom was ready . . . or so he thought.

At the first session, which was intended to be an introduction and overview to the program so that participants could decide if they were truly interested or not, seven people attended. Tom had planned for and designed his program primarily for seminary students who were struggling and wrestling with their own faith identities in the midst of a diverse and pluralistic context. However, only one student from the seminary came. The rest were people from the community who had heard about the program through their churches. Tom had expected his constituents to be younger, perhaps in their mid-twenties to early thirties. Most of these non-seminary participants were in their forties, fifties, and even sixties. Clearly, the anthropological model that Tom had so carefully constructed would have to be modified.

However, this wasn't the least of the unexpected occurrences that Tom had to face. A significant part of this first session, as appendix C shows, was spent having each participant share something about their personal backgrounds and why they were attending this program. Hearing their comments, Tom came to realize that two of the churches he sent flyers to had mis-advertised the program. Instead of the program being presented as a "spiritual identity exploration program" through contemplative practices, these churches had announced that it was an "introductory class on contemplative traditions." As a result, six of the seven people in attendance at this first session were there expecting this alternative class that Tom had not prepared.

Despite all of this, Tom proceeded with the first session as originally planned and explained what the course's planned intention and directions were, apologizing for the mis-advertising. After this session, Tom took a major step back and questioned how the program should proceed from here. Looking back to the planning stages, he now remembered that he had some thoughts and feelings that the program, as he originally designed it, did not fully resonate within him. In other words, as Tom was discerning the program's foci, and detailing how the program would be carried out, he now recalled that there were affective movements within him that were not fully consoling and affirming of the directions he was developing.

At that time, though, he did not pay these feelings too much attention since the planning and preparations seemed to be going so well and were so comprehensive. Now, however, he was beginning to wonder if he shouldn't have prayerfully sat with these stirrings earlier on. We can see here that an over reliance on models, methodologies, and strategies can sometimes draw our attention away from other ways of knowing that our discernment processes may prompt us to additionally consider.

The Bush Wilts: Growing Doubts about the Course's Direction

Despite the unanticipated realities of this first session, and these alternative inner stirrings, Tom decides to continue with the first phase of the program as planned. He did revisit his anthro-cosmologies but he could not yet see how changes to them might alter the overall design of his program. Also, since he had already presented an overview of the program, Tom felt compelled to go forward with this plan out of a felt obligation to those people who continued to attend. Nevertheless, Tom felt much less confident now about the program's current trajectory.

This first phase of the course was three weeks of autobiographical reflections. Here, participants—now four to five people depending on the week—were encouraged to look back over their lives and to divide it up into chapters. These weeks were crucial for Tom as he came to learn more about each of these participants: their past histories, their vocational and religious journeys, and their hopes and dreams for the future. Throughout it all, Tom's doubts about the originally planned program continued to grow. In his own journaling about the program, which is one of the monitoring approaches he utilized, Tom notes "fears of [the upcoming] Stage and Personality Theories being too theoretical, too dull—fears of [the participants] loosing interest/passion in our journey." Tom is thankful for the generativity that these autobiographical reflections did foster among the group, as evidenced by the passionate sharing and stimulating conversations that they were having together. However, he is also afraid that the

From Mustard Seeds to Apple Trees

next originally planned phase of the program—theoretical reflections on stage theories—will loose this vitality. Yet, Tom is still at a loss for what to do about it. As a result, he continues to monitor, discerningly evaluate, discuss these issues with his support group, and pray.

The Mustard Bush Dies: Tom's Turning Point

Tom has committed, as we heard, to an "integrative discernment" process. This means that Tom is reflecting on how he perceives God to be moving in the material that they are engaging, the small group dynamics that are emerging, the reflections of each participant, and with his own inner movements. This discernment process, as we shall now see, eventually empowers him to find the new direction that his program needs in order to continue in vital and transformative ways.

His original anthro-cosmologies are no longer completely valid. It has become obvious from the autobiographical reflections that the participants, who are much older and more experienced than he had expected, are well settled in their own identities and do not seem to need the kinds of life reflections that Tom originally thought might be helpful for them. In other words, as we may recall, Tom was expecting a group who was still struggling with questions of who they were and what all of this diversity that surrounds them means for their lives. However, none of the members actually attending each session were wrestling in these ways, as evidenced by their autobiographical sharing.

Tom has also noted that this group enjoys talking about their own faith journeys as well as hearing from one another. They are also curious about the contemplative practices they have been engaging and the traditions that these practices have come from. These, in addition to the inner stirrings that Tom has become increasingly aware of in himself as the program has progressed, lead him toward considering changing the program in major ways.

For Tom, the turning point of his ongoing integrative discernment came in the fourth session of the program. They had just finished with their autobiographical reflections and Tom began presenting the stage theories that he had originally planned to. Toward the end of his presentation, however, one of the participants raised their hand and asked, "Are we going to be talking more about how to get closer to God? Because I feel like that's what I need to be focusing on more right now." Looking at the others in the group, Tom sees nodding heads and asks, "Would you like to know more about contemplative ways of doing this?" The unanimous response was yes. For Tom, this was the permission that part of himself had been looking for; permission to fundamentally change the direction of their time together each week. The subsequent changes that Tom makes not only resonate with what he feels inside himself, but they also fit more closely with the participants who are attending and the dynamics that have emerged in their small group.

New Seeds Germinate and Grow: Tom Reenvisions His Program

The next day after this session, Tom sits down to pray through all that the group has been through to date. He recalls that most of the participants had originally attended hoping for a course that would introduce them to a contemplative way of life. He notes that their own journeys have led them to a place in their lives where they yearn for a deeper, more intimate, and experiential relationship with God.

Tom also thinks about his own beginning vocation in contemplative spiritual formation and his desires to share these practices and traditions with others. He revisits the fact that the core models, particularly the anthro-cosmological models, are not accurate and therefore the program he originally designed based on them does not fit with the participants who are actually attending. Instead, this group collectively yearns for more tangible practices and ways of deepening their relationship with God.

THE APPLE TREE TAKES ROOT: TOM REVISITS HIS CORE MODELS

Revisiting his core models, Tom realizes that while his theology still seems to hold he does need to modify his ideals, anthro-cosmologies, and theories of change. Beginning with his ideals, he still wants for them to have a closer explicit relationship with God. However, self-exploration and knowledge no longer holds the centrality that it originally did. Now, both he and the group are more interested in deepening their spiritual life through a contemplative worldview. Tom's core ideals therefore shift now toward helping the group to know what such a spiritual worldview is, according to the Western Christian tradition, and how to tangibly live it out in one's daily life. Tom also realizes that there must be an experiential emphasis on this ideal, as his participants yearn for a deeper and more personal relationship with God.

Tom still affirms the three ideals that were originally set, though now with a focus on contemplative spirituality. He will continue to try and foster a "safe, affirming, and supportive environment." He will strive to help participants to learn the material—now contemplative worldviews and ways of living—that they are engaging with. And he will continue to work to help them grow in their own intrapersonal spiritual development, only now from a more fully contemplative perspective. In this way, Tom modifies the ideals that he has for his program.

Turning next to his anthro-cosmologies, Tom essentially has to drop his original model and start anew. Perry's model, which captured some of the developmental changes that young students traverse through at liberal arts colleges, does not accurately capture the population that he is working with. As Tom has now only two weeks within which to completely redesign his program, he decides to primarily rely on his own contextual experiences with the group. Having just completed the sharing of each of their autobiographies, Tom feels that he now knows them well enough to reformulate this model.

For him, as we have heard, these are middle-aged to older persons who are well established in their lives and vocations. Some have grown children and are approaching retirement while others are building a family and progressing through the middle years of their careers. All of them, as evidenced by their autobiographical reflections, have a great deal of self-knowledge and are emotionally well developed; meaning that they are able to articulate their histories and feelings with both depth and confidence.

The most dominant dynamic that Tom notes, however, is their yearning to deepen their experiential religious life with God. While each of them has grown up and are still attending Protestant churches, they long for practices and ways of living life that are more explicitly oriented toward God in deeply personal ways. As they each expressed in the introductory session, they are interested in contemplative traditions because they are wondering if these might have something to offer them along these lines. With this newly modified anthro-cosmology, Tom further reflects on how this program might be reenvisioned.

Next, Tom looks back at his theories of change and realizes that these too, also being based on Perry's model, must go. Now, the theories of change that seem most pertinent are those that focus on enculturation such as are found in John Westerhoff's book, *Will Our Children Have Faith?*[11] Such theories assert that we come to be transformed by being fully

---

11. However, Tom did not explicitly turn to this book or any other text as a resource for his new change theory. However, he did note the existence of these kinds of

immersed in the ways of life of our communities.[12] If Tom's group longs for a deeper way of life with God, and they do so from a contemplative perspective, then perhaps enculturation is an adequate model for understanding some the dynamics for how this can transpire.

Viewing Christian faith as a story, Westerhoff asserts, "Unless the story is known, understood, owned, and lived, we and our children will no have Christian faith."[13] Tom decides that this more adequately represents the kinds of changes that God now wants to foster with this group. By helping them to "know, understand, own, and live" the contemplative way, they will grow in the experiential ways that they are longing for. Tom therefore adopts such an enculturation model as his new theory of change.

Finally, the theological considerations that Tom made did not change all that significantly. He still affirms the incarnational nature of God, but his application of it has changed. Rather than being more focused on the "spiritual identity" of each person, his focus now shifts to emphasizing the activity of the Spirit through the learning of a particular way of being with God (i.e., the contemplative path). Tom affirms that the group's longings for a deeper and more experiential relationship are "godly movements." He also affirms the contemplative ways of Western Christianity as being valid ways to deepen such a life. Tom therefore finds further confirmation of these emerging directions through his theological reflections.

The Tree Branches Out: Reassessing His Interventions

In light of these modified core models, Tom then reassesses the interventions that he is using. Since they have been following a set format for four weeks now, Tom decides to initially focus these reflections on discerning whether or not this format will still work for this newly emerging program. With enculturation into a contemplative way of life being the new horizon, Tom realizes that these elements are valuable. Education, reflection, sharing, and experiential engagement with contemplative practices can facilitate such enculturating changes.[14] Looking back at the core models

---

theories. Instead, Tom elected to rely most heavily on his own experiences, as well as on the contextual data that he was continuing to gather.

12. Westerhoff, *Will Our Children Have Faith?*, 16.
13. Ibid., 34.
14. Ibid., 23, 38, 49–50.

above, Tom further affirms these essential interventions and decides to retain them.

However, Tom does change their order. With the emphasis of the program now shifting to be more on learning and experiencing the contemplative way than on personal reflections, he makes the following changes. First, Tom decides to now open each session with the contemplative practice, making this the heart of the program. The group will then briefly reflect on their experiences with this practice, raising questions and learning from one another's experiences. Following this, Tom will then spend the second half of class teaching the group about a specific aspect of contemplative traditions. With these model modifications and slight changes in how they will engage the interventions, Tom then moves to finalizing the newly revised program.

The Apple Tree Blossoms: Tom Recreates and Implements His Program

Based upon all of this, Tom decides to refocus the program toward contemplative ways of living as discussed above. Appendix D shows the revised syllabus that Tom constructs as a result of these discerning reflections. We can see that Tom has completely restructured part 2 of the program toward the exploration of Western Christian contemplative traditions. With Tom's seminary education focusing on contemplative spirituality, he draws together some of these resources to present to the group.

Using our praxis-based methodologies as a framework for how to present this material, he decides to cover contemplative ideals, cosmologies, anthropologies, interventions, theories of development, monitoring, and discernment. Tom finds these topics to comprehensively cover contemplative spiritualities. He decides to present these elements to his participants through the metaphor of a journey: the ideals represent the horizons toward which we tend; the approaches are the means by which the Spirit moves us there; the anthropologies, cosmologies, and theories of change are maps to help guide our trip; and monitoring and discernment help us to stay on track. For each one of these areas, he then discerns which resources to present and how to go about teaching each one so that they progressively move toward the new ideals in an enculturating way.

Stepping back, Tom feels deeper levels of inner peace with this new program and moves forward with confidence. Before finalizing his decision to implement this program, he contacts the group and asks for feedback on what he has prepared. The group unanimously approves the new direction and its content. They then spend the next six weeks learning about these contemplative perspectives, engaging in their practices, and reflecting on them as both individuals and as a group. The discussions they have continue to be vital and engaging as they struggled with such topics as the nature of sin/suffering and God's relationship to it according to contemplative authors as well as how these traditions view one's deepening relationship with the Divine. Tom's monitoring and discerning evaluations confirm, as they continue on, that this was a good direction to change to. The program therefore proceeds as planned without any further alterations on a major scale.

In their final evaluations, the participants reported great appreciation for the exposure that they received through the program. Some of them stated that they were deeply impacted by the practices that they engaged for it was through these experiences that, one wrote, helped her to face her own "negative feelings without being engulfed by them or reacting to them." All of them expressed appreciation for the program and the contemplative ways of seeing and engaging with their own lives that were presented in the program.

Overall, Tom's newly discerned direction resonated with his own inner movements, they fit with the backgrounds and yearnings of each participant, and it continued to nurture the small group dynamics that emerged. Hence, even though there were major changes to the content of the program, Tom still realized the ideals that were originally discerned. Even though it was a lot to encounter, Tom reportedly felt the presence and guidance of God all along the way.

Post-Program Reflections:
Tom Looks Back and Moves Forward

Looking back, in his final report, Tom reflected on the trajectory of the program, its unexpected changes, and the significance of it for both future programs and his own unfolding vocation. In particular, Tom noted the initial inner stirrings that were present but overlooked during the original planning and preparation stages and what the implications of this were for his own approaches to discernment. He realized that he must pay more attention to these stirrings early on and what their possible implications might be at every step of the way. Tom also took the time to look ahead and reflect on what his experiences of the program might mean for his vocation. Tom feels pulled between the possibility of pursuing a doctoral degree or returning to congregational ministry. Ultimately, Tom returned to congregational ministry, making contemplative retreats a significant portion of his formative focus.

Closing Reflections: The Centrality of Discernment

We can see in these reflections how Tom continues on living spiritual praxis. Even though this particular program is finished, life still goes on. These sorts of ongoing reflections and discernment are important not only while we are engaging with specific programs, but also long after they are completed. The cycles of spiritual praxis therefore occur at many levels and in many ways, ever inviting us into a way of life that fosters sacred vitality.

Tom's journey through the duration of his program, from planning and preparation to major overhaul and revising, provide us with one way that our three praxis-based methodologies might be embodied. As we have seen, not every step will necessarily be engaged in the same way each time, nor will their order be exactly as presented. In Tom's case, for instance, he found it much more convenient to simultaneously embody some of the exploration and analysis and design and implementation methodologies as he reflected on his core models and the possible interventions that they might suggest for his program. It is therefore up to each practitioner to discerningly decide how to engage with each of these methodologies.

Spiritual discernment, as we have heard from the very beginning of this book and seen throughout, is therefore absolutely central to our work. Theories and planning strategies should not displace ongoing, in vivo discernment for a practitioner. Once a model is constructed or a theory is professed, it is essentially "dead." It is dead in the sense that is ceases to be related to the ever changing dynamics of our local contexts, at least until we revise this model in light of such changes as Tom did his own core models.

Hence, while our core models and the praxis methodologies that we have explored throughout this book can be helpful, they are not intended to replace the holistic and contextually rooted processes of spiritual discernment that we explored in our first chapter. The Spirit is continuously alive as we minister and our spiritually forming vocation must move with and be moved by this unending life. Tom's case is therefore not only an example of how we might embody our methodologies but also of this all

PART TWO: Methodological Movements

important formation fact: theistic spiritual formation rises and falls on moment-by-moment discernment of God's life and work in our midst. We must therefore give such discernment a central place to our craft for it can take us toward ends that we might never have anticipated from the beginning, just as it did for Tom.

Conclusion

Living Spiritual Praxis in Retrospect

AN URBAN PREACHER DISCERNS the closing call of the Spirit with a congregation. A senior minister explores some of the dynamics of a hurting relationship. An associate pastor designs a course for lay leaders. A public school teacher alters his class on literature. And a seminary student journeys through unexpected valleys and heights as he implements a contemplative formation program. For Montague, Francis, Min, Matt, and Tom, the life and work of a formator can be thrilling, challenging, and unpredictable. And, yet through methodologies such as have been presented in these pages, we can discern the help and guidance that we need in order to navigate the trajectories of this exciting vocation. In these final pages, we reflect on the journey that we have been through, cycling back around through each movement for such is the nature of our work; such is living spiritual praxis.

Finding God in All That Is:
Notes on Spiritual Discernment

Western Christian theistic spiritual formation is but one worldview through which to approach the broader vocation of human transformation. As we saw both with our reflections on spiritual discernment and with our exploration and analysis theological reflections, it is one that intentionally seeks to perceive and pursue the movements of the Sacred in our midst. Such theistic discernment, as Tom came to experientially realize, is the very core of our craft as it can lead us in directions that we might never have anticipated.

PART TWO: Methodological Movements

As formators, working in most ministerial contexts, we are invited to partner with the Spirit's formative movements as God works with the individuals, relationships, and communities to which we are called. Not only does the Divine continually shape and transform the inner person, but also the space that lies in between couples and small groups. We can also incarnationally find God's life to be active in the political, social, and economic dynamics of our congregations as Montague learned. And, as we saw with Min and Matt as well as with Tom's modified program, this Spirit is equally alive in the subjects that we learn and in the knowledge that we acquire.

In short, I am asserting, a central part of the nature of theistic spiritual formation is to discerningly unite with God's leading life as it lives and moves and has its Being in every part of creation. From physical to psychological, from sociological to epistemological, there is no place that we cannot perceive the movements of divine life in accordance with our religious and theological traditions. As we heard in the last chapter and throughout this book, our formative work therefore rises and falls on spiritual discernment.

CYCLES IN PRAXIS: OUR THREE METHODOLOGIES

With this discerning foundation in place, we then turned to the praxis-oriented pragmatics of program development. With theory, practice, and reflection—for the purposes of transformation—we have come to see through each of our three methodologies just how praxis-oriented spiritual formation can be. Again and again, for each of our methodological movements, these three praxis elements interact with one another in ways that inform and transform the programs we are seeking to develop. External resources, theological reflections, clarifying interventions, modifying our models, et cetera, all embody theory, practice, and reflection to one degree or another.

Each of our three methodologies also collaborated to help us partner more transformatively with God's life in our communities. Reflecting on these, we can note just how intermingled these methodologies are. The exploration and analysis methodologies enable us spiritually discern the strong foundational insights and understandings that God needs us to have. The design and implementation methodologies then empower us to stand firmly on these foundations and more clearly perceive the means by which the Spirit will form the people we are working with. Sometimes, however, our explorations here might prompt us to return to the previous movement as we seek to learn more about our community and how to engage with them. Finally, the assessment and modification methodologies compel us into the cyclical and ongoing nature of walking with God as our program unfolds and moves along on its sometimes unpredictable paths. Figure 12 below shows these movements and their feedback nature.

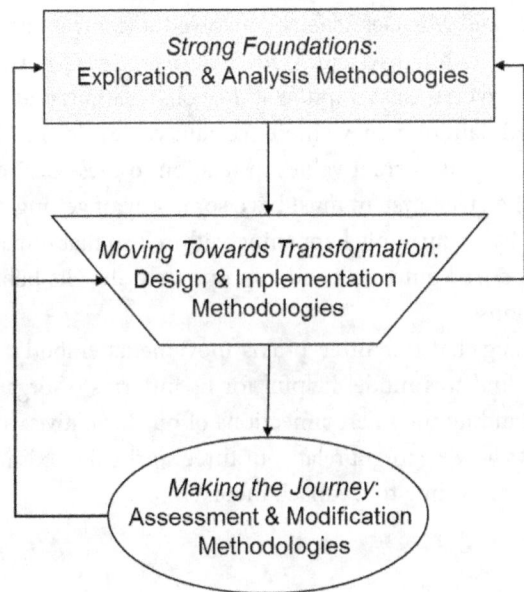

Figure 12. Our Three Methodologies and Their Cyclical Nature

Round and round, we might be led to engage with portions of these methodologies as our program progresses toward the ideals that lie ever before us. Program development, as we have encountered it here, is therefore one of a cyclical nature. It is about discerning direction, taking action, and assessing the fruits that come to bear. Ultimately, it is one of feedback.

Reflections on Feedback: A Framework for Our Craft

We have already seen how action researchers and practical theologians think about and engage in praxis, as shown in the figure above. However, I offer one alternative way of representing and understanding the praxis nature of spiritual formation program development based on our discussions throughout this book. Overall, the purpose of these reflections is to help us to gain a better feel for the nature and essence of these three methodologies and our formative work more generally.

At its heart, when conceived of as praxis, program development is essentially a feedback back system.[15] Feedback theory has had wide ranging applications in such fields as engineering, theater and acting, and neuroscience-based approaches to formation.[16] In its most fundamental and simplified essence, "feedback processes," write professors of psychology Charles Carver and Michael Scheier, "involve the control and regulation of certain values within a system."[17] It is referred to as "feedback theory" because it is based on the assumption and/or observations that in order for a system to maintain or achieve these "certain values" it must have some way of monitoring its current values in relation to these desired ones. In other words, the given system must have some way of getting continuous feedback on what is currently happening within it so that it may compare this with the desired outcomes and appropriately alter its behaviors and actions in response.

Recognizing that our three praxis movements embody such feedback, we may find this model helpful for us in terms of organizing and better understanding the interconnections of our formative work. Figure 13 below shows how we might relate our three spiritual praxis movements to one another according to feedback theory.

---

15. For discussions on the nature of feedback and its application to human systems, see such texts as: Carver and Scheier, *On the Self-Regulation of Behavior*, ch. 2.

16. For examples of texts in these fields, see: Franklin et al., *Feedback Control of Dynamic Systems*; Bilgrave and Deluty, "Stanislavski's Acting Method and Control Theory," 329–40; Dispenza, *Evolve Your Brain*, 292, 303, 326, 439–42.

17. Carver and Scheier, *On the Self-Regulation of Behavior*, 10.

Living Spiritual Praxis in Retrospect

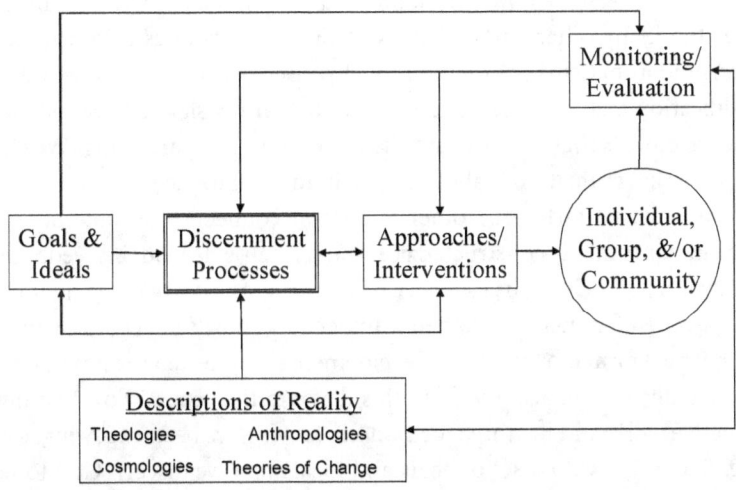

Figure 13. A Proposed Feedback Framework

From this diagram, we can begin to see how our three methodologies are interrelated. The first exploration and analysis movement is largely concerned with the descriptions of reality and the ideals that we discerningly set forth. The design and implementation movement is directly related to the approaches and interventions shown in this figure. Finally, the assessment and modification movement is also clearly captured by this architecture with its monitoring and evaluation feedback. Overall, then, this feedback framework provides us with a diagrammatic way of better understanding how each of the praxis methodologies might be depicted as being related to one another.

We can also see that discernment is a central part of the process, as we have heard throughout. In order for this discernment to be more fruitful, it requires the input of almost every part of our work: the ideals we are striving for, the interventions we are using, the core models that inform our work, and the feedback we have available to us via our monitoring and evaluation systems. Each of these inputs can and should therefore be a part of our individual and communal discernment processes.

We can also note how our core models play a foundational role not only for our discernment processes, but also for the ideals we choose, the interventions we drawn from, and the monitoring and evaluation techniques we implement. This framework therefore helps to see just how foundational these descriptions of reality are. It is therefore with much care intentionality that we must engage in our exploration and analysis methods.

Next, we can see how our monitoring and evaluation feedback influences the many other parts of our system. Not only does it inform our discernment, but this information is also used—as our assessment and modification methodologies showed—to further revisit and reassess both the core models that we have and the interventions we are using. We can also note that evaluation is always made in relation to the goals and ideals that we have set forth. The other important connection to note here is how our contextually constructed core models rely solely on this feedback, thereby further helping us to realize its importance for work. Seeing these linkages therefore helps us to better understand how each component of our spiritual formation program development is connected to one another.

Finally, we can also see from this diagram the general flow that our formative work, and the three methodologies we have been exploring, can take. Beginning with a set of goals and ideals that we discern God to be inviting us toward, we then discern—in light of all of the information that we have available to us—how we should go about pursing these ideals. The result, as we found with our design and implementation methodologies, was a set of approaches and interventions that we then implemented with the people and communities we are called to work with. But our efforts do not stop here, following the flow of this architecture, because we must continue to monitor and evaluate the results of our work, which is then fed back into our discernment processes thereby fueling the ongoing and cyclical nature of the "living spiritual praxis" that we are seeking to embody. This architecture therefore helps us to see how each of our three sets of methodologies, and of the components related to them, are interconnected and practically realized in our spiritually forming craft.

Discerned Simplicity: Returning for a Final "KISS"

This proposed framework can also help us to realize something that we have come to see as we journeyed through part 2 of this book: spiritual formation program development can be a very complex and detailed set of processes! As we saw with each one of our case examples, the busy life of a formator who is working in a ministerial context just does not permit her or him to engage in every single one of these steps to the full extent that they have been presented herein. This book is intended to present the "foundations" for such program development, not the "mandatory requirements" of it.

Living Spiritual Praxis in Retrospect

How, then, do we know what is needed and what is not? This is where, once again, the KISS principle comes into play. We must remember that the primary focus for each of our spiritually forming programs is to "partner with God's formative life and leadings in our local contexts." This means, for each of our three methodologies, that we must ever discerningly perceive the extent to which the Spirit is inviting us to engage in or modify each one of the sixteen steps presented herein.

How much detail is needed for the core models that we have synthesized? How many different interventions do we really need to consider? Which assessments and modifications do we need to focus most of our time and attention on? Questions such as these can help to guide our spiritual discernment processes as they are applied to each one of these steps. Discernment, as we heard, is therefore not intended to be a one-time and discrete practice that we apply here and there. Rather, it is intended to become a way of life that ever more fully harmonizes us within and to the Spirit. We therefore need to continually seek to KISS the sacred as we discern the extent to which we are invited to engage in each of these steps. Sometimes this will mean embodying all of them to the fullest and, more often, this will mean modifying them to fit with what God is doing locally.

The End of the Beginning

As we have now come to the end of these explorations, we simultaneously come to a beginning—or continuation—of our program development efforts. With the life of the Spirit being so fully and unendingly active in every part of creation, each one of us has been, knowingly or not, engaged in the kinds of spiritually discerning living that our praxis-oriented fields encourage us to embody. Theories and models—such as the theologies we hold—impact and guide our lives, action and practice transforms our world, and discerning reflection leads us along various paths.

For program development in the field of theistic spiritual formation, such ways of living and being truly can transform ourselves and the people we are called to work with. With these foundations in place, we may continue in our work to move with God toward these ends. As we do, the cycles will continue, feedback will bring transformation, and the dance that ever more fully unites our world with the ones that God foresees will continue to unfold as we continue on living spiritual praxis.

Appendix A

Various Steps to Discernment

THE FOLLOWING ARE A list of steps that seven of our authors on discernment recommend. It is upon our synthesis of these that the five discernment processes recommended in chapter 2 are based.

- 1) Daniel Wolpert's "Examining Spirits" Practice (Wolpert, *Leading a Life with God*, 172–73)
  - Step 1) "Choose a period of time to examine in prayer"
  - Step 2) "Allow your mind to wander through that period of time. Some questions you might ask yourself about that period include:
    - What are you most/least grateful for during that time?
    - When did you feel a sense of love, peace, joy, life (the gifts of the Spirit)?
    - When did you feel exhausted, dead, drained, angry, mean?
    - What specific events, thoughts, or experiences draw your attention?
    - What aspects of that time repel you?
    - What things feel out of place, uninteresting?
    - Ask yourself, When did I notice God during this time? What felt like a time of God's absence?"
  - Step 3) "As some answers to these questions arise, notice what they suggest to you about the future. How is God calling you into being? Toward what actions, activities, or attributes is God drawing you?"

Appendix A

- Step 4) "Repeat this prayer at regular intervals in order to see how God is working in your life."

* 2) Wilkie and Noreen Cannon Au's Steps (Au and Au, *Discerning Heart*, 60–64)
  - Step 1) "Identify the decision that faces us or the issue we need to resolve"
  - Step 2) "Examine the underlying values (human, Christian, spiritual) and personal concerns involved"
  - Step 3) "Strive for Ignatian indifference"
  - Step 4) "Take time to pray over the matter, paying attention to how we are being drawn or led"
    - "we ask for God's guidance and try to be sensitive to how we are being drawn when the matter is brought to prayer . . . God can influence us through our thoughts as well as through our feelings of consolation and desolation in prayer"
  - Step 5) "Make a choice based on both the results of our "head work" and our "heart work""
    - ""Head work" includes weighing the matter with our reasoning process . . . "Heart work" entails sitting with the choice that our reasoning has determined to be the best and checking for affective confirmations"
  - Step 6) "Discuss the matter with a spiritual companion"
    - "someone who is committed to helping us be truthful, patient, and persevering in our search for God's call"
  - Step 7) "Dialogue with those who will be intimately affected by the decision being made"
    - Step 8) "Live out our decision with courage, hope, and trust"

* 3) Richard Hauser's Steps (Hauser, *Moving in the Spirit*, 68–81)
  - Step 1) "formulation of the proposition to be reflected upon" (p. 68)
  - Step 2) "using our minds to reflect on the proposition" (p. 70)

Various Steps to Discernment

- - - "we want to call up into our awareness all the reasons that incline us against the proposition and all the reasons that move us toward accepting the proposition"
    - List pros and cons
  - Step 3) "observing the direction of our will when we reflect on the reasons for and against the decision" (p. 73)
    - "as we gain illumination from the Spirit on the reasons for and against the proposition, we simultaneously find our will being moved by the Spirit in one or the other direction"
  - Step 4) "center on our feelings: we ask the Lord to give us the feeling of sensible consolation on the alternative that is more for God's greater glory" (p. 74)
  - Step 5) "confirmation of the decision that has been made…this means accepting the tentative decision as God's will and living with the decision over a period of time" (p. 76)
    - "we want to observe our inner experience of mind, will and feeling to see whether they continue to be drawn toward the decision. If the decision is truly from the Lord, usually our minds will find more reasons to support it, our wills will be held toward the decision and the feeling of consolation will accompany our thoughts on our decision."

- 4) Valerie Isenhower and Judith Todd's Movements: (Isenhower and Todd, *Living into the Answers*, chaps. 4–10)
  - Movement 1) Naming and Framing
    - "We start by naming "the issue" we are facing that calls for a decision . . . Naming the issue is how we identify it." (p. 51)
    - "As you proceed to clarify the issue or decision you are focusing on, start by describing all the parts within it for which you desire God's guidance." (p. 53)
    - "In framing the issue, first we try to identify the broad, overarching questions" (p. 55)
  - Movement 2) Centering
    - "we need to become aware of the values and assumptions that affect our process of discernment. This chapter provides

Appendix A

guidance for centering ourselves in God's yearning for us and uncovering presuppositions that shape our life." (p. 59)

- ◊ "One important aspect of centering ourselves for spiritual discernment involves our core values. They are the values we have develop over the years that serve as pillars of our faith and life... Our values are critical to us as we live our lives. As guiding principles, they instruct us on how we live." (p. 59–60)

- ◊ "We name our core values so that they can be instructive to us and available to God for change." (p. 63)

- ▫ "Ignatian indifference can be described as a state of inner freedom openness, and balance. It does not incline us more toward one option than another... Shedding involves letting go of our agendas and becoming indifferent to any choice except what God wants." (pp. 63–64)

- Movement 3) Remembering
  - ▫ "Remembering helps us know where we've been and who we were... Looking at the path we have trod in order to arrive at this place, remembering when we have called on God, when we have felt God's presence acting in our lives, and when we have felt God's absence are important steps in knowing where God is leading us." (pp. 67–68)

- Movement 4) Listening
  - ▫ "We will gather data and opinions that gave an impact upon our decision making…Here we will pull together both factual information and feelings." (p. 77)
    - ◊ "The chart [on page 80] helps you sort out the voice: voices with facts and data, voices of other people, interior voices and feelings, and voices from other sources. Continue to categorize information you discover about the subject of your discernment." (p. 78)
      - » Two columns: Voices and Feelings (p. 80)
    - ◊ "The Holy Spirit is active in our process, so be prepared to listen to words from unexpected places and unexpected people." (p. 86)

- Consolidating: "At this point, simply look back over your experience in data gathering and notice the major trends or pieces of information that rise to your attention." (p. 89)
    - Ponder them (p. 90)
- Movement 5) Path Building
    - "At this stage in your journey, you need to look at the possible paths available based on all the information you have gathered to date. It is time to let your imagination loose, to be creative and not limit God's possibilities. Don't discount anything. Let your dreams range as widely as possible." (p. 93)
        - "The information you have gathered probably sorts itself into several major categories we can call "paths." Each path represents a different direction you could take to resolve your issue or to make your decision . . . Before you choose among the options—or paths—consider each one in turn." (p. 93)
        - "Does the path draw you nearer to God or move you farther away? Does the path keep you centered on Christ? Any choice you uncover should lead you into a deeper relationship with God." (p. 98)
- Movement 6) Sifting
    - "You are finally ready to sift all the data and allow a direction to emerge, pointing toward a decision and resolution of your issue." (p. 101)
        - "It is a time to step back and look at the whole picture in an inactive way. It is a time to let go of control and see what rises to the top." (p. 102)
        - "Read over the information you have gathered about all the paths. Which one stirs positive emotions in you? Right now focus on looking for the path that brings you closer to God." (p. 103)
- Movement 7) Resting
    - "Spiritual discernment teaches us to wait before acting . . . We need to live with the results of our discernment process for a while." (p. 109)

Appendix A

- ◊ "This final circle, focused on resting calls us to enter a Sabbath period in which the information gathered in the previous circles sinks into our understanding and becomes clear." (p. 111)
- ◊ "In this final stage, reflect on the entire process, allowing the feelings of consolation or desolation to sink in at a deeper level." (p. 112)

* 5) Ackerman's Stages of Discernment (Ackerman, *Listening to God*, 84–91)
  - Stage 1) Application of Spiritual Doctrine
    - "For individuals, starting places for telling their story and beginning to discern God are reading scripture devotionally and making a simple inventory of the day . . . For congregations, it's important to reread and study what God has to say about the church."
  - Stage 2) Recognize Feelings
    - "This second stage of discernment calls for recognizing feelings and deciding what to do with them. By "feelings" the Jesuits and John Calvin usually meant the things going on inside us that were not the product of our reason: insights, intuitions, emotions, movements that might be toward God or away from God."
    - "At stage 2, we also have to make decisions after we are in touch with our inner life. We need to make a commitment to follow God no matter what our feelings are."
  - Stage 3) Interpreting Feelings
    - "Interpreting feelings means a direct experience of God. Here we are able to ask, "So what is God saying in all this?" . . . Stage 3 is illumination—meaning that we know the truth."

* 6) Parker's Model of the Discernment Process (Parker, *Led by the Spirit*, 190–98)
  - Step 1) "A time for attending to the intuitive, affective dimensions of discernment and decision making."
  - Step 2) "A time for attending to and describing claims to experiences of Spirit leading. This element basically involves the sharing

of experiences, moving discernment and decision making from an individual experience to a communal endeavor in the process."

- Step 3) "Enriching the description of Spirit leading experiences from multiple perspectives. This element deepens the reflective aspect of the discernment and decision making and begins an evaluative moment as well."
  - "This expansion and enrichment is to elevate to a more conscious level both the positive and negative elements to be found in these experiences."
  - "Pentecostals should enrich the description and assessment of these practices by expanding this element to include perspectives from outside the Pentecostal tradition."
- Step 4) "Evaluation of these experiences . . . A Pentecostal would be most aware of this element in those times when a judgment is made on the basis of norms drawn from within the Pentecostal tradition."
  - "Ideally, discernment and decision making expand the evaluative element to include criteria drawn from other perspectives."
  - "At some point the evaluative criteria by which Spirit leading experiences are judged must be made publicly accessible."

* 7) Edwards steps (Edwards, *Living in the Presence*, 100–101)
  - Step 1) "Relax your body and mind in whatever way this best happens for you"
  - Step 2) "Be in touch with your desire for God's will. Ask to be shown what you need to realize about that will as you and the situation are ready to receive it."
  - Step 3) "Place before God some area of your life where you feel an internal desire for action . . . Notice the images, thoughts, and feelings that rise. Note their relation to your own ego desires and fears, and to any sense of God's desire for you . . . Note the possible consequences for yourself and others in moving one way or another, as well as their consonance with Christ's way as revealed in Scripture."

Appendix A

- Step 4) "Now release yourself to God as best you can and be simply present with a quality of open, trusting awareness."
- Step 5) "End with a surrender of your discernment process to God, asking that whatever action is taken be consonant with the divine will."

Appendix B

An Introduction to the Basics of Modeling

THROUGHOUT THIS BOOK, WE see the central role models have for spiritual formation program development. We may have already heard a working definition of what a model is, but what does it really mean more precisely and where does it come from? What are the intended purposes of such models and what are they to be used for? How are models constructed and what are their components? Are there limitations to what models can do for us? If so, what are they and why do these limits exist? Each of these questions is relevant if we are to seek to use such models with greater intentionality and effectiveness in our vocation.

Also important are the underlying worldviews and assumptions that undergird the models we use. Of particular importance for spiritual formation is the difference between secular models and theistic models. In this appendix, we will therefore explore these questions and cosmologies as they relate to the use of models for our field. Before closing this appendix, I will outline the four sets of methods that I assert practitioners need to have in order to more effectively incorporate models into their craft. Overall, this appendix is intended to provide some of the core basics that we need in order to make models are more integral part of spiritual formation.

Appendix B

SURVEYING, FOUNDATIONS, AND PLANS: DEFINITIONS AND PURPOSES OF MODELS

As we have heard or will hear in chapter 4, before any house building project begins, a solid foundation must first be laid. As it relates to understanding how models and theories are constructed, we must first explore what we mean, more precisely when we use these terms. It will also be helpful to know what some of the primary purposes of models are so that we gain more insight into their nature and uses. Before addressing these topics, however, we begin by exploring some of the terminologies that have been used in relation to various kinds of models.

Surveying the Landscape: What's in a Term?

There are many terms that try and capture a certain way of seeing and representing our world. Examples include "myths," "metaphors," "models," "theories," "analogies," "concepts," and "claims" to name a few. Myths have been understood as representing some part of the cosmos, providing structure and meaning to the communities that embrace the myth.[1] Concepts have been defined as being "generalizations from particulars" and, like myths, they give some kind of greater coherence and meaning.[2] The term, model, has been used to denote an "interpretative description of a phenomenon."[3] Claims, alternatively, are used in rhetoric and are intended to capture the point or position that one is taking in an argument.[4] Such wide ranging terms have been defined and used in many different ways, with some authors noting the differences and nuances between them.[5] Yet, these terms are also sometimes used interchangeably.[6] Indeed, it seems, that there also seem to be some similarities, some common characteristics, between these various terms.

1. Barbour, *Myths, Models and Paradigms*, 5.
2. Cohen et al., *Research Methods in Education*, 14.
3. Bailer-Jones, "Models, Metaphors, and Analogies," 108, 124.
4. Murphy, *Reasoning and Rhetoric in Religion*, 6.
5. For definitional differences between models and theories, see: Britt, *Conceptual Introduction to Modeling*, 16; Cohen et al., *Research Methods in Education*, 13; Craver, "Structures of Scientific Theories," 65. For differences between myths, models, and analogies, see Barbour, *Myths, Models and Paradigms*, 12, 27.
6. This is particularly true for the terms "models" and "theories." For discussions of such interchangeability, see: Cohen et al., *Research Methods in Education*, 13; Jaccard and Jacoby, *Theory Construction and Model-Building Skills*, 29.

An Introduction to the Basics of Modeling

Laying the Foundations

While such terminological distinctions are sometimes necessary depending on one's application, for our purposes here we are more simply seeking to capture the more essential nature of what some of them mean. Specifically, we are interested primarily in the terms "model" and "theory," but also "concepts," which are considered to be a fundamental part of the first two terms.[7] To help us to do this, we begin by outlining what some of the core characteristics are that have been ascribed to models and theories. From these brief explorations, we will then be able to lay our own foundations by putting forth a working definition of what a model/theory is. Finally, in their fuller form as we shall see, models have at least four levels to them.

Core Characteristics

There are several characteristics that models, theories, and concepts are asserted to have. They are described as being "building blocks" for how we understand and engage the world.[8] Such building blocks are also intended to be generalizable to some degree.[9] For instance, the word "tree" can refer to any number of different kinds of trees. But we don't just use words when we create models, for we can also use pictures, numbers, sounds, et cetera to symbolically stand for something else.[10] In a sense, then, models and theories are simply abstract representations about particular aspects of the world that surrounds us.[11] They are intended to represent the things we see and the experiences we have both internally and externally.[12]

As a result, models essentially summarize what we think we know about our world; they give us a unique kind of access to it.[13] As one set

---

7. Jaccard and Jacoby, *Theory Construction and Model-Building Skills*, 10–11.

8. Ibid., 11.

9. Ibid.

10. Barbour, *Myths, Models and Paradigms*, 7; Basmadjian, *Mathematical Modeling of Physical Systems*, 1; Cohen et al., *Research Methods in Education*, 13; Jaccard and Jacoby, *Theory Construction and Model-Building Skills*, 29; Sagan, "Can We Know the Universe?," 6–7.

11. Barbour, *Myths, Models and Paradigms*, 37.

12. Ibid., 6; Jaccard and Jacoby, *Theory Construction and Model-Building Skills*, 12, 29.

13. Bailer-Jones, "Models, Metaphors, and Analogies," 108, 124; Britt, *Conceptual Introduction to Modeling*, 4.

Appendix B

of authors write, "Theories, then, are human inventions that attempt to explain the workings of nature."[14] For instance, in spiritual formation we often have our own ideas about what human nature is and what it is comprised of. A common contemporary model of human nature is one that asserts that people are made up of a "mind," a "body," and a "spirit."[15] It is a model that helps us to understand more clearly what we think we know about ourselves and one another.

Once we have such a theory about our world, we are then better able to evaluate what we believe, to question and examine it in more detail, and to critique and change it if necessary.[16] From such explorations, we are therefore able to build an ever more coherent understanding of reality.[17] Just as we heard above with myths, models bring greater meaning, lead us to focus on certain parts of reality more than on others, and they organize how we understand and engage our world.[18] These characteristics, then, form the solid foundations for helping us to better understand what models and theories are and some of the ways that they might be used.

A Working Definition

Now we are in a position to offer our own definition of a theory or model (which is itself a model/theory). Using these two terms interchangeably, *a model/theory is a theoretical construct that seeks to more coherently represent some specific phenomena in our world and its various internal and external relationships.* They are, as we've seen, building blocks that are often generalizable to some extent and symbolically summarize what we think that we know about some experienced or perceived part of our world. Myths and stories accomplish this in a narrative form, metaphors do so by comparing different symbols, and claims pursue these ends through the means of logic. But at their core, they all accomplish the task of helping us

---

14. Hatton and Plouffe, introduction to part 2, vii.

15. For examples of such a model, see: Hauser, *Moving in the Spirit*, 27; Van Kaam, *Fundamental Formation*, 60; Wilber, *Integral Spirituality*, 203.

16. Britt, *Conceptual Introduction to Modeling*, vii, 2; Murphy, *Reasoning and Rhetoric in Religion*, 51.

17. Cohen et al., *Research Methods in Education*, 12; Hatton and Plouffe, general introduction to *Science and Its Ways of Knowing*, vii.

18. Barbour, *Myths, Models and Paradigms*, 7; Britt, *Conceptual Introduction to Modeling*, 2; Cohen et al., *Research Methods in Education*, 12; Van Kaam, *Scientific Formation*, 89.

An Introduction to the Basics of Modeling

to better and symbolically represent and offer specific insights into some part of creation.

Four Components of a Model

We can see, as we have in the chapters of this book, that models are intricate part of our world, and certainly the field of spiritual formation. Whenever we have an idea about how do to something, such as what it means to eat lunch with our friends and what that should be like, we are creating theories about the world around us.[19] Such models pervade our existence. However, applying our KISS principle here, models often have four essential components to them.

First, models typically identify and define the specific parts of the world that they are attempting to represent.[20] In our example of a human nature model above, these specific parts would be the "mind," "body," and "spirit." If we choose to adapt such a model for use in our own spiritual formation programs, we would then need to clarify what, more precisely, we mean when we use these terms.

Secondly, models will sometimes clarify the relationships between these various parts.[21] While not all models that we encounter may do this, it can be very helpful at times to sort this out. So, for instance, we might ask: what is the nature of the relationship between the mind and the body? Throughout the centuries, various answers have been given for this question ranging from the claim that they are not connected at all, as was the case with Descartes, to the assertion that the mind is only a manifestation of body, as is the case with a philosophic school of thought known as "reductionism."[22] Regardless of where we stand in relation to these views, the important thing to note here is that it is sometimes very important to clarify what the relationships are between the various parts that our model identifies and focuses on.

Though it is rarer, a model will also sometimes offer a summary of what the overall nature or dynamics of the phenomenon is. For instance, we could ask: How are the mind, body, and spirit of a person integrated

---

19. In this example, such models are referred to as "schemas" by cognitive researchers; see Matlin, *Cognition*, 157.

20. Jaccard and Jacoby, *Theory Construction and Model-Building Skills*, 30.

21. Ibid., 137.

22. For a more detailed discussion of these and other views, see Clayton, *Mind and Emergence*, ch. 1.

Appendix B

together? How do they collectively interact to make up the more essential and holistic nature or personality of a person? This third component of a model therefore seeks to capture not just the individual parts, nor just the various interrelationships between them, but also the overall and more global aspects of the phenomenon being represented.

Finally, a fourth component to models might involve the relationship between each of the previous levels and the larger context of which it is a part. How is the body connected to the environment and what is the nature of this relationship? What contextual factors influence the relationship between the mind and the body? How is the person, as a whole, influenced by the social situations they find themselves within? Each of these questions are relevant to this fourth component that models sometimes address as a part of their formulations.

Taken together, these four components of a model help us to understand a given phenomenon, such as human nature, in much greater detail. Figure 14 below depicts these four components for the example we have been working with.

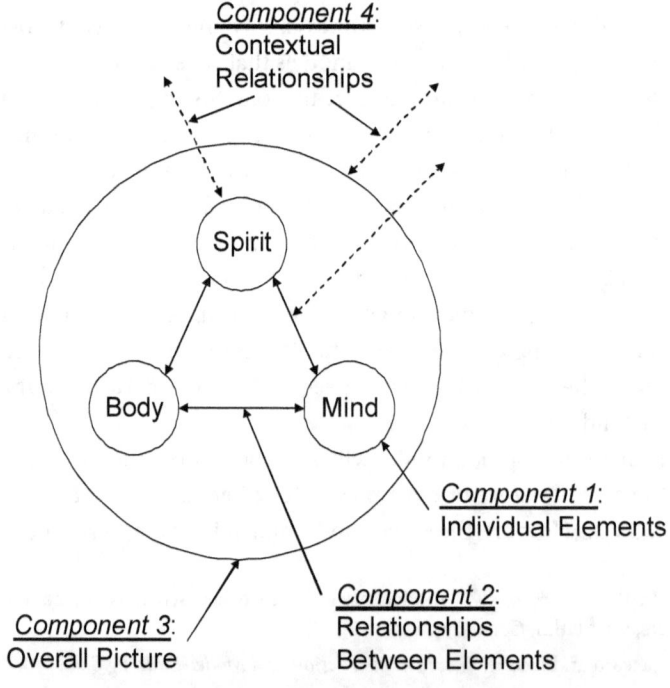

Figure 14. Four Components of Models

256

An Introduction to the Basics of Modeling

Working with a Master Plan: Primary Purposes of Models

Before we can continue on and learn how models are constructed, it will first be helpful to clarify what some of their primary and intended purposes are. From our working definition, it may seem obvious: their primary purpose is to symbolically represent some part of our world. While this is true, there are actually two specific purposes that models have in relation to such representations: description and prediction. In a nutshell, the former has to do with understanding what already is while the latter has more to do with what could be. These purposes provide us with a better understanding, a master plan if you will, of how models can be and are utilized.

Description

The first and more obvious purpose is related to the picture of reality that any particular model provides us with. As theologian Ian Barbour explains, "its chief use is to help one understand the world."[23] In this capacity, models give us additional insights into how our world works, they interpret events for us, and they call our attention to distinct parts of the world that we might not have noticed before as closely.[24] They also help us to classify, segregate, and delineate different parts of a particular phenomenon.[25] For instance, in the model of human nature we have been considering, a mind is not the same as a body or a spirit; they are distinct from one another. Theories and models are also asserted to unify what we think we know about something and they provide us with a more coherent understanding of our world.[26] All in all, then, one of the primary purposes of models is to describe some part of the world around us with greater clarity, precision, and coherence.

Prediction

If that were all that models were used for, however, then models might have more of a static impact on our world. Simply learning that human

---

23. Barbour, *Myths, Models and Paradigms*, 30.
24. Ibid., 7, 49, 64, 140.
25. Jaccard and Jacoby, *Theory Construction and Model-Building Skills*, 14.
26. Barbour, *Myths, Models and Paradigms*, 180; Cohen et al., *Research Methods in Education*, 14.

beings are the composite of mind, body, and spirit may not be as useful for us if we do not have some way of utilizing this information. In the Western Christian tradition, for instance, a core theory is that encountering the Gospel will evoke an "experience of forgiveness, love and grace in [one's] personal life."[27] This claim, it is asserted, is one upon which Christians can seek to base their lives. A second purpose for models, then, is one that is recognized in the sciences and it is related to a model's predictive capacity; its ability to dynamically influence our present and future lives.[28]

In this way, models can be used to help us solve problems when they provide us with specific insights into why something is the way that it is.[29] For instance, it has been asserted that the observed behaviors of others can influence our own choices.[30] If someone else acts in selfish ways and receives negative consequences, then we learn from their experiences. In effect, these observed behaviors become descriptive models to us that help us to better understand how things work and subsequently influence how we personally behave. As a result, models and theories can have an effect on the attitudes we have, the behaviors we choose, and the general directions that we head in.[31] It is through the understandings and insights that models give us, then, that we can try and predict possible future outcomes.

In spiritual formation, such predictive powers are an intricate part of the nature of our work. Intentionally fostering the spiritual growth of a person or community presupposes that we have some understanding, some model, of what is being formed and how to go about nurturing it. Without such theories, we are left in the dark, for instance, as to which practices to choose, the manner by which to engage them, and when the best moments might be for utilizing them. This second purpose of models therefore encompasses a substantial part of our work as spiritual formators.

However, we must remember, such predictions can only be as accurate as our models. As we shall see in more detail below, a model is only an approximation of some finite part of reality and may therefore not accurately anticipate outcomes. A child may see a friend steal something and

---

27. Barbour, *Myths, Models and Paradigms*, 179.

28. Jaccard and Jacoby, *Theory Construction and Model-Building Skills*, 3; Worrall, "Philosophy of Science," 32.

29. Basmadjian, *Mathematical Modeling of Physical Systems*, 1; Jaccard and Jacoby, *Theory Construction and Model-Building Skills*, 15.

30. McCallum and Lowery, *Organic Disciplemaking*, 87–89.

31. Barbour, *Myths, Models and Paradigms*, 16, 51, 58, 180.

An Introduction to the Basics of Modeling

not get caught, but that does not necessarily mean that they won't either. Or, just because someone else has a profound conversion experience does not necessarily mean that we will ourselves. Models, therefore, may give us insights into how into our world works, and we can and often do make predictions based upon them, but that does not necessarily guarantee that these predictions will be accurate for our own lives and the communities we are seeking to formatively work with. Nevertheless, we can still use models for both understanding and prediction and these two purposes, which comprise our master plan, provide us with the direction we need to better understand how such theories might be used in spiritual formation.

Construction 101: Understanding How Models Are Built

Now that we have a more thorough understanding of what the essential nature and purposes of theories and models are, we can briefly explore how models are constructed. As we shall can see throughout this book, understanding these basics is necessary in order for us to more effectively utilize models in our spiritual formation program development. It is in this section that we will seek to gain a clearer understanding of where models come from; i.e., of the processes by which we come to assert the theories and claims that we do. Not only is this important for how we engage in ministry, but also for our lives more generally.

Two Levels to Consider

Basically, there are two levels that model and theory construction works at. The first is at the level of the model itself. It is the claims that we are making about the phenomena that we are attempting to capture with our model. The model of human nature that we have been using as an example throughout this appendix is an example of this first level. We make a statement, "Human nature is comprised of a mind, a body, and a spirit," and then we might spend sometime unpacking their relationships and the overall dynamics as we have heard. This first level therefore has to do with our unpacking the details of the model itself and all of its various interconnections and dynamics. This level primarily has to do the claims that our models and theories are explicitly making.

The second level that we must consider in model construction is the foundation upon which the model and its various details are based.

Appendix B

This is the level upon which the first is built. Often, in everyday use, it is a hidden or unspoken level for the theories we proclaim and models that implicitly and explicitly guide our lives. For example, we may believe, knowingly or unknowingly, a negative stereotype about a certain group of people thereby avoiding interacting with that group as much as possible. The stereotype itself would be the model or claim that is guiding our life, the first level discussed above. This second level would then be the experiences, influences, education, reasoning, et cetera that have contributed to the formation of this biased and stereotyped belief. This second level of models is therefore the underlying foundations upon which the model is built.

When we think about how models and theories are constructed, then, we must address these two levels of consideration: the claims of our models and the foundations upon which they are based. The foundations that our models are based upon turn out to have at least two components to them: sources and warrants. Figure 15 below shows how these three are related to one another and we will now explore each of these in more detail.

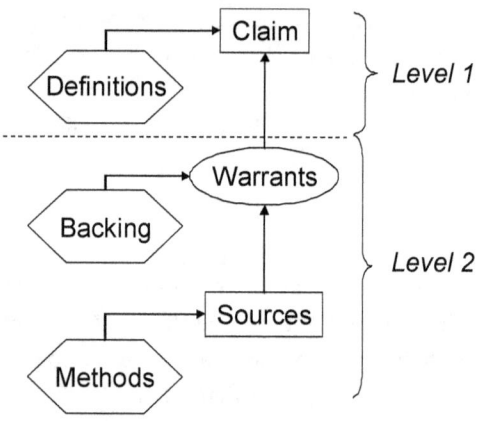

Figure 15. Three Parts of Model Construction

Level 1: Claims/Definitions

As we have already heard, the claims of a model are some part, or whole, of the model itself; i.e., some component of the model (like the "mind" for a model of human nature) or some relationship between components in the

An Introduction to the Basics of Modeling

model (such as how the mind is related to the body). What is important to note about these claims, is that whenever we make them we need to be very clear about what we are talking about.[32] Such clarity helps us and others to better understand what it is, more precisely, we are talking about.[33]

For example, our field is directly oriented towards "spiritual formation." But what does that mean exactly? Take the term "spiritual," for starters. One spiritual care and counseling researcher reviewed more than 2,300 articles on spirituality in his field and found that there was no consensus as to what this term means more precisely.[34] So, if we are working for the "spiritual" formation of an individual or community, what it is exactly that we are forming?

It is therefore very important in the construction of models that we be very clear in the definitions and meanings of the claims that make up our models and theories. These claims, it was noted above, comprise the first level at which model construction takes place; it is the level at which most of us interact with the theories that make up our world.

Level 2: Sources/Methods

However, as we noted, it is not enough to stop at the first level. While we may have a theory of human nature and then begin to base our spiritual formation programs upon it, it behooves us to probe and understand it more deeply. We must work to be more explicit about the foundations upon which our beliefs and claims are based. Doing so, can not only help us to identify and guard against biases and stereotypes, as we've heard, but it can also help us to better utilize our models.

The first part of these foundations are the sources and methods from which our models are derived. The sources can be very narrow, as they are with scientific methods, or they can be based upon any one or combination of the various other ways of knowing that we, as humans, have available to us. The important KISS point to remember for model construction is that we should be clear about the sources upon which our claims are based and, secondarily, the methods that we use to access those sources because both of these make up the solid "bedrock" of our theories.[35]

---

32. Jaccard and Jacoby, *Theory Construction and Model-Building Skills*, 88.
33. Booth et al., *Craft of Research*, 122.
34. O'Connor, "Research Methods in Spirituality and Health Care," 151.
35. Booth et al., *Craft of Research*, 131.

Appendix B

One commonly used source in our contemporary Western world is modern science. In scientific methods, there are two commonly used sources: empirical observations and the means of logic.[36] Scientists use the five senses, which are generally agreed upon and accessible to their community, and make inductive and deductive logical claims to build and test their theories. However, the primary and final source of validation and/or falsifiability is empirical observation; with how well the theory reliably fits with the observable data that has been collected.[37]

However, such empirical sources are not the only ones upon which to build our models. Reason and logic, as we have heard, are used by scientists but also by philosophers to generate new hypotheses and theories.[38] Overall, the goal is to generate new ideas and possibilities and it is, theologian and philosopher Nancey Murphy tells us, "limited only by the failure of our imaginations."[39]

Our imaginations can also be fueled by any number of other sources.[40] These other sources can, and often do – particularly in religious and theological traditions – become the basis for models about reality. As discussed in chapter 1, I have provided a brief overview of some of the various ways of knowing.[41] Figure 16 below again shows this mapping.

---

36. Barbour, *Myths, Models and Paradigms*, 29; Cohen et al., *Research Methods in Education*, 5; Hatton and Plouffe, general introduction to *Science and Its Ways of Knowing*, vii–viii ; Jaccard and Jacoby, *Theory Construction and Model-Building Skills*, 26; Kneller, "Method of Inquiry," 18; Pirsig, "On Scientific Method," 8; Van Kaam, *Scientific Formation*, 89; Woodward, "Explanation," 44.

37. Barbour, *Myths, Models and Paradigms*, 44; Bauer, "So-Called Scientific Method," 26; Jaccard and Jacoby, *Theory Construction and Model-Building Skills*, 27; Cohen et al., *Research Methods in Education*, 5; Worrall, "Philosophy of Science," 20, 22.

38. Cohen et al., *Research Methods in Education*, 6; Jaccard and Jacoby, *Theory Construction and Model-Building Skills*, 39; Murphy, *Reasoning and Rhetoric in Religion*, 43–46.

39. Jaccard and Jacoby, *Theory Construction and Model-Building Skills*, 71; Murphy, *Reasoning and Rhetoric in Religion*, 45.

40. Braud, "Integral Inquiry," 47; Cohen et al., *Research Methods in Education*, 18; Gardner, *Frames of Mind*, 60–61; Huebner, "Spirituality and Knowing," 170–72; Moser et al., *Theory of Knowledge*, 24, 41.

41. Kyle, "Putting God Under the Microscope."

An Introduction to the Basics of Modeling

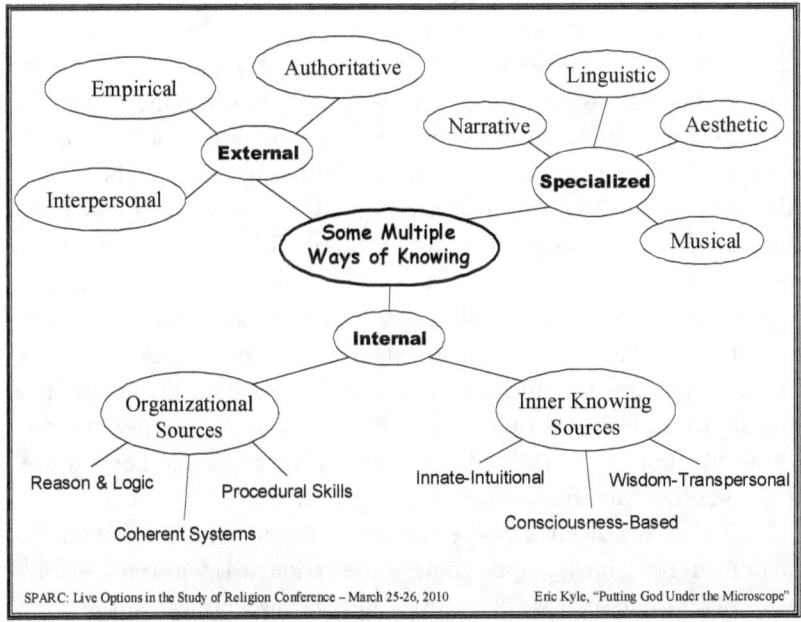

Figure 16. A Mapping of Some of Our Ways of Knowing

From this mapping, we can see that there are any number of possible sources upon which to build models. We can look to authoritative sources, such as political and religious leaders, to dictate what we believe.[42] We can make our claims based upon inner movements, such as conversion experiences or intuition.[43] Or, as some have asserted, we can turn to transpersonal and wisdom, or "whole-being," sources for inspiration and insights into the nature of some part of reality.[44] In other words, the number of possible sources is quite large.

Again, we must remember, the overall aim of these discussions is for us to be explicit about the sources that we base our models on. While, for scientific credibility, some of these alternative ways of knowing might not be accepted as "valid," they can and should, I believe, still be used as the basis for our models. To reiterate, the primary KISS aim of them to better capture some phenomena that we are interested in and thereby empower

42. Moser et al., *Theory of Knowledge*, 4–5.

43. Barbour, *Myths, Models and Paradigms*, 125; Arnheim, "Double-Edged Mind," 77.

44. Braud, "Integral Inquiry," 51; Bourgeault, *Wisdom Way of Knowing*, 27; Huebner, "Spirituality and Knowing," 162; Radin, *Conscious Universe*, 2.

us to better understand them and work with them so that we might be more effective in our formative craft. If the models we construct and utilize accomplish this, then they are "valid" for use in our specific context and local ministries, regardless of the sources upon which they are based.

Before we move on to the final part of explorations of how models and theories are constructed, we must first briefly note another aspect that is related to these many different kinds of sources and that is the methods by which these sources are accessed. It has been observed that "each science has its own techniques," or methods, for making empirical observations.[45] Even these well-defined and elaborate methodologies are sometimes disputed within and among scientific communities.[46] What is important to note for our purposes is that in identifying the sources that undergird the claims we are making with our models, we must also give some attention to the methods by which we are accessing those sources because others may question these methods as well.[47]

For instance, let us suppose that one wanted to better understand human nature by drawing upon some of the various wisdom-transpersonal ways of knowing such as "alternative states of consciousness, imagination, and intuition," some of which are based on traditional religious approaches to meditation and contemplation.[48] And out of these experiences, one then built their model of the relationship between mind and body. In sharing this model, it would be helpful for this modeler to let others know how they came to this theory because others may question the methods by which they did so. In building our models, then, there are any number of diverse sources upon which to base our claims. Not only does it help to be explicit about which of these sources we are drawing from, but also about the methods by which we used to access them.

Level 2: Warrants/Worldviews

So, we have the various claims/definitions that our models are making and we have the sources/methods upon which they are based outlined and defined. We're finished right? Not exactly. Quoting from another source in her book, *Reasoning and Rhetoric in Religion*, Murphy notes the following story,

45. Keller, "Feeling for the Organism," 14.
46. Bogen, "Experiment and Observation," 128.
47. Booth et al., *Craft of Research*, 117.
48. Anderson, "Intuitive Inquiry," 70, 82, 88.

An Introduction to the Basics of Modeling

A national sensationalist tabloid once published the theory that the wife of a famous entertainer was the descendant of aliens. A key piece of evidence supporting the theory was that the lady had slightly lower than average blood pressure. Now lower than average blood pressure is indeed empirical data, but there is no reason to connect it with alien ancestry. Real science requires that there be some rational connection between explanatory theory and empirical data.[49]

Just because we have a piece of data obtained from a source via some method, does not necessarily mean that it directly supports the claim that is being made. There is something more that is needed, something that will link the data to the claim as shown in figure 15. That link, that reason for believing that the data directly supports part of our model, is called a warrant.[50]

Warrants are not always needed, especially when the link is an obvious one.[51] When they are needed, however, one common way to build a warrant is based upon methods of reasoning. In their book, *The Craft of Research*, Booth, Colomb, and Williams outline one of these logical approaches. "The logic behind all warrants," they write, "is that if a generalization is true, then so must be specific instances on it."[52] The basic idea here is that if we can show that our claim is a specific instance of a more general claim, then it is a valid warrant.[53] For instance, as we heard in chapter 3, we can assert the general principle, "where there's smoke, there's fire,"[54] and then make the more specific claim that there must be a fire somewhere in our house because we see smoke coming from it. In this case, our claim is that our house is on fire, the data is the smoke that we see coming from it, and the warrant is the general principle just mentioned.

Such reasoning can also go the other way, and that is by starting from particular sources and then generalizing from there. For instance, we may observe that a child in our Sunday school classroom prefers red licorice to black ones and then generalize from there to make the claim that all children have the same preference. This kind of reasoning is known as

49. Murphy, *Reasoning and Rhetoric in Religion*, 13.

50. Booth et al, *Craft of Research*, 114, 152; Murphy, *Reasoning and Rhetoric in Religion*, 14.

51. Booth et al., *Craft of Research*, 115. Murphy, *Reasoning and Rhetoric in Religion*, 18.

52. Booth et al., *Craft of Research*, 114.

53. Ibid., 153–56, 160, 164.

54. Ibid., 155.

inductive reasoning while the smoke/fire kind of reasoning above is known as deductive reasoning.[55] As we can see from these examples, it is the warrant that seeks to link the claims that we are making to the supporting sources we are drawing from. It is the glue that binds the claims of a model to its foundational data.

However, not all warrants are considered to be "strong" and different communities have different ideas as to what is an acceptable warrant and what is not.[56] As a result, warrants themselves may need to be turned into claims that then need to be further backed by sources and other warrants.[57] Yes, what may start out as a simple model can quickly become a very complex set of interconnected claims, warrants, and sources, each of which has their own definitions, backing, and methods. Indeed, the world of modeling is complicated endeavor as figure 17 below shows. Not only do we need to be explicit about the claims and foundations for the "mind" and the overall model of human nature, for instance, but the warrants for these might also need further support and justification.

---

55. Pirsig, "On Scientific Method," 8.

56. Booth et al., *Craft of Research*, 154, 157–59; Murphy, *Reasoning and Rhetoric in Religion*, 31.

57. Murphy, *Reasoning and Rhetoric in Religion*, 14–18, 23.

An Introduction to the Basics of Modeling

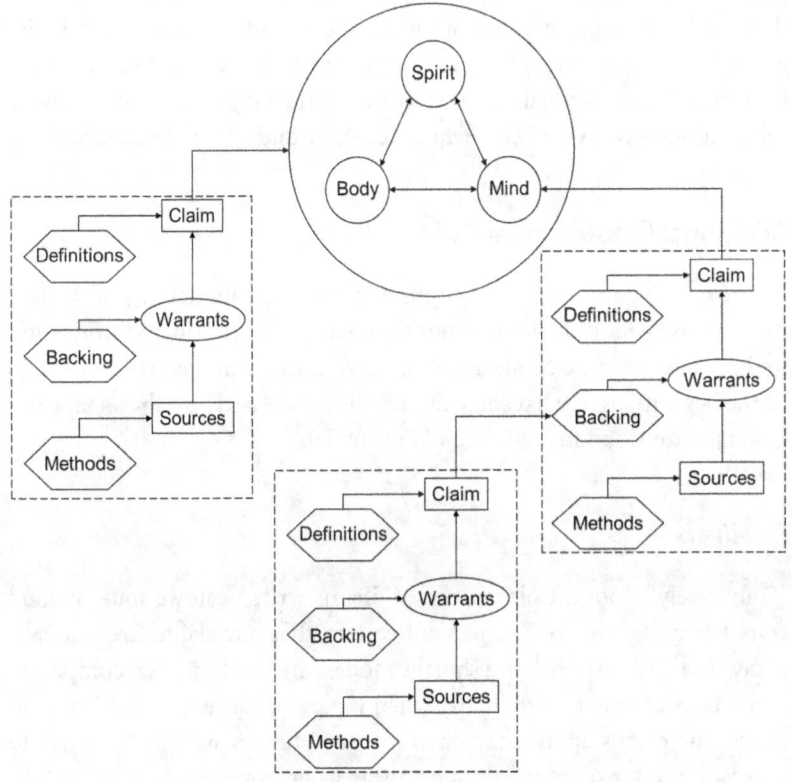

Figure 17. An Example of Complex Modeling Foundations

In light of this, once again invoking the KISS principle, we can again return to our working plan, which are the primary purposes of our models and theories: description and prediction. As long as the models we are using, regardless of the sources they are drawn from or the warrants that are being used to help justify them, accurately help us to better understand and work with the people and communities of our local ministerial contexts, then they are valid. We will know that they are valid because our formative programs will progress towards the ideals that we set as we have discussed throughout this book. However, we must also remember that the more intentional and explicit we are with the claims/definitions, warrants/worldviews, and sources/methods of our models, they better the chances will be that they will be accurate and helpful for us in our craft.

Finally, as we shall hear more fully below when we discuss the limitations of models, we also need to be aware of the worldviews that the

Appendix B

person/community constructing the model has. As models are created, they tend to be representative of their contexts and cultures to certain degrees. We must therefore be very clear in our understanding of the where the model has contextually come from and who has generated it. Knowing their unique worldviews can help us to better understand their models.

Additional Considerations

Before moving on to our discussions of some of the limitations of models, there are two additional assertions that need to be considered in relation to the models that we create and use. These considerations are intended to be the beginnings of what some of these limits are and how they shape our understanding and formulation of our models.

Qualifiers

"Only rarely," Booth, Colomb, and Williams write, "can we state in good conscience that we are 100 percent certain that our claims are unqualifiedly true."[58] As we shall see shortly, models are rarely, if ever, completely accurate. As a result, particularly when we are not sure as to the extent to which our claims apply, they often include phrases such as "we wish to suggest," "in our opinion," "some appear to be," or words like "certainly, undoubtedly presumably, probably, apparently, possibly, perhaps."[59] These hedges are known as qualifiers and they have the intention of letting others know the extent to which we are certain about various aspects of our theories. Such qualifiers are important because of the inherent limitations that all theories have.

Rebuttals & Alternate Theories

When constructing any model, we must also consider the fact that there are many different possible models that can be constructed in relation to any given phenomena.[60] Such an assertion is articulated most clearly by David Britt, who has written a book on modeling for the social sciences, when he claims, "For any given set of facts or patterns of relationships,

---

58. Booth et al., *Craft of Research*, 128.
59. Ibid.; Murphy, *Reasoning and Rhetoric in Religion*, 32.
60. Murphy, *Reasoning and Rhetoric in Religion*, 45.

An Introduction to the Basics of Modeling

there are a limitless number of theories that can plausibly explain them."[61] The important point here is the notion that just because we have a claim that is based upon strong sources accessed via accepted methods using generally agreed upon warrants, there may still be other viable models to consider.[62]

In addition to this, model and claim builders admonish, we must also continually be thinking about where the weak points in our models might be; i.e., where arguments, or rebuttals, against our claims might be made.[63] The idea here is for us to really analyze and question the strength of the theories we are working to construct and to really look closely for where our models may not be either accurate or useful. By doing so, we are seeking to improve, as much as possible, the accuracy of our models in representing certain aspects of our local context.

Use with Caution! Three Limitations of Models

With qualifiers and rebuttals to claims being a precursor, we can now more fully explore what some of the very real limits are that models have. It has been written that models and theories are to be "taken seriously, but not literally."[64] From our explorations of the both the characteristics and construction of models, we have already seen that models have inherent limitations. Specifically, there are three fundamental limitations that practitioners must be aware of in their construction and use of models in spiritual formation program development.

Models Only Capture a Finite Part of Reality

The first primary limitation of models is that they can ever and only capture some finite part of creation. Think of how vast the universe is right now at this very moment with all of the galaxies that we have discovered and the complexities that are contained within the human body. Now, think of all of the dynamic motion and change that is occurring in all of this literally on a moment-by-moment basis. Is it really possible for any one single model to represent all of this vastness? My claim, and the claim

---

61. Britt, *Conceptual Introduction to Modeling*, 14.
62. Booth et al., *Craft of Research*, 112, 139–40.
63. Ibid., 113, 139–41; Murphy, *Reasoning and Rhetoric in Religion*, 36.
64. Barbour, *Myths, Models and Paradigms*, 7.

Appendix B

of others such as famed scientist Carl Sagan, is that it is just not possible; creation is just too vast and complex.[65] As a result, all theories and models are inherently limited in that they can ever and only capture a finite part of reality.[66] As theorists James Jaccard and Jacob Jacoby assert in relation to our belief systems, "Indeed, if they possessed no such limitation, they would be forced to grasp all of the complexity of the ongoing world as it progressed, and that would be impossible."[67]

Models Are Only Approximations

The limitations of models, however, do not stop here. Not only do models capture a finite part of creation, but they are also asserted to be mere approximations of the parts of creation that they do represent.[68] "Precision is not what modeling is about," writes Britt, "modeling is about getting to the essence of the causal dynamics of a situation configured in time and space."[69] In other words, it is claimed, models can never fully capture all that makes up even a single phenomenon.

Take the most empirically studied element of the model of human nature that we have been considering in this chapter, the body. Even better, let us take one finite part of this complex organism say, neurons. There are an estimated hundred billion of them that each of us has,[70] so let us peer inside of just one of them for simplicity's sake. While neuroscientists have been able to uncover much of what a neuron is comprised of, there is still a great deal about them we just do not know.[71] As a result, models of these tiny parts of our body are only approximate. Is it possible, with time, that all that there is to know about even a single neuron will be known? Well, if we assert that part of what makes a neuron a neuron is its interactions with other neurons as well as the larger human organism of which it is a

---

65. Sagan, "Can We Know the Universe?," 5. For a similar claims, see: Basmadjian, *Mathematical Modeling of Physical Systems*, 14; Cohen et al., *Research Methods in Education*, 14.

66. Barbour, *Myths, Models and Paradigms*, 47, 67–68.

67. Jaccard and Jacoby, *Theory Construction and Model-Building Skills*, 23.

68. Hatton and Plouffe, general introduction to *Science and Its Ways of Knowing*, 2.

69. Britt, *Conceptual Introduction to Modeling*, 7.

70. Bear et al., *Neuroscience*, 45.

71. For instance, still relatively little is known about the functioning of what are called glia cells. Since these cells make up a major part of our brain, they are considered to be the "sleeping giant" of neuroscience. See Bear et al., *Neuroscience*, 24, 46.

An Introduction to the Basics of Modeling

part (which is, of course, interconnected with its environment),[72] I do not think so. In other words, the claim here is that, based upon the interconnectedness of creation, by trying to model any finite part with exact precision we are eventually lead back to the infiniteness of it all, which we have just seen is not possible to completely model.

As a result, all models are inherently approximations and this means, then, that the knowledge that is gleaned from our models will always have an uncertainty to them.[73] For spiritual formation, as with other all other fields, we must therefore use such theories and models with great care and caution. If we proceed believing that the information a model is giving us is 100 percent accurate, and it is not, then we may very well be led to act in ways that are more harmful than helpful in our local contexts. In Part Two of this book, the methodologies that we will explored are developed with these cautions in mind with the hopes that such potential hazards may be avoided.

Models Have the Inherent Interpretations of Their Creators

There is a story of the great sculptor, Michelangelo, rolling a large slab of marble down the street.[74] A boy stops and asks him something like, "What are you doing with that giant rock?" Michelangelo, with a glimmer in his eyes, looks at the rock and says, "My child, there is an angel in there waiting to be set free!" For one person, there may only be a slab of stone, but for another, there may be something more splendid and sacred. This story illustrates another limitation that is asserted of all models, and that is that they carry the inherent interpretations and worldviews of their creators.

In reflecting on these kinds of limitations, Barbour notes, "In the eighteenth century, Newtonian mechanics led to a mechanistic view of the world and a deistic understanding of God the cosmic clockmaker."[75] Such a claim asserts that the Newtonian interpretations of that era, of how the world was constructed and operated, led to a theology that was

---

72. An integral part of what makes up a neuron are the axons and dendrites it has that connects it to other neurons and parts of the body. See Bear et al., *Neuroscience*, ch. 2.

73. Barbour, *Myths, Models and Paradigms*, 98; Britt, *Conceptual Introduction to Modeling*, 15; Hatton and Plouffe, introduction to part 2, 59; Murphy, *Reasoning and Rhetoric in Religion*, 54; Van Kaam, *Scientific Formation*, 83.

74. For a variation of this story, see Lutheran Social Services, "Can You Find the Angel in the Rock? Honoring Elizabeth Dinges."

75. Barbour, *Myths, Models and Paradigms*, 2.

Appendix B

compatible with it.[76] In the sciences, it has been widely argued that all theories carry with them such inherent perceptions and biases.[77] One of the reasons given for such influences are the ways in which we have been formed and taught to see things as well as the assumptions that have been passed on to us.[78] "As things are conceived," one theorist writes, "so are they seen."[79] Another reason for this is the communal processes by which a model is accepted, rejected, or simply ignored. These, too, are asserted to sometimes be influenced by the biases, assumptions, and interpretations of that community.[80]

A third limitation of all models is therefore that they can have the tendency to embody the interpretations of their theorists. This limitation further supports the claims of the second limitation because such interpretive influences may be further obscuring the model's accuracy and usefulness thereby further rendering it a loose approximation of reality. However, such interpretations might also help in the formulation of a model. For instance, if we were to construct a model of human nature that applied to a group of second generation Chinese American youth, the interpretations of a theorist who shared these cultural distinctions and experiences might actually make the model more valid. The important thing to remember in relation to this third limitation, then, is the two levels of model construction discussed above. In other words, if we are explicit about the sources and warrants that undergird the claims we are making, then these interpretations should come to the surface so that they might be better evaluated. All models have limitations, so we must always proceed with caution in using them.

---

76. Ibid., 168.

77. Bauer, "So-Called Scientific Method," 36; Britt, *Conceptual Introduction to Modeling*, 11–12; Hatton and Plouffe, general introduction to *Science and Its Ways of Knowing*, 1–2; Maslow, *Motivation and Personality*, 1; Sagan, "Can We Know the Universe?," 3.

78. Barbour, *Myths, Models and Paradigms*, 9–10, 96, 113, 123; Britt, *Conceptual Introduction to Modeling*, 6, 13–14; Cohen et al., *Research Methods in Education*, 37; Jaccard and Jacoby, *Theory Construction and Model-Building Skills*, 30, 33.

79. Kneller, "Method of Inquiry," 14.

80. Bauer, "So-Called Scientific Method," 29; Bogen, "Experiment and Observation," 136.

Secular Versus Theistic Models

Given that our models contain the worldviews and perspectives of those who construct them, in the field of theistic spiritual formation we must consider how our own theological perspectives are embodied by the theories that we use for our craft. With there being so many different theories that are available from the secular sciences, we must be clear as to what some of the differences are in relation to how models are viewed from both theistic and secular perspectives. Such explorations, we can see throughout our praxis-oriented methodologies, will influence not only how we use models in relation to our theistically oriented craft, but also how we interact with secular theories. As an example of what the primary differences are between theistic and secular models, we turn in the final section of this appendix to one illustrative case example.

Simple Causality or Divine Direction? The Case Example of Evolution

The debates over evolution between secular scientists and creationists/Intelligent Design proponents continue to run hot these days with both sides taking ideological stances in relation to the interpretations that biological and geological empirical data are given.[81] The purpose of this section is neither to frame this debate nor to assert a stance in relation to it. Rather, we will be looking briefly at how two communities—mainstream secular science and a theological school known as panentheism—view evolution. The primary purpose of our explorations here is to draw out some of the differences between secular and theistic perspectives in relation to model construction.

Scientific Views

Secular scientific worldviews begin by noting the regularity that seems to be a part of creation and how it operates.[82] "It is an astonishing fact," Sagan notes, "that there are laws of nature, rules that summarize conveniently—not just qualitatively but quantitatively—how the world works."[83] Rules, or

---

81. Peters, *Science, Theology, and Ethics*, 8, 18.

82. Allport, *Personality*, 3; Carver, "Structures of Scientific Theories," 55; Machamer, "Brief Historical Introduction to the Philosophy of Science," 4.

83. Sagan, "Can We Know the Universe?," 6–7.

Appendix B

laws, are able to do this precisely because of the regularity by which much of nature seems to operate. For instance, if I am holding a book and let go of it, it will drop to the ground. In scientific terminology, as we all know, this is called the law of gravity and we can even write mathematical equations to represent how fast the book will fall. These predictions may then be tested experimentally. It is based upon such repeatability, therefore, that scientific methods are founded and these laws are asserted.[84]

Scientific worldviews have also noted and sought to uncover the causality of some of creation's dynamics.[85] The basic notion here is that elements of creation are interactively related to one another. If I roll a ball across a table towards another set of balls, we can causally expect those other balls to begin moving when they are struck. They are said to be causally connected because the first action was the direct cause of the second one.

Now, take these two fundamental views of science and apply them to the workings of evolution and we might expect one to conclude that creation progresses as a result of these regularities, or laws, by which it causally interacts within itself after the big bang.[86] Described succinctly by philosopher of science and theologian Philip Clayton, "To do science is generally to presuppose that the universe is a closed physical system, that interactions are regular and lawlike, that all causal histories can be traced, and that anomalies will ultimately have physical explanations."[87] If these assumptions and worldviews are true, it can be asserted, then there is no need for any external causally acting entity, such as a God.[88]

As a result, the theories and models of science in relation to evolution can remain fully secular; meaning that they do not need to explicitly address or discuss the place or role of an externally intervening God. One can, as mainstream science does, simply point to the regularly occurring cause and effect relationships to describe the "natural" workings of creation and the unfoldings of evolution.

---

84. Hoagland, "Preface from *Toward the Habit of Truth*," 119; Kneller, "Method of Inquiry," 24; Machamer, "Brief Historical Introduction," 3; Peacocke, *Paths from Science towards God*, 16.

85. Craver, "Structures of Scientific Theories," 66, 71; Powell, *Participating in God*, 56–57.

86. Knight, *God of Nature*, 1.

87. Clayton, *Adventures in the Spirit*, 186.

88. Ibid., 77; Peacocke, *Paths from Science towards God*, 34, 70, 75, 83, 93, 146.

Panentheistic Perspectives

If we start with the same assumptions as to the law-like and causal behavior of creation, is this secular scientific perspective the only worldview that we can take? As creationists and intelligent design proponents have publically proclaimed, the answer is no. In addition to their voice, however, there are alternative perspectives that might be considered. One of these is known as "panentheism."

In its most basic form, panentheism is "the belief that God, while above the world, is at the same time within the world, everywhere present as the heart of its heart, the core of its core."[89] The primary and paradoxical claim of panentheists is therefore that God is at one and the same time completely transcendent to creation whilst simultaneously being supremely immanent "within and through" every part of it.[90] Such a foundation, especially the immanent assertions of panentheists, alters how the workings of creation are perceived.

Not satisfied either with claims that God regularly and supernaturally intervenes to suspend the "natural and causal laws" of creation or that God is completely separate from its workings,[91] panentheists support the notion that it is through these regularities and laws that God acts in creation.[92] "God creates," one panentheist writes, "through natural processes that enable a life-bearing universe to evolve."[93] God is therefore understood to be the "the creative spirit and the ultimate order" that undergirds creation's processes.[94] In discussing his own quantum approach to panentheism, physicist-turned-theologian Robert John Russell asserts that it "offers a robust version of 'theistic evolution,' namely that biological evolution, from the perspective of Christian theology, is 'how God creates life.'"[95] The result is a theistic view of evolution that is contrasted with

---

89. Ware, "God Immanent Yet Transcendent," 158–59.

90. Brierley, "Naming a Quiet Revolution," 8–9. Clayton, *Adventures in the Spirit*, 106, 118, 151; Peacocke, *Paths from Science towards God*, 57; Smith, *God, Energy and the Field*, 12.

91. Griffin, *Reenchantment without Supernaturalism*, 135; Knight, *God of Nature*, 111; Peters, *Science, Theology, and Ethics*, 7.

92. Clayton, *Adventures in the Spirit*, 211; Griffin, "Panentheism," 43; Knight, *God of Nature*, 23; Peacocke, *Paths from Science towards God*, 138; Russell, *Cosmology*, 15.

93. Edwards, "Relational and Evolving Universe," 201.

94. Barbour, *Myths, Models and Paradigms*, 139; Griffin, *Reenchantment without Supernaturalism*, 139; Knight, *God of Nature*, 85.

95. Russell, *Cosmology*, 20.

Appendix B

secular scientific versions. It is one that, unlike secular theories, seeks to explicitly identify how God is related to the dynamics under consideration; in this case evolution.

The Providential Fork in the Road: Theologizing Science

These discussions therefore illustrate a fundamental difference between what I term to be "secular" and "theistic" models. The primary difference that I want to highlight here is that theistic models explicitly endeavor to clarify how God is a part of the phenomena that we are seeking to approximate with our models. Secular models, alternatively, make no explicit attempt to do this.

This is important for the field of "Theistic Spiritual Formation," which I have more simply termed as "spiritual formation" in this book, because our primary goal is to seek to intentionally nurture more of God's manifesting life within and to the individuals and communities that we are called to work with in our ministries. In order to do this, however, we need to have a clear idea of: (1) how God's Life is present within/to the people we are working with (description), and (2) how more of this Life may be nurtured (prediction). Our models therefore need to be theistic models; i.e., they need to clarify how we currently believe that God's Life is present to the phenomena that we are formatively working with and seeking to represent with our model.

This poses a particular challenge for spiritual formators who are seeking to work with secular models, such as those taken from mainstream sciences. We might choose, for example, to utilize some of the insights from Freud's psychodynamic theories related to ego, id, and superego.[96] If we did, however, as theistic spiritual formators we would have the additional challenge of further clarifying how God is a part of them; i.e., to translate these secular theories into theistic models. As we found in chapter 3, there are ways of doing this, and these ways are an integral part of our spiritual praxis methods. In order to engage with them, however, we must first acknowledge the kinds of models we are working with—be they secular or theistic—and whether the theologies they depict are in accordance with our own.

---

96. Freud, *Ego and the Id*.

Closing Reflections

This appendix has been an attempt to help us to further clarify what models are and how they are constructed. As theoretical representations of some part of creation, models can give us unique insights into the nature of reality. They can draw our attention to patterns and phenomena that we might have otherwise missed without them. Not only do theories help us to better understand how things are, they also have the potential to help us anticipate what might happen in the future. It is based upon such insights that our work in spiritual formation can be honed and improved as our three methodologies illustrate.

However, we must also recognize the inherent limitations that all models have. As mere approximations of reality, the insights they provide can never be fully accurate or comprehensive. It behooves us to approach the use of such theories with much caution and discernment. We must therefore understand how the models we are utilizing were constructed so that when we go to apply them, we might do so with greater wisdom.

Appendix C

Tom's Original Program

Finding Our Way: Detailed Syllabus

Self-Explorations: Getting to Know Ourselves

Fall Semester

- *Introductions, Program Overview* (1 week)
  - Purpose:
    - To introduce participants to the program as a whole, its goals and anticipated trajectories. This is also intended to be a time when participants get to know one another, and we covenantually begin establishing a safe space.
    - It is also for students to gain a better understanding of themselves through a personal engagement with various autobiographical, stage theories, and personality related tools. Participants should also then be better enabled to help others in their self-explorations and growth.
  - Group Sharing:
    - Name, relation to Seminary (if any), why they signed up for the program, and what they hope to get out of it; any religious/spiritual affiliations?
    - *Narrative exercise*: Take a few moments to think about who you are as a person—your gifts, your likes, the life you have lived, the people you have been blessed to know, the jobs

you've had, etc.—and think of an animal that best seems to represent who you are at your core. Write your name on your nameplate and draw this animal. Share with the group the info from above and the animal you chose and how this animal captures something of your essence.

- *Content to Be Presented*:
  - Overview of the program and its elements (weekly format, reflections, and spiritual practices)
  - A general introduction and overview of Autobiographies
- *Reflective Exercise for the Coming Week*:
  - Reflecting on the first part of their life for their autobiography
- *Contemplative Practice*:
  - Compassion Practice generally: I will be introducing this practice at this point because doing an autobiography can bring up some unresolved issues and painful memories. I therefore would like them to have some of the tools to engage these as they arise

✺ *Autobiographies* (3 weeks)

- *Purpose*:
  - Who we are today is partly the product of the experiences that we have had. In this portion of the program, participants will be invited to reflect on their journeys to date through the use of autobiographical reflections.
- *Week 1*: First Half of Life
  - *Group Sharing*:
    - ◊ Sharing what they have come up with over the last week in relation to the first half of their life.
  - *Content to Be Presented*:
    - ◊ How autobiographies can be used to guide others (individuals and small groups) to reflect on their own journeys.
    - ◊ Golden Shadow work
  - *Reflective Exercise for the Coming Week*:
    - ◊ Reflecting on the second half of their life

Appendix C

- ▫ *Contemplative Practice*:
    - ◊ Applying the Compassion Practice to Golden Shadow work—There may be times in their autobiographical reflections that they come across memories of unfulfilled yearnings. This practice is intended to help them to contemplatively sit with these movements and reflect on their latent invitations.
- Week 2: Second Half of Life
    - ▫ *Group Sharing*:
        - ◊ Sharing what they have come up with over the last week in relation to the second half of their life.
    - ▫ *Content to Be Presented*:
        - ◊ Reflecting on one's autobiography as a whole, looking for themes, storylines, dominating symbols, etc and what they might suggest for us
        - ◊ The "gift" of enemies
    - ▫ *Reflective Exercise for the Coming Week*:
        - ◊ Reflecting on our journey as a whole
    - ▫ *Contemplative Practice*:
        - ◊ Compassion Practice for Enemies—just as Golden Shadows might arise as we do this work, so too will Dark Shadows, sometimes in the form of "enemies" we have encountered. Through this practice, participants will be invited to sit with these enemies and the healing invitations that come with them.
- Week 3: Overarching Themes, Stories, and Images of our Life
    - ▫ *Group Sharing*:
        - ◊ Sharing what they have come up with over the last week in relation to the their life as a whole
    - ▫ *Content to Be Presented*:
        - ◊ In light of these autobiographies, we now begin to transition to stage theories of development beginning with Erikson's.
    - ▫ *Reflective Exercise for the Coming Week*:

Tom's Original Program

- ◊ How do you see the dynamics described by Erikson's stages at work in our life history? Are there any unresolved or underdeveloped aspects of a healthy personality that you see in yourself? For instance, is your autonomy or basic trust underdeveloped? Why? How can you more fully nurture it?
- *Contemplative Practice*:
  - ◊ Lectio Divina with Erikson's stages—Which one stands out for you most? What do you hear God saying to you as you sit with this stage?

* *Stage Theories* (2 weeks)
  - *Purpose*:
    - While stage theories can be restrictive, and even outright wrong, the dynamics they capture can sometimes be helpful for us in understanding the journeys that we have been on and how we have experienced life to date. These theories, which are still widely used today, can also help us to better understand others.
  - Week 1: Erikson's Stages of Healthy Ego Development
    - *Group Sharing*:
      - ◊ Reflections on Erikson's stages and our own journeys to date
    - *Content to Be Presented*:
      - ◊ Kegan's stages
      - ◊ Also a brief overview of other stage theories: Fowler, Teresa of Avila's, and Monastic (Purgative, etc)
    - *Reflective Exercise for the Coming Week*:
      - ◊ Similar reflections on Kegan's stages and our own life journeys—Where am I in this journey according to Kegan's stages? Do I seem to favor individuality or interpersonal relationships more in the whole of my journey? And/Or: do any of the other theories call to me?
    - *Contemplative Practice*:

Appendix C

- ◊ Active Imagination with one of Kegan's stages—choose the stage that most speaks to you and do the Active Imagination Practice with it by picturing yourself in this stage: what might your behaviors look like? What might you do if you were in this stage? Etc.
  - Week 2: Kegan's Evolving Self
    - *Group Sharing*:
      - ◊ Reflecting on our life's journey in light of Kegan—and some of the others if they feel so moved
    - *Content to Be Presented*:
      - ◊ Now we begin our transition to personality type theories. I will give a brief talk about each of the indicators of the Myers-Briggs system (I-E, S-N, T-F, J-P)
      - ◊ I will then discuss David Keirsey's presentation and organization of Myers-Briggs, covering the two types, Idealists and Artists, first.
      - ◊ Is there a neurophysiological basis for MB?
    - *Reflective Exercise for the Coming Week*:
      - ◊ Reflect on how we see these two types being a part of our life—Where in my life have I embodied these two types? Is either of them particularly strong or weak for me? Do I feel an invitation to develop one of these types more?
    - *Contemplative Practice*:
      - ◊ Julia Cameron's Morning Pages and Artist's Date, and/or a creative art project of some kind

- ✳ *Personality Types Systems* (4 weeks)
  - Purpose:
    - Personality type theories, like stage theories, can be both helpful and restrictive. One of the helpful contributions is that they can help us to see different parts of our selves that we may not have noticed before. In this portion of our program, we will be reflecting how each of the personality traits/structures identified by Myers-Briggs and the Enneagram systems are operative in our own lives.

Tom's Original Program

- Week 1: Myers-Briggs' Idealists and Artists (The "Right-Brained" Types)
  - Group Sharing:
    - Reflecting on how and where we see ourselves embodying the Idealists and Artisan types.
  - Content to Be Presented:
    - Myers-Briggs' types—the Rationalists and Guardians
  - Reflective Exercise for the Coming Week:
    - Reflect on how we are Rationalists and Guardians and where we have and do embody them in our lives
    - Reflect on which of the type indicators we have seemed to most embody throughout our lives in light of our autobiographies
    - Take the Myers-Briggs inventory test
    - What MB Type am I according to the test? Do I agree with it? Does knowing this help me to better understand my autobiography, the decisions I have made, and how I have experience life in general? Are there any changes in my life I feel moved to make in light of this?
  - Contemplative Practice:
    - Mapping Version of the Compassion Practice, or some other Scholastic/Intellectual/Ordering-based Spiritual Practice
- Week 2: Myers-Briggs' Rationalists and Guardians (The "Left-Brained" Types)
  - Group Sharing:
    - Sharing on our Rationalists and Guardians selves
    - Sharing on what our MB Type might be and some of its possible implications for our lives
  - Content to Be Presented:
    - We will now be transitioning from the Myers-Briggs system to the Enneagram. I will offer a brief overview of the Enneagram system and some of its dynamics (intuiting,

283

Appendix C

feeling, and thinking groups) and how it differs from MB. Then I will briefly introduce types 2–5.

- *Reflective Exercise for the Coming Week*:
  - ◊ Reflect on how and where we see the dynamics of types 2–5 are and have been a part of our life. Do we seem to embody one of these more than the others? When do each of these seem to be dominant for us – when we're happy? Sad? When? Where? Do we seem to use these different types when we are in different roles in our lives?
- *Contemplative Practice*:
  - ◊ Ignatian Contemplation, or Praying with our emotions

- Week 3: Enneagram 2–5
  - *Group Sharing*:
    - ◊ Sharing our 2–5 type dynamics
  - *Content to Be Presented*:
    - ◊ Types 6–1
    - ◊ The integrating and disintegrating movements between the types (for instance, 1s go to a 4 when under pressure, and they go to a 7 when things are going well; give them the diagram that shows this).
  - *Reflective Exercise for the Coming Week*:
    - ◊ Reflecting on our 6–1 type dynamics as we did 2–5.
    - ◊ Which type, and its associated dynamics, do we seem to most embody? Do I "self-identify" as any one of these types? Does this help me to better understand my autobiography, the decisions I have made, and how I have experienced life in general? Do I feel invited to make any changes in light of this?
  - *Contemplative Practice*:
    - ◊ Walking Meditation (some other form of body-centered prayer) or some form of intuiting prayer

- Week 4: Enneagram 6–1
  - *Group Sharing*:
    - ◊ Sharing our 6–1 type personality dynamics

- ◊ Reflecting on which of the Enneagram types we think we might most embody and some of its possible implications for our lives
- ▫ *Content to Be Presented*:
  - ◊ We will now be transitioning to the final phase of this first part: a brief introduction to Holmes' Parts Work
- ▫ *Reflective Exercise for the Coming Week*:
  - ◊ Creating a parts map/drawing: Where and how have these different parts been active in our lives? How has each benefitted and limited us? Which ones are out of balance?
  - ◊ Watch the different parts that arise in us as the week unfolds: Do these parts seem to be fixed, or are there parts that come and go? Do the parts seem to have parts?
- ▫ *Contemplative Practice*:
  - ◊ Parts work practice of getting to know each part – name, age, gender, species, fears, longings, job, etc.

* *Holmes' Parts Work* (2 weeks)
  - *Purpose*:
    - ▫ Now that we have reviewed different stage theories and personality type systems, we will now experience a less structured way to view the various parts of our inner lives and psyches through the Parts Work/Internal Family Systems theories and practices.
  - *Week 1*: Mapping our Parts
    - ▫ *Group Sharing*:
      - ◊ Sharing our part maps
    - ▫ *Content to Be Presented*:
      - ◊ Inviting the sacred, and sacred guides, to be with us as these various parts take over the "living room" of our psyches.
    - ▫ *Reflective Exercise for the Coming Week*:
      - ◊ (see Spiritual Practice)

Appendix C

- ◊ Questions to reflect on and share: Who was/were some of the sacred guides that arose for us? What did the sacred do? How did the parts respond? Is this a beneficial practice? Does it help us to deal with issues that arise in our daily life? Do you feel that healing genuinely occurred through these encounters?
- *Contemplative Practice*:
  - ◊ Parts Work practice of inviting the sacred to address the parts as issues arise throughout our week
- Week 2: Encountering the Sacred to be with our Parts
  - *Group Sharing*:
    - ◊ Sharing our experiences from Parts Work and inviting the sacred
    - ◊ Maybe do the group part sharing exercise that Holmes did with us when he was here
  - *Content to Be Presented*:
    - ◊ Recap of the Part I and the journey that we have been on throughout the semester together
  - *Reflective Exercise for the Coming Week*:
    - ◊ Go back over all that we have done from the beginning of the semester—What have I learned about myself? What did I learn that was new? What was further affirmed and elaborated on? What will I do differently in my life in light of all of this?
  - *Contemplative Practice*:
    - ◊ Ignatian Examen—Where were the movements of life as I look back over this semester's journey? Where were the movements of desolation? What is God inviting me into in light of all of this?

* *Closing, Part I Wrap-Up* (1 week)
  - *Purpose*:
    - To bring the semester to a close
    - To honor and celebrate the short journey that we have been on together

- *Group Sharing*:
    - Sharing what we have gained from this first part of the program
    - To celebrate one another as God's gift to us and to the world!

Appendix D

Tom's Revised Program

Finding Our Way: An Introduction to a Contemplative Way of Life for Laity

Wednesdays 7:15–9:00 pm

Course Description

This course will explore some of the practices, worldviews, and teachings of a contemplative way of life. In addition to reflecting on our own life's journey, it will focus on some of the contemplative practices that have been used throughout Christian history as well as a few contemporary ones. This course will also explore some of the core worldviews, theologies, and theories of development that contemplative traditions have fostered. Overall, the primary goal is to offer you an experiential introduction to contemplative living.

Objectives

By the end of this course, participants will:

* Be exposed to a broad range of Contemplative Practices

* Know the basic principles and traditions of a Contemplative Way of Life

* Reflectively review their life's journey from a contemplative and developmental perspective

* Be exposed to the diversity present in our class

Facilitation

To pursue these goals, we will be engaging in the following:

* *Contemplative Practices*—each week we will engage in one practice as a class; you also be invited to continue the practice throughout your week

* *Lecture*—Where appropriate, I will be presenting the material of each week's theme

* *Readings*—For most weeks, I will provide you with readings relevant to the week's theme and discuss their content during our time together. While not required, you are invited to read these at your leisure and come to class with your questions and reflections.

* *Group Sharing & Reflections*—participants will be invited to share their own experiences with the practices and any reflections on the material we are engaging

Course Schedule

* Week 1: *Introduction & Program Overview*
  - *Purpose*:
    - To introduce participants to the program as a whole, its goals and anticipated trajectories. This is also intended to be a time when participants get to know one another, and we covenantually begin establishing a safe contemplative space.
  - *Contemplative Practice*:
    - *Compassion Practice*
  - *Selected Readings From*:

Appendix D

- Walter Burghardt, "Contemplation: A Long Loving Look at the Real"
- Thomas Merton, *The Inner Experience*
- *New Westminster Dictionary of Christian Spirituality*, "Contemplation"
- *'Homework' for the Coming Week*:
  - Reflect on the first part of your life for your autobiography

PART I: *Exploring Our Own Journey*

- Week 2: *The First Half of Life*
  - *Purpose*:
    - Who we are today is partly the product of the experiences that we have had in the past. In this portion of the program, you will be invited to contemplatively reflect on the first half of your life's journey to date through the use of structured autobiographical reflections.
  - *Contemplative Practice*:
    - *Praying a Sacred Moment*
  - *'Homework' for the Coming Week*:
    - Reflect on the second part of your life for your autobiography

- Week 3: *The Second Half of Life*
  - *Purpose*:
    - We continue our autobiographical reflections by exploring the second half of our journeys.
  - *Contemplative Practice*:
    - *Beholding Practice*
  - *'Homework' for the Coming Week*:
    - Reflect on your journey as a whole, what overarching themes, images, metaphors, or stories seem to emerge for you?

- Week 4: Overarching Themes & Images
  - Purpose:
    - We complete these contemplative explorations of our life journeys by now stepping back and looking at it as a whole to see what emerges.
  - Contemplative Practice:
    - Ignatian Awareness Examen
  - Selected Readings From:
    - James Fowler, *Stages of Faith*
    - Robert Kegan, *The Evolving Self*
  - 'Homework' for the Coming Week:
    - Choose one of these theories of stage development. How do you see the dynamics described by its stages at work in your life history?

PART II: Exploring the Contemplative Journey

- Week 5: Exploring Contemplative Ideals
  - Purpose:
    - Having considered our own journeys, we now begin our explorations of a contemplative way of life. In this first session, we will be considering the ideals towards which contemplative traditions would have us orient our entire lives around.
  - Contemplative Practice:
    - Jungian Active Imagination
  - Selected Readings From:
    - Gerald May, *Will and Spirit*
    - Teresa of Avila, *The Interior Castle*
    - Julian of Norwich, *Showings*
    - Jean-Pierre de Caussade, *The Sacrament of the Present Moment*
    - Nicolas of Cusa, *On the Summit of Contemplation*

Appendix D

- Masao Abe, *Zen and Western Thought*
- Pseudo-Dionysius, *The Mystical Theology*

* Week 6: *Contemplative Worldviews—Creation*
  - *Purpose*:
    - Contemplative living is intended to impact every part of our lives. In this session, we will consider two competing views of creation that contemplative traditions have asserted.
  - *Contemplative Practice*:
    - *Ignatian Contemplation*
  - *Selected Readings From*:
    - Walter Wink, *Engaging the Powers*
    - St. Isaiah the Solitary, *On Guarding the Intellect*
    - T. L. Osborn, *Healing the Sick*
    - Marshall Rosenberg, *Nonviolent Communication*
    - Marjorie Hewitt Suchocki, *God Christ Church*
    - Lao Tzu, *Tao Teh Ching*
    - Pierre Teilhard de Chardin, *Hymn of the Universe*
    - William Shannon, *Silence on Fire*

* Week 7: *Contemplative Worldviews—Humanity*
  - *Purpose*:
    - We continue our explorations of contemplative worldviews by now looking at one view of human nature that is contemporarily found.
  - *Contemplative Practice*:
    - *'Parts Work' Contemplation*
  - *Selected Readings From*:
    - Tom Holmes, *Parts Work*
    - Kraybill, Evans, & Evans, *Peace Skills*
    - Howard Zehr, *Restorative Justice*

Tom's Revised Program

- ✳ Week 8: *Contemplative Approaches to Spiritual Formation*
  - *Purpose*:
    - Having the horizons towards which to head and the lenses to guide our journeys, we will now take a look at some of the contemplative approaches and specific kinds of practices that are intended to help us along our way.
  - *Contemplative Practice*:
    - Lectio Divina
  - *Selected Readings From*:
    - (Handout: *Spiritual Formation Approaches/Supports*)

- ✳ Week 9: *Contemplative Stages of Development*
  - *Purpose*:
    - A core part of Western Christian contemplative traditions has included reflections on the nature and stages of development that one traverses as we grow. In this session, we will consider two such views.
  - *Contemplative Practice*:
    - Walking Meditation in a Labyrinth
  - *Selected Readings From*:
    - Teresa of Avila, *The Interior Castle*
    - Richard of St. Victor, *The Mystical Ark*
    - (Handout: *Some Notes on Human Transformation*)

- ✳ Week 10: *Contemplative Monitoring & Discernment*
  - *Purpose*:
    - How do we really know if we are progressing in our spiritual journeys? How do we know if we are headed in the right direction? The contemplative traditions offer ample ways to both monitor and discern the steps one takes along their path.
  - *Contemplative Practice*:
    - Focusing Prayer

Appendix D

- *Selected Readings From:*
  - (Handout: *Spiritual Formation Texts from Christian History*)
  - Richard Hauser, *Moving in the Spirit*
  - (Handout: *Some Notes on Monitoring & Discerning*)

* Week 11: *Closing & Wrap-Up*
  - *Purpose:*
    - To bring our time together to a close
    - To honor and celebrate the short journey that we have been on!
  - *Contemplative Practice:*
    - *Ignatian Awareness Examen*
  - *Selected Readings From:*
    - (Handout: *Closing/Wrap-Up* [a summary of our course])
  - *Group Sharing:*
    - What have you gained from this first program?
    - Where were the movements of life and vitality for you?
    - Where might your journey go from here?

Bibliography

Ackerman, John. *Listening to God: Spiritual Formation in Congregations*. Herndon, VA: Alban Institute, 2001.
Allport, G. W. *Personality: A Psychological Interpretation*. New York: Holt, 1937.
Altizer, Thomas J. J. *The New Gospel of Christian Atheism*. Aurora, CO: Davies Group, 2002.
Anderson, Rosemarie. "Intuitive Inquiry: A Transpersonal Approach." In *Transpersonal Research Methods for the Social Sciences: Honoring Human Experience*, edited by William Braud and Rosemarie Anderson, 69–94. Thousand Oaks, CA: Sage, 1998.
Arnheim, Rudolf. "The Double-Edged Mind: Intuition and the Intellect." In *Learning and Teaching the Ways of Knowing: Eighty-Fourth Yearbook of the National Society for the Study of Education*, edited by Elliot Eisner, 77–96. Chicago: National Society for the Study of Education, 1985.
Au, Wilkie W., and Noreen Cannon Au. *The Discerning Heart: Exploring the Christian Path*. New York: Paulist, 2006.
Azeemi, Khwaja Shamsuddin. *Muraqaba: The Art and Science of Sufi Meditation*. Translated by Syed Shahzad Reaz. Houston: Plato, 2005.
Bailer-Jones, Daniela M. "Models, Metaphors, and Analogies." In *The Blackwell Guide to the Philosophy of Science*, edited by Peter Machamer and Michael Silberstein, 108–27. Malden, MA: Blackwell, 2002.
Barbour, Ian G. *Myths, Models and Paradigms: A Comparative Study in Science and Religion*. New York: Harper & Row, 1974.
———. *Religion and Science: Historical and Contemporary Issues*. Rev. ed. New York: HarperCollins, 1997.
———. *When Science Meets Religion: Enemies, Strangers, or Partners?* San Francisco: HarperSanFrancisco, 2000.
Barrick, Marilyn C. *Sacred Psychology of Love: The Quest for Relationships That Unite Heart and Soul*. Corwin Springs, MT: Summit University Press, 1999.
Basmadjian, Diran. *Mathematical Modeling of Physical Systems: An Introduction*. New York: Oxford University Press, 2003.
Bauer, Henry H. "The So-Called Scientific Method." In *Science and Its Ways of Knowing*, edited by John Hatton and Paul B. Plouffe, 25–37. Upper Saddle River, NJ: Prentice Hall, 1997.
Bauman, Lynn C. "Spiritual Formation through the Liturgy." In *The Christian Educator's Handbook on Spiritual Formation*, edited by Kenneth O. Gangel and James C. Wilhoit, 99–110. Grand Rapids: Baker, 1998.
Bear, Mark F., et al. *Neuroscience: Exploring the Brain*. 3rd ed. Philadelphia: Lippincott, Williams & Wilkins, 2007.

Bibliography

Beitler, Michael A. *Strategic Organizational Change: A Practitioner's Guide for Managers and Consultants*. 2nd ed. Greensboro, NC: Practitioner Press International, 2006.

Best, John W., and James V. Kahn. *Research in Education*. 8th ed. Boston: Allyn & Bacon, 1998.

Bidwell, Duane R. "Formation through Parallel Charting: Clinical Narratives and Group Supervision." In *The Formation of Pastoral Counselors: Challenges and Opportunities*, edited by Duane R. Bidwell and Joretta L. Marshall, 143–54. Binghamton, NY: Haworth Pastoral, 2006.

Bidwell, Duanne R., and Joretta L. Marshall. "Formation: Content, Context, Models and Practices." In *The Formation of Pastoral Counselors: Challenges and Opportunities*, edited by Duane R. Bidwell and Joretta L. Marshall, 1–7. Binghamton, NY: Haworth Pastoral, 2006.

Bilgrave, Dyer P., and Robert H. Deluty. "Stanislavski's Acting Method and Control Theory: Commonalities Across Time, Place, and Field." *Social Behavior and Personality* 32 (2004) 329–40.

Bisman, Cynthia D., and David A. Hardcastle. *Integrating Research Into Practice: A Model for Effective Social Work*. Belmont, CA: Brooks/Cole, 1999.

Blaising, Craig A. "Spiritual Formation in the Early Church." In *The Christian Educator's Handbook on Spiritual Formation*, edited by Kenneth O. Gangel and James C. Wilhoit, 21–36. Grand Rapids: Baker, 1998.

Bogen, James. "Experiment and Observation." In *The Blackwell Guide to the Philosophy of Science*, edited by Peter Machamer and Michael Silberstein, 128–48. Malden, MA: Blackwell, 2002.

Booth, Wayne C., et al. *The Craft of Research*. 3rd ed. Chicago: University of Chicago Press, 2008.

Bourgeault, Cynthia. *The Wisdom Way of Knowing: Reclaiming an Ancient Tradition to Awaken the Heart*. San Francisco: Jossey-Bass, 2003.

Bracken, Joseph A. *The Divine Matrix: Creativity as Link between East and West*. Maryknoll, NY: Orbis, 1995.

Braud, William. "Integral Inquiry: Complementary Ways of Knowing, Being, and Expression." In *Transpersonal Research Methods for the Social Sciences: Honoring Human Experience*, edited by William Braud and Rosemarie Anderson, 35–68. Thousand Oaks, CA: Sage, 1998.

Braud, William, and Rosemarie Anderson. *Transpersonal Research Methods for the Social Sciences: Honoring Human Experience*. Thousand Oaks, CA: Sage, 1998.

Brierley, Michael W. "Naming a Quiet Revolution: The Panentheistic Turn in Modern Theology." In *In Whom We Live and Move and Have Our Being: Panentheistic Reflections on God's Presence in a Scientific World*, edited by Philip Clayton and Arthur Peacocke, 1–15. Grand Rapids: Eerdmans, 2004.

Britt, David W. *A Conceptual Introduction to Modeling: Qualitative and Quantitative Perspectives*. Mahwah, NJ: Erlbaum, 1997.

Burghardt, Walter J. "Contemplation: A Long Loving Look at the Real." *Church*, winter 1989, 14–18.

Cameron, Julia. *The Artist's Way: A Spiritual Path to Higher Creativity*. 10th anniversary ed. New York: Penguin, 2002.

Carver, Charles S., and Michael F. Scheier. *On the Self-Regulation of Behavior*. Cambridge: Cambridge University Press, 1998.

Cassian, John. *John Cassian: The Conferences*. Translated by Boniface Ramsey. Mahwah, NJ: Paulist, 1997.
Clark, Robert. "Spiritual Formation in Children." In *The Christian Educator's Handbook on Spiritual Formation*, edited by Kenneth O. Gangel and James C. Wilhoit, 234–46. Grand Rapids: Baker, 1998.
Clayton, Philip. *Adventures in the Spirit: God, World, Divine Action*. Minneapolis: Fortress, 2008.
———. *Mind and Emergence: From Quantum to Consciousness*. Oxford: Oxford University Press, 2004.
———. "Panentheism Today: A Constructive Systematic Evaluation." In *In Whom We Live and Move and Have Our Being: Panentheistic Reflections on God's Presence in a Scientific World*, edited by Philip Clayton and Arthur Peacocke, 249–64. Grand Rapids: Eerdmans, 2004.
Clayton, Philip, and Arthur Peacocke, editors. *In Whom We Live and Move and Have Our Being: Panentheistic Reflections on God's Presence in a Scientific World*. Grand Rapids: Eerdmans, 2004.
Cobb, John B., Jr., and David Ray Griffin. *Process Theology: An Introductory Exposition*. Louisville: Westminster John Knox, 1976.
Cohen, Louis, et al. *Research Methods in Education*. 6th ed. London: Routledge, 2007.
Cooper-White, Pamela. "Thick Theory: Psychology, Theoretical Models, and the Formation of Pastoral Counselors." In *The Formation of Pastoral Counselors: Challenges and Opportunities*, edited by Duane R. Bidwell and Joretta L. Marshall, 47–67. Binghamton, NY: Haworth Pastoral, 2006.
Crabb, Larry. "Longing for Eden and Sinning on the Way to Heaven." In *The Christian Educator's Handbook on Spiritual Formation*, edited by Kenneth O. Gangel and James C. Wilhoit, 86–98. Grand Rapids: Baker, 1998.
Craver, Carl F. "Structures of Scientific Theories." In *The Blackwell Guide to the Philosophy of Science*, edited by Peter Machamer and Michael Silberstein, 55–79. Malden, MA: Blackwell, 2002.
Cunningham, J. Barton. *Action Research and Organizational Development*. Westport, CT: Praeger, 1993.
Damasio, Antonio. *The Feeling of What Happens: Body and Emotion in the Making of Consciousness*. San Diego: Harcourt, 1999.
Daugherty, Alane. *The Power Within: From Neuroscience to Transformation*. Dubuque, IA: Kendall Hunt, 2008.
Dawkins, Richard. *The Selfish Gene*. 30th anniversary ed. Oxford: Oxford University Press, 2006.
Deison, Peter V. "Spiritual Formation through Small Groups." In *The Christian Educator's Handbook on Spiritual Formation*, edited by Kenneth O. Gangel and James C. Wilhoit, 269–79. Grand Rapids: Baker, 1998.
Dettoni, John M. "What Is Spiritual Formation?" In *The Christian Educator's Handbook on Spiritual Formation*, edited by Kenneth O. Gangel and James C. Wilhoit, 11–20. Grand Rapids: Baker, 1998.
Diamond, Robert M. *Designing and Assessing Courses and Curricula: A Practical Guide*. 3rd ed. San Francisco: Jossey-Bass, 2008.
Dispenza, Joe. *Evolve Your Brain: The Science of Changing Your Mind*. Deerfield Beach, FL: Health Communications, 2007.

Bibliography

Dorsett, Lyle W. "The Pietistic Tradition in Evangelical Spirituality: A Bibliographic Essay." In *The Christian Educator's Handbook on Spiritual Formation*, edited by Kenneth O. Gangel and James C. Wilhoit, 296–306. Grand Rapids: Baker, 1998.

Dougherty, Rose Mary. *Group Spiritual Direction: Community for Discernment*. New York: Paulist, 1995.

Driskill, Joseph D. "Spirituality and the Formation of Pastoral Counselors." In *The Formation of Pastoral Counselors: Challenges and Opportunities*, edited by Duane R. Bidwell and Joretta L. Marshall, 69–85. Binghamton, NY: Haworth Pastoral, 2006.

Duncan-Andrade, et al. *The Art of Critical Pedagogy: Possibilities for Moving from Theory to Practice in Urban Schools*. New York: Peter Lang, 2008.

Edwards, Denis. "A Relational and Evolving Universe Unfolding within the Dynamism of the Divine Communion." In *In Whom We Live and Move and Have Our Being: Panentheistic Reflections on God's Presence in a Scientific World*, edited by Philip Clayton and Arthur Peacocke, 199–210. Grand Rapids: Eerdmans, 2004.

Edwards, Tilden. *Living in the Presence: Spiritual Exercises to Open Your Life to the Awareness of God*. San Francisco: HarperSanFrancisco, 1995.

Elias, John L. *The Foundations and Practice of Adult Religious Education*. Malabar, FL: Krieger, 1982.

Erasmus. "The Handbook of the Militant Christian." In *The Essential Erasmus*, translated by John P. Dolan, 28–93. New York: New American Library, 1964.

Felder, Trunell D. "Counsel from Wise Others: Forming Wisdom through Male Mentoring." In *In Search of Wisdom: Faith Formation in the Black Church*, edited by Anne E. Streaty Wimberly and Evelyn L. Parker, 89–107. Nashville: Abingdon, 2002.

Fowler, James W. *Stages of Faith: The Psychology of Human Development and the Quest for Meaning*. San Francisco: HarperSanFrancisco, 1981.

Francis, de Sales. *Introduction to the Devout Life*. Vintage Spiritual Classics. New York: Vintage, 2002.

Franklin, Gene F., et al. *Feedback Control of Dynamic Systems*. 3rd ed. Reading, MA: Addison-Wesley, 1994.

Freud, Sigmund. *The Ego and the Id*. Translated by Joan Riviere. London: Hogarth, 1927.

Gall, Meredith D., et al. *Educational Research: An Introduction*. 6th ed. White Plains, NY: Longman, 1996.

Gangel, Kenneth O. "Spiritual Formation through Public Worship." In *The Christian Educator's Handbook on Spiritual Formation*, edited by Kenneth O. Gangel and James C. Wilhoit, 111–29. Grand Rapids: Baker, 1998.

Gardner, Howard E. *Frames of Mind: The Theory of Multiple Intelligences*. New York: Basic Books, 1983.

Gilligan, Carol. "A Different Voice in Moral Decisions." In *From Christ to the World: Introductory Readings in Christian Ethics*, edited by Wayne G. Boulton et al., 172–76. Grand Rapids: Eerdmans, 1994.

Glasziou, Paul P., et al. *Evidence-Based Medicine Workbook*. London: BMJ, 2003.

Graham, Alice M. "Race and Ethnicity in the Formation of Pastoral Counselors." In *The Formation of Pastoral Counselors: Challenges and Opportunities*, edited by Duane R. Bidwell and Joretta L. Marshall, 87–98. Binghamton, NY: Haworth Pastoral, 2006.

Bibliography

Graham, Elaine L. *Transforming Practice: Pastoral Theology in an Age of Uncertainty*. Eugene, OR: Wipf & Stock, 1996.

Graham, Elaine L., et al. *Theological Reflection: Methods*. London: SCM, 2005.

Graham, Larry Kent, and Jason C. Whitehead. "The Role of Pastoral Theology in Theological Education for the Formation of Pastoral Counselors." In *The Formation of Pastoral Counselors: Challenges and Opportunities*, edited by Duane R. Bidwell and Joretta L. Marshall, 9–27. Binghamton, NY: Haworth Pastoral, 2006.

Green, Joel. *Body, Soul, and Human Life: The Nature of Humanity in the Bible*. Grand Rapids: Baker Academic, 2008.

Greenwood, Davydd J., and Morten Levin. *Introduction to Action Research: Social Research for Social Change*. 2nd ed. Thousand Oaks, CA: Sage, 2007.

Gregersen, Niels Henrik. "Three Varieties of Panentheism." In *In Whom We Live and Move and Have Our Being: Panentheistic Reflections on God's Presence in a Scientific World*, edited by Philip Clayton and Arthur Peacocke, 19–35. Grand Rapids: Eerdmans, 2004.

Greider, Kathleen J., et al. "Formation for Care of Souls: The Claremont Way." In *The Formation of Pastoral Counselors: Challenges and Opportunities*, edited by Duane R. Bidwell and Joretta L. Marshall, 177–95. Binghamton, NY: Haworth Pastoral, 2006.

Griffin, David Ray. "Panentheism: A Postmodern Revelation." In *In Whom We Live and Move and Have Our Being: Panentheistic Reflections on God's Presence in a Scientific World*, edited by Philip Clayton and Arthur Peacocke, 36–47. Grand Rapids: Eerdmans, 2004.

———. *Reenchantment without Supernaturalism: A Process Philosophy of Religion*. Ithaca, NY: Cornell University Press, 2001.

Groome, Thomas H. *Christian Religious Education: Sharing Our Story and Vision*. San Francisco: Jossey-Bass, 1999.

Hatton, John, and Paul B. Plouffe. General introduction to *Science and Its Ways of Knowing*, edited by John Hatton and Paul B. Plouffe, vii–x. Upper Saddle River, NJ: Prentice Hall, 1997.

———. Introduction to part 2, Developing a Theory. In *Science and Its Ways of Knowing*, edited by John Hatton and Paul B. Plouffe, 59–60. Upper Saddle River, NJ: Prentice Hall, 1997.

Hauser, Richard J. *Moving in the Spirit: Becoming a Contemplative in Action*. New York: Paulist, 1986.

Hawking, Stephen. "My Position." In *Science and Its Ways of Knowing*, edited by John Hatton and Paul B. Plouffe, 7–11. Upper Saddle River, NJ: Prentice Hall, 1997.

Hesslefors-Arktoft, Elisabeth, and Annika Lindskog. "Connecting Theory and Practice? A Discussion about Praxis-Related Criteria for Examinations Tasks and Degree Projects in Teacher Education." In *Examining Praxis: Assessment and Knowledge Construction in Teacher Education*, edited by Matts Mattsson et al., 77–96. Rotterdam: Sense, 2008.

Hoagland, Mahlon. "Preface from *Toward the Habit of Truth*." In *Science and Its Ways of Knowing*, edited by John Hatton and Paul B. Plouffe, 118–24. Upper Saddle River, NJ: Prentice Hall, 1997.

Huebner, Dwayne E. "Spirituality and Knowing." In *Learning and Teaching the Ways of Knowing: Eighty-Fourth Yearbook of the National Society for the Study of*

Bibliography

    Education, edited by Elliot Eisner, 159–73. Chicago: National Society for the Study of Education, 1985.

Hull, Bill. *The Complete Book of Discipleship: On Being and Making Followers of Christ*. Colorado Springs: NavPress, 2006.

Hunt, T. W. "Teaching People to Pray." In *The Christian Educator's Handbook on Spiritual Formation*, edited by Kenneth O. Gangel and James C. Wilhoit, 189–98. Grand Rapids: Baker, 1998.

Isenhower, Valerie K., and Judith A. Todd. *Living into the Answers: A Workbook for Personal Spiritual Discernment*. Nashville: Upper Room, 2008.

Jaccard, James, and Jacob Jacoby. *Theory Construction and Model-Building Skills: A Practical Guide for Social Scientists*. New York: Guilford, 2010.

Jackson, Jonathan, Jr. "Forming a Spirituality of Wisdom." In *In Search of Wisdom: Faith Formation in the Black Church*, edited by Anne E. Streaty Wimberly and Evelyn L. Parker, 154–66. Nashville: Abingdon, 2002.

Johansson, Inge, and Anette Sandberg. "What Knowledge Develops from Participation in Practitioner-Oriented Research?" In *Examining Praxis: Assessment and Knowledge Construction in Teacher Education*, edited by Matts Mattsson et al., 157–68. Rotterdam: Sense, 2008.

Kegan, Robert. *The Evolving Self: Problem and Process in Human Development*. Cambridge: Harvard University Press, 1982.

Keller, Evelyn Fox. "A Feeling for the Organism." In *Science and Its Ways of Knowing*, edited by John Hatton and Paul B. Plouffe, 136–43. Upper Saddle River, NJ: Prentice Hall, 1997.

Kemmis, Stephen, et al. "Reflections on 'Examining Praxis.'" In *Examining Praxis: Assessment and Knowledge Construction in Teacher Education*, edited by Matts Mattsson et al., 187–207. Rotterdam: Sense, 2008.

Kneller, George F. "A Method of Inquiry." In *Science and Its Ways of Knowing*, edited by John Hatton and Paul B. Plouffe, 11–25. Upper Saddle River, NJ: Prentice Hall, 1997.

Knight, Christopher C. *The God of Nature: Incarnation and Contemporary Science*. Minneapolis: Fortress, 2007.

Kornfeld, Margaret Zipse. *Cultivating Wholeness: A Guide to Care and Counseling in Faith Communities*. New York: Continuum, 2002.

Kretzmann, John P., and John L. McKnight. *Building Communities from the Inside Out: A Path Toward Finding and Mobilizing a Community's Assets*. Evanston, IL: Asset-Based Community Development Institute, Institute for Policy Research, Northwestern University, 1993.

Kyle, Eric J. "Putting God under the Microscope: Can There Be a Science of Spirituality?" Presentation to the Society of Philosophy and Religion in Claremont (SPARC), Second Annual Student Conference: Live Options in the Study of Religion, Claremont, CA, March 25, 2010.

Law, William. "A Serious Call to a Devout and Holy Life." In *William Law: A Serious Call to a Devout and Holy Life, The Spirit of Love*, edited by Paul G. Stanwood, 41–352. New York: Paulist, 1978.

Lawrenz, Mel. *The Dynamics of Spiritual Formation*. Grand Rapids: Baker, 2000.

Levine, Michael P. *Pantheism: A Non-Theistic Concept of Deity*. London: Routledge, 1994.

Lightner, Robert P. "Salvation and Spiritual Formation." In *The Christian Educator's Handbook on Spiritual Formation*, edited by Kenneth O. Gangel and James C. Wilhoit, 37–48. Grand Rapids: Baker, 1998.

Lockerbie, D. Bruce. "Living and Growing in the Christian Year." In *The Christian Educator's Handbook on Spiritual Formation*, edited by Kenneth O. Gangel and James C. Wilhoit, 130–42. Grand Rapids: Baker, 1998.

Machamer, Peter. "A Brief Historical Introduction to the Philosophy of Science." In *The Blackwell Guide to the Philosophy of Science*, edited by Peter Machamer and Michael Silberstein, 1–17. Malden, MA: Blackwell, 2002.

Mafico, Temba L. J. "Forming Wisdom: Biblical and African Guides." In *In Search of Wisdom: Faith Formation in the Black Church*, edited by Anne E. Streaty Wimberly and Evelyn L. Parker, 23–39. Nashville: Abingdon, 2002.

Mahoney, Michael J. *Human Change Processes: The Scientific Foundations of Psychotherapy*. New York: Basic Books, 1991.

Marshall, Joretta L. "Gender Identity, Sexual Orientation, and Pastoral Formation." In *The Formation of Pastoral Counselors: Challenges and Opportunities*, edited by Duane R. Bidwell and Joretta L. Marshall, 113–24. Binghamton, NY: Haworth Pastoral, 2006.

Maslow, Abraham. *Motivation and Personality*. 2nd ed. New York: Harper & Row, 1970.

Matlin, Margaret W. *Cognition*. 6th ed. Hoboken, NJ: Wiley & Sons, 2005.

Mattsson, Matts. "Degree Projects and Praxis Development." In *Examining Praxis: Assessment and Knowledge Construction in Teacher Education*, edited by Matts Mattsson et al., 55–76. Rotterdam: Sense, 2008.

———. "What Is at Stake?" In *Examining Praxis: Assessment and Knowledge Construction in Teacher Education*, edited by Matts Mattsson et al., 3–15. Rotterdam: Sense, 2008.

May, Gerald. *Will and Spirit: A Contemplative Psychology*. San Francisco: Harper & Row, 1982.

McCallum, Dennis, and Jessica Lowery. *Organic Disciplemaking: Mentoring Others into Spiritual Maturity and Leadership*. Houston: Touch, 2006.

McLeod, John. *Doing Counselling Research*. London: Sage, 1994.

Meye, Robert P. "The Imitation of Christ: Means and End of Spiritual Formation." In *The Christian Educator's Handbook on Spiritual Formation*, edited by Kenneth O. Gangel and James C. Wilhoit, 199–212. Grand Rapids: Baker, 1998.

Mezirow, Jack, editor. *Learning as Transformation: Critical Perspectives on a Theory in Progress*. San Francisco: Jossey-Bass, 2000.

Milavec, Aaron. *The Didache: Faith, Hope, and Life of the Earliest Christian Communities, 50–70 C.E.* New York: Newman, 2003.

Mischel, Walter, et al. *Introduction to Personality: Toward an Integrative Science of the Person*. 8th ed. Hoboken, NJ: Wiley & Sons, 2008.

Moberg, David O. "Guidelines for Research and Evaluation." In *Aging and Spirituality: Spiritual Dimensions of Aging Theory, Research, Practice, and Policy*, edited by David O. Moberg, 211–24. New York: Haworth Pastoral, 2001.

Morinis, Alan. *Everyday Holiness: The Jewish Spiritual Path of Mussar*. Boston: Trumpeter, 2008.

Moser, Paul K., et al. *The Theory of Knowledge: A Thematic Introduction*. New York: Oxford University Press, 1998.

Bibliography

Mucherera, Tapiwa N. "Pastoral Formation of Counselors in Intercultural Studies." In *The Formation of Pastoral Counselors: Challenges and Opportunities*, edited by Duane R. Bidwell and Joretta L. Marshall, 99-111. Binghamton, NY: Haworth Pastoral, 2006.

Murphy, Nancey C. *Reasoning and Rhetoric in Religion*. Valley Forge, PA: Trinity, 1994.

Neuendorf, Kimberly A. *The Content Analysis Guidebook*. Thousand Oaks, CA: Sage, 2002.

Nhat Hanh, Thich. *Calming the Fearful Mind: A Zen Response to Terrorism*. Berkeley, CA: Parallax, 2005.

O'Connell, Timothy. *Making Disciples: A Handbook of Christian Moral Formation*. New York: Crossroad, 1998.

O'Connor, Thomas St. James. "Research Methods in Spirituality and Health Care." In *Spiritual Care and Therapy: Integrative Perspectives*, edited by Peter L. VanKatwyk, 141-51. Waterloo, Ontario: Wilfrid Laurier University Press, 2003.

Ogden, Greg. *Transforming Discipleship: Making a Disciples a Few at a Time*. Downers Grove, IL: InterVarsity, 2003.

Olomo, Aina. *The Core of Fire: A Path to Yoruba Spiritual Activism*. Brooklyn, NY: Athelia Henrietta, 2002.

Palmer, Parker J. *The Courage to Teach: Exploring the Inner Landscape of a Teacher's Life*. 10th anniversary ed. San Francisco: Jossey-Bass, 2007.

Parker, Evelyn L. "Singing Hope in the Key of Wisdom: Wisdom Formation of Youth." In *In Search of Wisdom: Faith Formation in the Black Church*, edited by Anne E. Streaty Wimberly and Evelyn L. Parker, 74-88. Nashville: Abingdon, 2002.

Parker, Stephen. *Led by the Spirit: Toward a Practical Theology of Pentecostal Discernment and Decision Making*. Sheffield, UK: Sheffield Academic, 1996.

Payne, Leanne. "Personal Healing and Spiritual Formation." In *The Christian Educator's Handbook on Spiritual Formation*, edited by Kenneth O. Gangel and James C. Wilhoit, 213-24. Grand Rapids: Baker, 1998.

Pazmino, Robert W. "Nurturing the Spiritual Lives of Teachers." In *The Christian Educator's Handbook on Spiritual Formation*, edited by Kenneth O. Gangel and James C. Wilhoit, 143-53. Grand Rapids: Baker, 1998.

Peacocke, Arthur. *Paths from Science towards God: The End of All Our Exploring*. Oxford: Oneworld, 2001.

Pears, Angie. *Doing Contextual Theology*. London: Routledge, 2010.

Perry, William G. *Forms of Intellectual and Ethical Development in the College Years: A Scheme*. San Francisco: Jossey-Bass, 1999.

Peters, Ted. *Science, Theology, and Ethics*. Aldershot, UK: Ashgate, 2003.

Phillips, Timothy R., and Donald G. Bloesch, "Counterfeit Spirituality." In *The Christian Educator's Handbook on Spiritual Formation*, edited by Kenneth O. Gangel and James C. Wilhoit, 60-73. Grand Rapids: Baker, 1998.

Phinney, Jean S., and Doreen A. Rosenthal. "Ethnic Identity in Adolescence: Process, Context, and Outcome." In *Adolescent Identity Formation*, edited by Gerald R. Adams et al., 145-72. Newbury Park, CA: Sage, 1992.

Piper, John. "God Is Most Glorified in Us When We Are Most Satisfied in Him." In *The Christian Educator's Handbook on Spiritual Formation*, edited by Kenneth O. Gangel and James C. Wilhoit, 74-85. Grand Rapids: Baker, 1998.

Bibliography

Pirsig, Robert. "On Scientific Method." In *Science and Its Ways of Knowing*, edited by John Hatton and Paul B. Plouffe, 7–11. Upper Saddle River, NJ: Prentice Hall, 1997.

Powell, Samuel M. *Participating in God: Creation and Trinity*. Minneapolis: Fortress, 2003.

Prabhupada, A.C. Bhaktivedanta Swami. *Dharma: The Way of Transcendence*. Los Angeles: Bhaktivedanta Book Trust, 1998.

Radillo, Rebecca M. "A Model of Formation in the Multi-Cultural Urban Context for the Pastoral Care Specialist." In *The Formation of Pastoral Counselors: Challenges and Opportunities*, edited by Duane R. Bidwell and Joretta L. Marshall, 167–76. Binghamton, NY: Haworth Pastoral, 2006.

Radin, Dean. *The Conscious Universe: The Scientific Truth of Psychic Phenomena*. New York: HarperEdge, 1997.

Reamer, Frederic G. *Social Work Research and Evaluation Skills: A Case-Based, User-Friendly Approach*. New York: Columbia University Press, 1998.

Reddie, Anthony G. "Forming Wisdom through Cross-Generational Connectedness." In *In Search of Wisdom: Faith Formation in the Black Church*, edited by Anne E. Streaty Wimberly and Evelyn L. Parker, 57–73. Nashville: Abingdon, 2002.

Reid, Daniel. *A Complete Guide to Chi-Gung: Harnessing the Power of the Universe*. Boston: Shambhala, 2000.

Russell, Robert John. *Cosmology: From Alpha to Omega; The Creative Mutual Interaction of Theology and Science*. Minneapolis: Fortress, 2008.

Ryken, Leland. "The Puritan Model of Spiritual Formation." In *The Christian Educator's Handbook on Spiritual Formation*, edited by Kenneth O. Gangel and James C. Wilhoit, 49–59. Grand Rapids: Baker, 1998.

Sagan, Carl. "Can We Know the Universe? Reflections on a Grain of Salt." In *Science and Its Ways of Knowing*, edited by John Hatton and Paul B. Plouffe, 3–7. Upper Saddle River, NJ: Prentice Hall, 1997.

Sandelowski, Margarete, and Julie Barroso. *Handbook for Synthesizing Qualitative Research*. New York: Springer, 2007.

Schipani, Daniel S. *Religious Education Encounters Liberation Theology*. Birmingham, AL: Religious Education Press, 1988.

Schmuck, Richard A. *Practical Action Research for Change*. 2nd ed. Thousand Oaks, CA: Corwin, 2006.

Schreck, Alan. "Principles of Church Renewal." In *The Christian Educator's Handbook on Spiritual Formation*, edited by Kenneth O. Gangel and James C. Wilhoit, 154–63. Grand Rapids: Baker, 1998.

Seymour, Jack L. "Approaches to Christian Education." In *Mapping Christian Education: Approaches to Congregational Learning*, edited by Jack L. Seymour, 9–22. Nashville: Abingdon, 1997.

Siegel, Daniel J. *The Mindful Brain: Reflection and Attunement in the Cultivation of Well-Being*. New York: Norton, 2007.

———. *Mindsight: The New Science of Personal Transformation*. New York: Bantam, 2010.

Smith, Adrian B. *God, Energy and the Field*. Ropley, UK: Hunt, 2008.

Smith, Yolanda Y. "Forming Wisdom through Cultural Rootedness." In *In Search of Wisdom: Faith Formation in the Black Church*, edited by Anne E. Streaty Wimberly and Evelyn L. Parker, 40–56. Nashville: Abingdon, 2002.

Bibliography

Stevens, Jose, and Lena Sedletzky Stevens. *Secrets of Shamanism: Tapping the Spirit Power within You.* New York: Avon, 1988.

Suchocki, Marjorie Hewitt. *God, Christ, Church: A Practical Guide to Process Theology.* Rev. ed. New York: Crossroad, 1989.

Swinton, John, and Harriet Mowat. *Practical Theology and Qualitative Research.* London: SCM, 2006.

Sztompka, Piotr. *The Sociology of Social Change.* Oxford: Blackwell, 1993.

Thunberg, Lars. *Microcosm and Mediator: The Theological Anthropology of Maximus the Confessor.* 2nd ed. Chicago: Open Court, 1995.

Torrell, Jean-Pierre. *Spiritual Master.* Vol. 2 of *Saint Thomas Aquinas.* Translated by Robert Royal. Washington, DC: Catholic University of America Press, 1996.

Townsend, Loren. "Theological Reflection and the Formation of Pastoral Counselors." In *The Formation of Pastoral Counselors: Challenges and Opportunities,* edited by Duane R. Bidwell and Joretta L. Marshall, 29–46. Binghamton, NY: Haworth Pastoral, 2006.

Van Kaam, Adrian. *Fundamental Formation.* Formative Spirituality 1. Pittsburgh: Epiphany Association, 2002.

———. *Scientific Formation.* Formative Spirituality 4. New York: Crossroad, 1987.

Ware, Kallistos. "God Immanent Yet Transcendent: The Divine Energies according to Saint Gregory Palamas." In *In Whom We Live and Move and Have Our Being: Panentheistic Reflections on God's Presence in a Scientific World,* edited by Philip Clayton and Arthur Peacocke, 157–68. Grand Rapids: Eerdmans, 2004.

———. *The Orthodox Way.* London: Mowbrays, 1979.

Westerhoff, John H. *Will Our Children Have Faith?* New York: Seabury, 1976.

Whitney, Donald S. "Teaching Scripture Intake." In *The Christian Educator's Handbook on Spiritual Formation,* edited by Kenneth O. Gangel and James C. Wilhoit, 164–73. Grand Rapids: Baker, 1998.

Wilber, Ken. *Integral Spirituality: A Startling New Role for Religion in the Modern and Postmodern World.* Boston: Integral, 2006.

Wilhoit, James C. "Following the Lord's Pattern of Prayer." In *The Christian Educator's Handbook on Spiritual Formation,* edited by Kenneth O. Gangel and James C. Wilhoit, 174–88. Grand Rapids: Baker, 1998.

Willard, Dallas. *Renovation of the Heart: Putting on the Character of Christ.* Colorado Springs: NavPress, 2002.

———. "The Spirit Is Willing: The Body as a Tool for Spiritual Growth." In *The Christian Educator's Handbook on Spiritual Formation,* edited by Kenneth O. Gangel and James C. Wilhoit, 225–33. Grand Rapids: Baker, 1998.

Williams, Margaret, et al. *Research in Social Work: An Introduction.* 2nd ed. Itasca, IL: Peacock, 1995.

Wilson, Edward O. *On Human Nature.* Cambridge: Harvard University Press, 1978.

Wimberly, Anne E. Streaty. *Soul Stories: African American Christian Education.* Rev. ed. Nashville: Abingdon, 2005.

Wimberely, Anne E. Streaty, and Maisha I. Handy. "Conversations on Word and Deed: Forming Wisdom through Female Mentoring." In *In Search of Wisdom: Faith Formation in the Black Church,* edited by Anne E. Streaty Wimberly and Evelyn L. Parker, 108–24. Nashville: Abingdon, 2002.

Wimberly, Anne E. Streaty, and Evelyn L. Parker. "In Search of Wisdom: Necessity and Challenge." In *In Search of Wisdom: Faith Formation in the Black Church,* edited by Anne E. Streaty Wimberly and Evelyn L. Parker, 11–21. Nashville: Abingdon, 2002.

Wolpert, Daniel *Leading a Life with God: The Practice of Spiritual Leadership*. Nashville: Upper Room, 2006.

Woodward, Jim. "Explanation." In *The Blackwell Guide to the Philosophy of Science*, edited by Peter Machamer and Michael Silberstein, 37–54. Malden, MA: Blackwell, 2002.

Worrall, John. "Philosophy of Science: Classic Debates, Standard Problems, Future Prospects." In *The Blackwell Guide to the Philosophy of Science*, edited by Peter Machamer and Michael Silberstein, 18–36. Malden, MA: Blackwell, 2002.

Wynn, Charles M. "Does Theory Ever Become Fact?" In *Learning and Teaching the Ways of Knowing: Eighty-Fourth Yearbook of the National Society for the Study of Education*, edited by Elliot Eisner, 60–63. Chicago: National Society for the Study of Education, 1985.

Yin, Robert K. *Case Study Research: Design and Methods*. 3rd ed. Thousand Oaks, CA: Sage, 2003.

Bibliography

Index

Ackerman, John, 3, 21, 22–24, 27, 28, 29, 31, 34–36, 38–39, 248, 295
Action Research, 10, 62, 63, 107, 182, 184, 186, 187, 191, 194, 197, 199, 202, 203, 208, 297, 303
Acts, Book of, 11
analogies, 148, 252
anthropology, 137, 202, 304
Aquinas, Thomas, 56, 102, 304
Aristotelian philosophy, 102
ascetical practices, 139, 149
assessment, 300, 301
authenticity, 38
awakening, 36, 82, 138, 139

Baptist, 2
Barbour, Ian, 94–99, 113, 120, 121, 252–54, 257, 258, 262, 263, 269, 270–72, 275, 295
Barrick, Marilyn, 2, 5, 115, 116, 122, 123, 126, 295
Barroso, Julie, 91, 97, 99, 106, 107, 112, 116, 127, 303
Beitler, Michael, 3, 63, 64, 133, 134, 136, 138, 141, 150, 153, 175, 177, 183, 185, 186, 190, 192, 195, 196, 296
beliefs, 11, 28, 84, 261
Bible, 2, 11, 44, 95, 99, 102, 162, 184, 205, 299
biblical literalists, 96, 120
Big Bang, 274

body, 4, 31, 94, 98, 155, 190, 240, 249, 254–59, 261, 264, 269, 270, 271, 284
brain, 114, 115, 238, 295, 297, 303
brainstorming, 10, 155, 158, 161, 211, 218
Britt, David, 89, 90, 94–96, 98, 99, 109, 116, 127, 128, 135, 189, 190, 191, 252–54, 268, 269–72, 296
Buddhism, 6

Carver, Charles, 238, 273, 296
centering prayer, 150, 153, 170, 185
chaos, 36
charisms, 219
chemistry, 15
Christian atheists, 5
Christianity, 6, 29, 58, 59, 98, 119, 192, 220, 230
Christology, 99
church revitalization, 47
claims, 56, 88, 93–96, 98, 108–10, 113, 115, 116, 119–21, 124, 129, 186, 187, 189, 191, 192, 194, 201, 248, 252, 254, 259–64, 266–70, 272, 275
Clayton, Philip, 11, 125, 255, 274, 275, 296–99, 304
close relationships, 7–9, 131
Cobb, John, 4, 125, 126, 191, 297
cognitive, 56, 255
community organizers, 4
companion, 27, 35, 39, 244
complimentary, 98, 99, 121

307

Index

concepts, 10, 14, 96, 252, 253
congregational development, 151
consolation, 28, 244, 245, 248
contemplation, 220, 284, 290, 291, 292, 296
contemplative practices, 85, 151, 221, 227, 288
contextual observations, 130
core models, 100, 133
cosmologies, 83, 139
counseling, 28
creation, 4, 25, 27, 28, 44, 54, 59, 83, 85, 95, 125, 138, 139, 188, 215, 218, 236, 241, 255, 269, 270, 271, 273–75, 277, 292
creator, 11, 31
cultures, 7
Cunningham, J. Barton, 62, 107, 297

decision-making, 21, 30, 34–36, 49, 50, 51, 53, 60
deductive, 95, 96, 262, 266
deity, 6, 300
demons, 83, 108, 109
descriptions of reality, 239
design, 7, 9, 72, 132, 178, 205, 211, 218, 273, 305
desolation, 244, 248, 286
Diamond, Robert, 3, 134, 135, 138, 141, 142, 153, 156, 177, 182–89, 191, 194–96, 198, 297
Didache, 21, 301
discernment, 13, 14, 19, 21–61, 68–70, 72, 73, 75, 78, 79, 84, 86, 105, 106, 109, 111, 113, 114, 120, 128, 129, 135, 136, 139, 140, 143, 156, 162, 168, 169, 173, 175, 176, 188, 193, 195, 198, 199, 201, 205, 208, 221–27, 231–36, 239–41, 245–50, 277

discipleship, 2, 9–11, 81–84, 86, 99, 139–41, 144–47, 152, 300, 302
Dispenza, Joe, 115, 116, 122, 238, 297
diversity, 2, 33, 34, 78, 119, 137, 160, 174, 213–16, 220, 227, 289
divine life, 10, 12, 236
Dougherty, Rose Mary, 21, 22, 25–27, 29, 31–33, 35, 298
dualism, 98
Duncan-Andrade, Jeffrey M., 62, 64, 90, 105, 108, 191, 298
dynamics, 7, 10, 11, 21, 30, 81–85, 138–40, 145–49, 152, 300

education, 3, 5, 7, 42, 43, 48, 58, 62, 114, 138, 155, 163, 186, 187, 217, 219, 221, 231, 260
ego, 24, 249, 276
Elias, John, 135–41, 150–55, 177, 182–92, 196, 298
empirical observation, 262
Erasmus of Rotterdam, 84
ethics, 273, 275, 298, 302
ethnographic, 62, 160
evolution, 95, 113, 273–76

faith, 50, 101, 187, 205, 214, 225, 227, 230, 246
fasting, 149
feedback, 9, 181, 237–39, 298
    framework, 239
    theory, 238
fields of formation, 4
forgiveness, 38, 149, 258
Fowler, James, 215, 281, 291, 298
Freire, Paulo, 58
frontal lobe, 115, 124, 129

Gardner, Howard, 34, 262, 298
Geist, 59
genetic, 5

Index

Gilligan, Carol, 88, 89, 92, 94, 101, 153, 298
goals, 10, 164, 166
gospel, 5, 258, 295
Graham, Elaine, 11, 56, 57, 59, 64, 82, 90, 101–3, 140, 145–50, 190, 192, 197, 201, 298, 299
Greco-Roman, 100
Greek philosophy, 102
Greenwood, Davydd, 62–64, 107, 190, 193, 197, 299
Griffin, David Ray, 4, 125, 126, 191, 275, 297, 299
Groome, Thomas, 10, 56, 57, 58, 59, 102, 117, 118, 122, 299
guru, 30
Gutierrez, Gustavo, 108, 192, 193

habits, 39, 42, 56, 148, 149
harmony, 9, 12, 37, 50, 89, 125, 126, 191
Hauser, Richard, 21, 23, 24, 27, 28, 31, 32, 36–40, 50, 51, 244, 254, 294, 299
healing, 10, 11, 81, 137, 141, 148, 152, 292, 302
Hegel, Georg Wilhelm Friedrich, 59
Hinduism, 6
holy pause, 51, 52, 177
Holy Spirit, 140
Hull, Bill, 2, 9, 10, 11, 81–86, 99, 100, 119, 139, 140–47, 152, 300
human nature, 5, 304
human transformation, 293
humanity, 28, 81, 137, 292, 299
humility, 11, 147, 149

ideals, 9, 85, 86, 134, 141, 214, 291
identity, 27, 32, 115, 120–28, 145, 191, 214–18, 225, 230
Ignatian, 28, 36, 42, 244, 246, 284, 286, 291, 292, 294

imagination, 148, 247, 264
immanence, 28
implementation, 7, 9, 72, 132, 175, 178, 205, 211, 218, 220
incarnational, 11, 125, 218, 230
indifference, 36, 42, 244, 246
inductive, 95, 121, 262, 266
ineffable, 187
inscrutable, 187
integration, 11, 49, 50, 97, 99, 121, 191
intellectual, 56, 80, 82
interconnections, 238
interpersonal, 85, 137, 151
interventions, 9, 10, 133, 134, 149, 166, 173, 194, 211, 219, 230
intrapersonal, 215, 229
Isenhower, Valerie, 21–51, 156, 163, 245, 300
Islam, 6

Jaccard, James, 109, 252–62, 270, 272, 300
Jacoby, Jacob, 109, 252–62, 270, 272, 300
Jesus, 2, 10, 12, 38, 100, 141, 147
Jewish, 99, 100, 119, 301
Judaism, 6
justice, 9, 59, 88, 119

Kegan, Robert, 5, 215, 281, 282, 291, 300
KISS Principle, 15, 16, 17, 70, 73, 97, 100, 114, 116, 131, 133, 141, 143, 155, 181, 196, 197, 211, 240, 241, 255, 261, 263, 267
knowledge, 15, 28, 56–59, 77, 138, 141, 144, 145, 152, 155, 162, 163, 165, 169, 212, 219, 223, 228, 229, 236, 271
Kohlberg, Lawrence, 88, 89, 92, 94, 101

Index

Lartey, Emmanuel, 64, 67, 71
Lawrenz, Mel, 10, 11, 81–85, 138–40, 145–52, 300
leadership, 9, 36, 47, 49, 50
learning, 5, 295, 299–305
lecture, 150, 165, 169, 174, 177
Levin, Morten, 62–64, 107, 190, 193, 197, 299
Lewin, Kurt, 136, 138, 140
liberation, 57, 58, 59, 192, 303
liturgies, 148
logic, 254, 262, 265
love, 1, 2, 11, 32, 38, 88, 116, 125, 147, 243, 258
Luke, The Gospel of, 117

Mark, The Gospel of, 15, 117, 295
Marriage, 70–72, 111, 115
Marxism, 58, 108, 192
Matthew, The Gospel of, 117
May, Gerald, 11, 88, 90, 92, 291, 301
meditation, 264
mentors, 50, 100, 186
metaphors, 148, 252, 254, 290
metaphysics, 96, 102
metasummaries, 91
Michelangelo, 271
mind, 4, 24, 33, 70, 84, 85, 88, 90, 94, 98, 115, 128, 138, 141, 142, 145, 151, 155, 190, 200, 243, 245, 249, 254–61, 264, 266, 271
mindfulness, 148, 151
ministers, 2
Moberg, David, 184, 187, 301
modifications, 97, 99, 121, 181, 195–97, 203, 206, 231, 241
monastic, 21
Morrell, Ernest, 62, 64, 67, 90, 105, 108, 191
Mowat, Harriet, 62–67, 71, 101–7, 110, 119, 190, 191, 304

Murphy, Nancey, 95, 252, 254, 262, 264, 265–71, 302
myths, 252, 254

narratives, 148
native/shamanistic, 6
neocortex, 115
neurons, 270, 271
neuro-psychology, 129
neuroscience, 115, 270
New Testament, 38
non-theistic, 300

Old Testament, 117
omnipresent, 27
organism, 137, 270
organizational development, 3
otherworldly, 187, 188

panentheistic, 124, 125
pantheism, 6, 300
paradigm-dependent, 96
Parker, Stephen, 10, 21, 23–40, 81, 84, 138, 140, 144–53, 248, 298, 300–305
Paul of Tarsus, 38
Pears, Angie, 64, 65, 89, 90, 97, 108, 119, 189–97, 302
pedagogies, 135, 151, 165, 174, 175, 200, 204, 206
pentecostal, 28, 37, 249, 302
Perry, William, 215–17, 220, 229, 302
personality types, 34, 219
person-centered, 7
philosophers, 98, 262
physics, 15, 95
practical theology, 10, 62–67, 101, 102, 105, 107, 110, 119, 190, 191, 302
praxis, 1, 4, 13–15, 19, 22, 24, 39, 54–62, 65, 67–79, 86, 103, 131, 133, 174, 177, 180, 181

praxis (cont.), 188, 189, 194–97, 198, 201, 203, 207–12, 217, 222, 231–41, 273, 276
prayer, 26, 32, 35, 36, 39, 43, 45, 108, 129, 147, 148, 152, 153, 185, 195, 224, 243, 244, 284
predictive models, 189, 201, 258
process theology, 4, 125, 297, 304
Protestant, 21, 229
psychological, 5, 88, 135, 222, 236
psychosocial, 80
Puritans, 85, 139

quadri-lectic, 194

Rahner, Karl, 99
rational, 28, 56, 265
reconciliation, 32
redemption, 81, 85
reductionism, 255
reflection, 57, 60, 84, 101, 102, 168, 174, 190, 197, 299, 303, 304
relativism, 216
religious education, 7, 56–59, 102, 117, 135–41, 150–55, 182–87, 190, 192, 196, 298, 299, 303
religious experiences, 33
religious traditions, 13, 47, 68, 71, 87, 89, 147, 157, 194, 218
responsive action research, 198
retreat, 8, 32, 70, 71, 72
revitalization, 1, 47, 78, 193
Roman Catholic, 99

sacred texts, 13, 23, 27, 87
Sagan, Carl, 253, 270–73, 303
salvation, 10, 81, 85, 140, 301
Sandelowski, Margarete, 91, 97, 99, 106, 107, 112, 116, 127, 303
Scheier, Michael, 238, 296
Schipani, Daniel, 57–59, 303

Schmuck, Richard, 107, 182–87, 191, 194, 197, 199, 202, 203, 207, 208, 303
scientific materialists, 94, 95, 96, 120, 121
self-differentiation, 111
self-knowledge, 11, 145, 221
selfless, 116
self-realization, 115, 123–26, 191
self-sacrifice, 88
Seymour, Jack, 7, 8, 303
signs of grace, 38
sin, 83, 137, 232
Smith, Yolanda, 11, 142, 145, 148, 151, 275, 303
sociological, 5, 236
solitude, 146
soul, 41, 98
spirit, 2, 3, 7–14, 21–44, 48–61, 69–73, 78–81, 84, 87–89, 97, 103, 105, 114, 125, 126, 132, 134, 136, 140–42, 154, 155, 173, 176, 177, 180, 181, 187, 188, 197, 199, 201, 204, 211, 214, 219, 223, 224, 230–36, 241–49, 254, 274, 275, 291, 294, 297–304
spiritual development, 33, 229
spiritual doctrine, 248
spiritual formation, 2–4, 7–14, 19, 21, 39, 54–56, 60, 61, 69, 73, 75, 80–84, 87, 88, 92, 130, 133, 141–48, 155, 163, 181–84, 187, 188, 197, 207–12, 220, 228, 237, 240, 241, 254, 258, 259, 269, 271, 273, 276, 277
spiritual growth, 134, 136, 145, 146, 184, 215, 258
spirituality, 10, 11, 80–84, 137–39, 145–48, 254, 261–63, 290, 298–304
stage theories, 221, 227, 278, 285
stillness, 146, 168

Index

Suchocki, Marjorie, 125, 126, 191, 292, 304
superego, 276
Swinton, John, 62–67, 71, 101, 102, 105, 107, 110, 119, 190, 191, 304
symbols, 148, 254, 280
Synoptic, 117
synthesizing, 9, 68, 91, 93, 97, 99, 106, 107, 112, 116, 127, 303

Taoism, 6
theater, 238
theistic, 3, 4, 6, 9–13, 22–25, 35, 53, 58, 60, 61, 64, 68, 71, 115, 124, 126, 134, 136, 140, 187, 197, 198, 218, 234–36, 241, 251, 273–76
theological, 5, 6, 11, 13, 22–25, 33, 46, 47, 51, 61, 64–67, 71, 78, 85–89, 99, 101–3, 115, 124–26, 137, 140, 152, 172, 188, 190–93, 201, 218, 230, 235, 236, 273
theology, 4, 11, 25, 57–59, 64, 65, 82, 89, 90, 97, 108, 119, 126, 145, 148, 150, 189–93, 197, 273, 275, 292, 296, 299–304
theories of change, 81, 138

theory of multiple intelligences, 34
Todd, Judith, 21–27, 29–40, 49, 51, 156, 163, 245, 300
transcendent, 6, 187, 275
transpersonal, 107, 295, 296
triangulation, 109, 112
Trinity, 12, 302, 303

United Methodist Church, 41, 50

validation, 262
Vatican II, 108
vocation, 7, 19, 53, 60, 61, 73, 174, 208, 228, 232–35, 251

Walton, Heather, 101, 103, 190
Ward, Frances, 101–3, 190
warrants, 93–97, 109, 113, 119–21, 193, 194, 201, 260, 265–69, 272
ways of knowing, 9, 28, 29, 118, 254, 263, 270, 295, 299, 300, 303, 305
Westerhoff, John, 229, 230, 304
whole-being, 263
Wolpert, Daniel, 21, 23, 27, 31, 35–40, 243, 305
worship, 148, 174, 195

www.ingramcontent.com/pod-product-compliance
Lightning Source LLC
Chambersburg PA
CBHW050619300426
44112CB00012B/1579